For Kay,
- just one birder
the one who led -
whooping cranes, Ev

Evelyn Copeland

LONESOME GLEE

LONESOME GLEE

TALES FROM THE BIRDING TRAILS

Evelyn Copeland

VANTAGE PRESS
New York

FIRST EDITION

Published by Vantage Press, Inc.
516 West 34th Street, New York, New York 10001

Manufactured in the United States of America
ISBN: 0-533-11739-9

Library of Congress Catalog Card No.: 95-90913

0 9 8 7 6 5 4 3 2 1

For Marjory and Eleanor
who first brought birding to my attention
and all the other birders
who have befriended Mack and me along the way

It is a lonesome Glee—
Yet sanctifies the Mind—
With fair association—
Afar upon the wind

A bird to overhear
Delight without a Cause—
Arrestless as invisible—
A Matter of the Skies.

—Emily Dickinson

Contents

Foreword

Birds, not rooted to earth, are among the most eloquent expressions of life.

—Roger Tory Peterson

Announcing my retirement from teaching in 1974, I sent my colleagues a bulletin titled "Going Fishing." In retrospect I realize it should have been "Going Birding." I have recounted in *But a Brown Bird Sang* how, after retiring to Florida, I gradually became a birder. This companion volume relates some of the adventures encountered on the road and along the trails in the years of birding that followed.

A note on vocabulary may be in order. *Bird* like *fish* is both a noun and a verb. As a fisherman fishes for fish, so a birder (not birderman) birds for birds. A fisherman goes fishing; a birder goes *birding*. In both sports the big one sometimes gets away. A bird (a species) seen for the first time is a *life bird* or a *lifer*. A *life list* is a compilation of *lifers*. Other than for the birds themselves, the vocabulary is as simple as that.

What was not so simple in writing these tales was deciding what to leave out. As I contemplated a seasick day off the Outer Banks of North Carolina, excursions to Guadalupe, and Davis Mountains, an aborted invasion of Big Bend in Texas, and Yellow-billed Magpies on the golf course in Solvang, California, I had to continually remind myself I was not writing the

Encyclopaedia Britannica of birds. Though it may seem a fine point, these tales are not so much about birds as about two beginning birders setting out in search of birds and what happened along the way.

The travels related here are limited to North America, which, according to the American Birding Association's official list, has 896 of the world's 8,700 species of birds. And, to extend the statistics a little further, Mack and I are two of the U.S.A.'s twenty million birders. We may even outnumber fishermen.

I owe thanks to so many of those twenty million birders we have met along the trails that I hesitate to be specific. But in hesitating I would be amiss in not thanking Bob Bradley for the memorable day in Arizona that started with LeConte's Thrasher and just kept going; Steve Buettner, former birding neighbor now with ABA in Colorado Springs; Bonnie Chartier, friend and guide in Churchill; Wally and Jenny Kate Collins of Boulder and the greater United States; Pat and Gale DeWind, generous hosts to both birds and birders in Salineno, Texas; Kim Eckert, who placed the marker in the path pointing our way to the Ferruginous Pygmy Owl; Ben Fawver in Coos Bay for our day on the Oregon coast; Betty and Art Forchgott in South Miami, who cheerfully welcome any birder in search of the Spot-breasted Oriole; Red and Louise Gambil, tireless guides of countless birders at Bentsen State Park; Dave Jasper, our guide at Cave Creek Canyon; Ken Knowles in Newfoundland; Linda Northrop for her dauntless search for the Ferruginous Pygmy Owl; Jeff Sohlstrom and his mother, Maryanne, for twelve Oregon lifers; Dick Walker, who initiated the Alaska adventure; and by no means least, though last, Florence McDermott, the Mack in these tales, who not only shared with me the joys and trials of birding but also read or listened to raw manuscripts and made many helpful suggestions, not the least of which was the reminder that both warblers and readers seek shelter from wind. To these and all who remain unnamed, this book is dedicated.

Astolat
Lake City, Florida
28 July 1995

LONESOME GLEE

In the Beginning Was the Bird

Within my Garden rides a Bird
Upon a single Wheel—
Whose spokes a dizzy Music make
As 'twere a traveling Mill—

—Emily Dickinson

"No," the man on the phone said, "ya wunt b'able t' drive yer motor home to Mile High."

"Will I be able to rent a car?"

"Some days ya can't park a bike up there. But if y'aren't comin' fer four weeks, I'd wait on a car."

True, we wouldn't get to Arizona for another month, but I wanted to be sure of a reservation at Apache Pointe Ranch. It is the closest campground to the hummingbirds at Mile High.

"Do you want a deposit? A credit card number?"

"No, I've got yer name. Copeland?"

"Right. You'll be sure to save us a space? With hookups?" I asked perhaps a little anxiously.

"Don't worry, lady. I'll save you the best in the lot," he assured me.

"I don't know what kind of camp ground we're getting into," I told Mack, who is sharing this adventure with me. "It sounds pretty casual, but we *do* have a reservation."

Mile High is a cluster of half a dozen cabins and a dozen and a half hummingbird feeders just outside the entrance to Ramsey Canyon Preserve. The preserve, with its own dozen

1

or more feeders, is owned and lovingly protected by The Nature Conservancy. The spot is renowned throughout bird-dom for the many species of hummingbirds these feeders attract. What better place to start a birding career?

Though we would bird along the way, Mack and I left Florida with our sights firmly set on Arizona. Mack's shnoodle Heidi didn't have her sights set on anything beyond her next meal, but wherever Mack goes, she is happy to go, too.

As Mack turned West onto Interstate 10, I sat, clean notebook in hand, pencil poised to record the first bird of the trip. That's the way the big birders do it. R-o-b-i-n I lettered on the unblemished page as neatly as I could in a jouncing motor home. I was as dedicated as an eager student on the first day of school. C-a-r-d-i-n-a-l . . .

"Crow," Mack called out.

"Crow?" I hesitated.

"It *is* a bird."

"Yes, I know. We must write down every bird we see. That's what a trip list is. But was it an American or a Fish crow?"

"American probably."

"Do we include probablies or only certainties? This may not be as easy as I thought."

"Why don't you add a question mark to the probablies?"

We'd never kept a list before, except the one recently completed of birds seen on the property at Astolat during the past year.

"Vulture," Mack said.

"Turkey or Black?"

Mack squinted into the sky on her left. "Errr, Black. It has white on the wing tips." Mack is good at driving with an eye and a half on the sky.

I added a Blue Jay, Mockingbird, and European Starling as I spotted them.

"Mourning Dove," Mack noted a little farther down the road.

In this fashion we made our way toward Tallahassee. Our birding career had started. I was leaving home to find birds that would never leave home to find me. Maybe as many as fifteen species of hummingbirds in one place. The thought was dizzying.

The second night we camped in Daingerfield State Park in eastern Texas.

"Any birds around?" I asked when I registered.

"Lots of birds," the man said, handing me the park's list of eighty-five, from American Coot to Yellow-billed Cuckoo. Pull-through campsites looped off the park road. We found one long enough to accommodate our thirty-six-foot Coachmen and set up camp under a canopy of trees beside a lake. Heidi joined us on exploratory ramblings while we waited for Jean and Barbara, who were coming from Dallas to spend the weekend with us. One trail circled the lake; others wandered through the woods.

Our trip list grew impressively during the weekend. We didn't count the birds we didn't see even though we recognized the evening Whip-poor-will and the Barred Owl that hooted in the night. We gave up trying to identify the Mallardlike ducks that bore hints of hanky-panky in their ancestry.

But Jean would not give up on the bird singing in the branches above the picnic table at breakfast. At first the song was our only clue. The flutelike quality left little doubt it was a thrush. But was the song "a series of loud phrases, each followed by a softer, guttural trill"? That would be a Wood Thrush. Or was it "a single high flutelike note followed by a rapid series of rising and falling notes"? That would be the Hermit Thrush.

"I could tell better if it would slow down," I said, "but I favor the Wood Thrush."

3

Jean and Mack thought it was the Hermit. Barbara said she was going fishing.

Finally Jean caught a glimpse of it among the leaves. "It has lots of spots on its breast," she reported.

"They both do," I said, studying the book. "It says the Hermit is seldom heard except on its breeding ground." Then I added, "And it doesn't breed in Texas."

"Hmmm." That from Jean.

Then Mack saw it. "Are the spots heavy or thin? Round or just little streaks?" I asked.

"It's hard to say."

"Is the tail brown or rusty?" Would that I could be so knowledgeable without the book in front of me.

"I can't see the tail. It's behind the leaves."

"What color's the back?"

"Brownish."

A Hermit Thrush would be the first lifer of the trip, but we must keep an open mind, pursue the identification objectively.

"I can see the tail now," Jean said. "It's rusty. It's definitely rusty. It's the Hermit's song, too. Hear that single high note it starts with?"

"I think it is a Two-eyed, Double-breasted Twitty Tit," Barbara called from the lake.

"Watch your mullets," Jean retorted.

"What do you think?" Mack asked. Jean and she thought it was a Hermit. I stuck with Wood because the Hermit doesn't breed in Texas, and it was July—and probably because I have a tin ear. Barbara abstained, and Heidi wouldn't take sides.

"Remember," Mack cautioned me, "birds don't read books or consult calendars."

I happily added Hermit Thrush to the trip list and beside it neatly lettered l-i-f-e-r.

Mack and I were both eager to be back on the road

Monday morning. But how many days would it take to cross Texas? Two hundred and fifty miles was a good day's stint. We liked to stop midafternoon with time to bird around the campground before dinner.

At Big Springs we found a Black-chinned Hummingbird, a Mississippi Kite, and what we confidently mislabeled a Tropical Kingbird. A few Western trips later, we would recognize the error and relabel it Couch's Kingbird. No one could deny, though, we made up in enthusiasm what we lacked in knowledge.

The next day in Monohan near those great Texas sand dunes, we correctly, I think, identified a Curve-billed Thrasher and a pair of Inca Doves. They are the ones that croon "whirlpool, whirlpool, whirlpool" all day long. I met, too, my first Scissor-tailed Flycatchers. Mack, being an Okie, already knew them well.

Shortly beyond Van Horn, our third Texas campground, a Greater Roadrunner streaked across the road. Running like a stretched-out floor mop, dragging its white-tipped tail on the pavement, it looked to me, in that startled flash, like a bedraggled squirrel. Roadrunners apparently use their wings only as a last resort, only when a situation becomes ultradesperate. This one slipped over the edge of the road and disappeared at the end of a culvert. I pulled onto the shoulder, grabbed my camera, and tiptoed to where he stood in anxious alert. I could see the blotches of blue and red behind his eye and the polka-dot effect of gray feathers showing through the brown crest. It *is* a comical bird, not by any conscious effort on its part but rather by Mother Nature's design. The crest pops up like an umbrella in a sudden storm. Its tail, as long as the body itself, jerks from horizontal to vertical and back in erratic twitches, as though communicating by Morse code. The instant we made eye contact, it gave one up-down jerk of the tail, and before I could cry, "Smile," it scurried into the mesquite.

As I added G-r-e-a-t-e-r R-o-a-d-r-u-n-n-e-r to the list, I wondered aloud, "Is there a Lesser Roadrunner?"

"Not that I know of," Mack said.

After one night in New Mexico, the scent of Arizona drew us like honey bears to honey. The trip list suffered, becoming shabby and sloppy:

Large Hawk (Unidentified)
Raven?
Sharp-shinned Hawk (Probably)
Falcon (Maybe)

Hawks were too hard. Excitement was mounting.

The next afternoon we drove through Sierra Vista (Sir Vista, the natives say), turned south on Highway 92, and drove six miles out of town to a sign on the right: Ramsey Canyon. Two miles up the canyon, an arrow pointed to the left to Apache Pointe Ranch.

"I hope he's saved us a campsite," I remarked. I was a fizz of anticipation.

About a quarter of a mile along the driveway (if that was what it was), the road split. The track to the left led past a corral, some sheds, a large house, and miscellaneous outbuildings—the ranch, I presumed. The one to the right ended abruptly in a large field.

"Which way do we go?" Mack asked.

"Where is the campground?" I wondered.

As we paused in indecision, a bird called. It was more of a call than a song, clear but not tuneful. "Where do you think it is?" Mack asked. We listened and traced it to the prickly pear cactus at the split in the road. Dead in front of us, ensconced among the cactus spines, was the source of this exuberance. Binoculars revealed a prominent white eyeline, heavily spotted breast, and a tipped-up tail.

6

"It has to be a wren," Mack said.

"But it's half again as big as our Carolina wrens."

"Of course!" A light went on in Mack's head. "It's a Cactus Wren. Sitting in a cactus. Get it?"

By then a man was coming toward us on foot from the direction of the corral.

Good, I thought. *Perhaps we can find out what's where.*

He spoke first, "Miss Copeland? I'm Paul and this is Lady," indicating the collie at his side. "Welcome to Apache Pointe Ranch."

Heidi was at the window, eager to meet Lady. After a few preliminaries, I asked, "Where is the campground?"

"Yer looking at it," Paul replied, pointing to the field.

"Where are the campers?" Mack wanted to know.

"We don't get many campers in July. Too hot, I guess."

"Well," I said, laughing, "which spot have you reserved for us?"

"Ya can take yer pick of 'bout a hundred right here. Or if ya prefer shade, I've fifty more behind the arena, but the ground's not as level. Ah'm sorry we don't have a rodeo fer ya folks tonight. Usually do on Friday, but not always in the summer. Do have a herd of Buffalo fer yer pleasure. Visit our art gallery, enjoy our museum, eat in the restaurant, and tomorrow night dance to the music of a live band. There'll be more'n a hundred cars out here tomorrow night," he said with considerable pride.

"Any birds?"

"Birds? Ya like birds? Then y'oughta camp in the timber yonder. Look it over."

I asked about the hummingbirds at Mile High. "Y'll hafta make a reservation to get onto the preserve tomorrow and Sunday. They're fussy up there. Don't like lots of folks on their trails. Y'can phone from the restaurant. Make yerselves't home. Y'll like the food in our restaurant." And he was gone.

We drove *yonder* to the *timber* but couldn't find a site level enough for the rig. So we returned to the field and selected a spot with water and electricity in full ninety-eight-degree Arizona sunshine.

"What about the hummingbirds?" Mack asked.

"Two things. First see whether we can get onto the preserve in the morning. If we can't, we'll jolly well sit here until we can even if it's the middle of August. It's too late this afternoon. They close at five. And second, find out how we're going to get up there short of walking."

"We could walk. It's only two miles. Doesn't it scorch your old tutu to be so close and yet so far?"

"Yeah, we *could* walk, BUT. We're going to be wearing those boots because we don't know about snakes. And I'll have a camera in addition to binoculars. I'm not sure I'd have steam enough in this heat to get home again."

"Don't forget my snacks."

"Right. What about Heidi?"

"She'll be all right here for two or three hours with the air conditioner on. If we can get up to the preserve by eight, I'd want to be back by lunch."

After several tries Mack reached The Nature Conservancy by phone. Yes, we could come at ten tomorrow morning.

"Ten? Don't the birds get up at dawn?"

"We monitor the number of visitors on weekends," the voice said coolly.

"At least something is cool around here," I commented. "Now let's ask Paul about transportation."

Paul'd be much obliged to run us up in his truck and fetch us any time before noon. He had some real estate matters to attend to after lunch.

"Now what?"

"Let's look for a Pyrrhuloxia," Mack suggested.

"A pair o' what?"

"A Pyrrhuloxia. Lane's guide says you aren't a birder until you can tell a Northern Cardinal from a Pyrrhuloxia, and Pyrrhuloxias should be here."

We ambled toward the trees, studying the bird guides as we went. Both species are the same size. Both sexes of both species have pointed crests. Their songs are almost indistinguishable. Only the male cardinal has a black bib. The cardinals' bills are red, the Pyrrhuloxias' yellow. But immature cardinals' bills are more yellow than red.

A crested bird with a red eye lit on a branch. It was gray with paler gray wing bars but no red feathers at all. And the bill was black. It didn't qualify for either.

"Besides," Mack said, consulting the book, "the Pyrrhuloxia doesn't have a red eye, just a red ring around a dark eye."

No red birds showed, either cardinals or otherwise. "I should be getting back to Heidi," Mack said. "She'll be wondering where dinner is."

On the way back, we made a short stop at the Mountain Gallery, which stood halfway between the museum in the main house and the arena. It was not an impressive building on the outside and rather crowded on the inside. Despite first impressions it boasted some credible Indian prints, some Remingtons and Catlins, and a modest display by local artists. Some Indian artifacts and modern ceramic pieces from the Western desert filled a display case running along one wall. Two women were framing a print in a corner set aside for that activity. The quality and so much activity on a ranch far from town surprised me.

As evening turned to night, our thoughts fixed on the morning, Ramsey Canyon hummingbirds at last.

Paul pulled up to the prickly pear cactus promptly at 9:50 the next morning. "Where's Lady?" Mack asked. "I thought you two were inseparable."

"I had to bribe her."

I clambered in beside Paul aware that my shorts and L. L. Bean boots looked a bit incongruous. Vivatars dangled from my neck. (This was long before the days of Zeiss and Bausch and Lomb.) I'd slung one camera over my shoulder. Pockets bulged with sunscreen and insect repellent. An auxiliary camera bag, buckled around my waist, hardly allowed for making a lap. Mack was equally bedecked, except she carried snacks instead of cameras. We were going birding—for two hours.

Five minutes later we dismounted at Mile High.

"Meet me at twelve," Paul said, departing. "Please be prompt. I can't park here."

"Fast as sparks shot from a fire" is how Marge Piercy, a contemporary poet, describes them. When I stepped from the truck, the darting sparks filled the air. Although I had done my homework, trying to fix in my mind the key distinctions of species most likely to be here, I stood dazzled by the comings and goings from feeder to feeder. It was little help to know the Blue-throated Hummingbird (or was it Broad-billed?) has double white lines on the face. My eyes couldn't move fast enough to fix on a face. But that inadequacy did not lessen the thrill of the moment. I basked in the brilliance of Mother Nature's darting jewels. When they crossed a shaft of sunlight, a black throat for briefer than a heartbeat turned brilliant blue, brown twinkled violet, gray flashed magenta. A fluster of kaleidoscopes!

Or as Emily Dickinson sees them

A Route of Evanescence
With a revolving Wheel—
A Resonance of emerald—
A Rush of Chochineal.

An Amazon myth says the hummingbird got its brilliance

10

when an inquisitive bird wanted to know what was on the other side of the sun. Flying straight through it, it gathered all the colors of the burning disc.

"Your jaw is hanging," Mack said quietly at my side.

"Oh, thanks," I said, coming back to reality. "Can you believe the number? Everywhere I look. The colors won't hold still. But what's what, anyway, and who's who?"

"I think one of the bigger ones is a Blue-throated. It has a broad white tip on its tail."

Fortunately others were watching with us. Between eavesdropping and starting a conversation with two who seemed knowledgeable, we learned we were watching two of the larger hummingbirds, the Blue-throated and the Magnificent.

"You can distinguish between the two by the forked tail of the Magnificent," one said. "Also the Magnificent has a green throat and violet crown."

"Which one is making that high-pitched whistle when it flies?" Mack asked.

"That's the whistling wings of the Broad-tailed. It's one of the smaller hummers, not much more than three and three-quarter inches. It is also the only Western hummingbird with a green crown."

"Have you seen an Anna's hummingbird yet?" the other man asked.

"Not to recognize it."

"It's not as common as the others here, but it is a common resident a little farther west. One's been at the feeder this morning."

We walked around to more feeders on a lower level. The hummers were just as numerous. "There's an Anna's now," our companion said. "It's drinking at the second feeder from the door. Well, it was. It just flew, but it will come back. The male's forehead and throat are red, a miniature Red-faced Warbler."

11

Eventually Mack and I made our way to the visitors center. We asked about the trails. We'd need a permit, a different color for each trail. With not much more than an hour to explore, we chose the main trail straight up the canyon. The path was wide and easy the first quarter-mile. A Black-and-White Warbler worked a tree near the path, a good trip bird. A little farther along, a flock of jays flew into some oaks. But what kind of jays? They were blue, but not Blue Jays. They had no crests, and although they had a jay accent, the voice was less raucous than that of Blue Jays. Without white spots on their throats or a white eyeline, they could not be Scrub Jays.

"Pinyon?" I suggested.

"We could hope, but there are no pinyon trees."

"They must be Gray-breasted Jays." And the ranger we met on the trail confirmed our guess. He also helped find a bird that had been calling in the trees, a noisy character for the little bird that Mack thought she had glimpsed through the foliage. When she described a brown bird with, she thought, a yellow breast, he asked whether we had ever seen a Kiskadee.

"Kiss-ka-dee?" I said syllable by syllable. "No, I've never even heard of one."

"Well, it wouldn't be a Kiskadee here, but the Sulphur-bellied Flycatcher is a less dramatic, smaller version of it, with prominent streaking on the breast. That is probably what you saw."

The trail soon grew steep and rocky. I began to question the wisdom of having toted my camera, and though I didn't admit it for a while, I would gladly have traded my L. L. Bean boots for a sun visor.

"What's up ahead?" I asked a youth who was skipping and jumping his way down the mountain.

"A vista you can't imagine," he took time to say. "You'll

come out of the trees and look back across the valley an incredible distance."

The trail zigzagged now, making hairpin turns to facilitate the ascent. We rounded three more hairpins, thinking each one would bring us to the rim of the canyon. A young couple came bounding down. They paused to speak.

"How much farther?" I managed to say.

"Not far."

My shin bones were blistering. "Shall we call it a day?" Mack asked.

"Let's go around one more turn."

"It's eleven-thirty. We can't go much farther."

"I don't know why I'm so pooped," I said as we paused to rest. A woodpecker flew into view. I made mental notes: brown back with no markings, lots of white around the face, spotted breast, about the size of a Hairy.

"It's a Strickland's Woodpecker," Mack decided, having summoned up enough strength to pull out her book. "Common resident in a limited range on pine-oak slopes at forty-five hundred to seven thousand feet," she read.

"We must be at seven thousand. No wonder I'm panting. Anyway, going down should be easier. We'd better get started."

"Shhh!" Mack put a finger to her lips. She pointed toward the pines just ahead. "It's a funny little warbler. The front half is all buffy, the back, gray with white wing bars."

We stood another moment, consulting Mack's book. "I think it has to be an Olive Warbler. They nest in sugar pine and fir forests above eight thousand feet."

"Eight thousand," I exclaimed. "It's a wonder I can stand up. Let's get going."

The way down wasn't any easier. The boulders were bigger, the pebbles more inclined to roll under my slightly too large boots. My blisters stung and my little toes killed me when I slid forward in my boots. We limped into the visitors center

13

with five minutes to spare. Relinquishing her trail pass, Mack asked, "Could we have seen an Olive Warbler?"

"If you were lucky."

"We were lucky."

"How high were we, say, halfway up the trail?" I asked.

"About five thousand feet."

"Oh, I thought it must have been at least ten."

We limped once more around the feeders where the sparks were still shooting despite the noonday hour.

Lady was in the navigator's seat when Paul pulled up. And she was not about to do us any favors, unbidden.

"Move over," Paul told her. She looked straight across her long collie nose as much as to say, *Where'd you find these two?*

"Just get in," Paul said. "She'll move over." I went first. Lady reluctantly gave up three inches.

She muttered under her breath, *This is a two-person truck.* Mack sat mostly on air, but we were soon back at campside, Lady never having once given us a sign of recognition. But Heidi was thrilled to see us.

By midafternoon we were refreshed and ready to visit the buffalo herd and look again for Pyrrhuloxia. The buffalo were a docile lot, except for a pair of calves whose curiosity at least suggested hospitality. We did finally find a pair of Pyrrhuloxia. Or were they strangely marked cardinals? No, the bills were yellow. The other crested birds—the ones with no red feathers—were Phainopeples. We found, too, before the afternoon was over, a Rufous-backed Robin and a Western Kingbird. The latter calls seductively, *C'm 'ere, c'm 'ere.*

"Do you want to stay another day or move on?" Mack asked as we ambled back to the rig.

"I'm ready to move on."

"What's next?" she asked.

"I think we can make Bog Springs campground in Madera Canyon tomorrow."

"Do we have a reservation?"

"No, but judging from this one, I doubt we'll need one."

The next morning we said good-bye to our fifty-acre campsite, the deer that wandered like pets throughout the ranch, and the Texas jackrabbits with their tall, translucent ears. Paul and Lady came to the Cactus Wren cactus to see us off, symbols of the best of the West as they stood against the backdrop of the rugged Huachuca Mountains. "Oh, give me a home where the buffalo roam . . . ," Heidi sang as we turned down the canyon road.

The drive to Madera Canyon, twenty-five miles south of Tucson, would be an easy run. We'd have time to stop at the Sonoita Creek Sanctuary near the village of Patagonia. Avoiding main roads, we hoped to see some birds along the way. The first to cross our path (and it did cross it) was a roadrunner that scuttled with the desperation of the farmer's wife who cut off the mice's tails with a butcher knife.

We rode on. The yucca was in bloom. Great spikes of white dotted the desert like giant candles.

"What was *that?*" I exclaimed when a patch from an artist's palette flashed by—red, yellow, blue. It was boldly marked, no subtleties. It lit for half a breath on a roadside yucca like a slightly off-side candle flame and was gone.

"I bet I can find that one in the book," I bragged. And I did—red head, yellow body, black tail, and black wings with white wing bars. A Western Tanager.

That afternoon in the Sonoita Creek Sanctuary, we found six lifers, two of which became benchmarks in the years of birding that have followed. We have seen Mountain Bluebirds since then, but never without saying, "Remember the one at Sonoita?" I thought a strip of sky had fallen. The blue of the Mountain Bluebird, perhaps because it is *all* blue with the blue washing into white on the belly, must come from dead center on the color spectrum. It is not bluish green or greenish blue

15

or indigo or slate. It is pure cerulean blue. It was a flight of seconds that we have remembered for years.

At the top of Mack's wish list that afternoon was a Yellow-billed Cuckoo. It should be there, but as the time approached to leave, it had not shown its face—or tail. We would identify it most easily by the three pairs of large white spots on the underside of the black tail.

"I must get back to Heidi," Mack had just said when we heard its hollow, wooden call, more guttural than that of the Black-billed we knew at home, but indisputably the voice of a cuckoo with its waterfall of rapid *kuk-kuk-kuk-kuks* petering out at the end like a rundown toy.

On the way to the RV, rejoicing in our good luck, Mack was accosted by a hummingbird. In the surprise of the moment, neither of us identified the species. It flew right to the cardinal on Mack's T-shirt, probing the red as it hovered. As long as one doesn't move, hummingbirds are no more disturbed by a person than by a tree stump. I read of one once that examined the inside of a man's ear "quite thoroughly." This one probed the folds of Mack's shirt while she stood motionless. Then, deciding she was not a flower, it vanished.

The sun was setting as our Coachmen groaned in low gear up, up, up into Madera Canyon. After the turnoff to Bog Springs Campground, the road rose even more precipitously. Mack was taking the whole road to maneuver the hairpin turns. The campground advertised pull-through sites and proprietors who feed birds and welcome photographers. The sites, all at the road's edge, looked like gussets bulldozed out to give the forest breathing spaces. In the gloaming they seemed indifferently leveled and all too short for our thirty-six-foot motor home. Nor did we see any spaces that we could pull into—and drive on through when we left, the kind of site we preferred.

"What do you suggest?" Mack asked as we reached the

top, the point at which the one-way loop now started to pitch downhill. The sun had set. Dark was overtaking us.

"Did you see any campers as we came up the mountain?" Mack asked.

"Not one."

"Well, let me back into this site here on the left for the moment. It's at least flattish. We may stick out in the road a little, but there's no traffic. Why don't you go read the bulletin board while I take Heidi for a walk?"

Two fellows we had talked to earlier at Sonoita Creek came up on their motorbikes while I was reading the Dos and Don'ts. *Do not build open fires. Do not wash dishes at the water fountain. Toilets on lower level. Deposit three dollars in envelope below and insert through slit in post.* The fellows weren't staying. They were looking for owls.

When Mack returned, she said that a couple with three children were tent camping at the foot of the steps leading to the toilets. "It's a dirt toilet," she reported with a bit of a sniff. She'd found no other campers and no camp host.

"Let's put our three dollars in the post and stay right here for the night," I proposed. "After supper we can listen for owls and tomorrow walk down to the hummingbirds at Santa Rita Lodge."

"Sounds good to me. Okay by you, Heidi?"

The setting was incredibly beautiful. We had climbed six thousand feet but still sat in a forested pocket surrounded by towering mountains. A nearly full moon turned the road into a silver stream. If any owls called or Whip-poor-wills sang, I slept too soundly to know.

"Why do you think we're the only campers?" I asked at breakfast.

"Beats me," Mack said.

We had come to Madera Canyon as we had to Ramsey, to see hummingbirds. Santa Rita Lodge, like Mile High, has many feeders. But whereas at Ramsey we still had to walk up to the hummers, here we had to walk down. After a leisurely breakfast, still awed by the beauty around us, I said, "Shall we walk down to the lodge? It's not much more than a half mile."

"Are you going to wear your boots?"

"No way."

Mack turned on the air conditioner for Heidi and we started out. The road was paved but so steep that I looked around for a walking stick. Before we reached the third campsite, I commented, "You know we'll have to walk back up here in the noonday heat. And it must be nearly a hundred already."

"Is there anywhere to park if we take the rig down?"

"Probably not at the lodge, but there's a picnic area between here and there. Let's take the rig that far."

We hit the jackpot at the lodge. The hummingbirds were being banded that morning. It is a very specialized activity that one has to be licensed to do. We'd be watching and talking with professional birders. Nets were strung near a couple of the many feeders around the little park. We watched how carefully the captor folded back the wings and held the bird as it was carried to the banding area, how deliberately the ring was slipped onto the wire-thin leg. We were allowed to stand close and ask questions.

"Why are you banding them?"

"We're trying to get an estimate of the various species feeding here. For instance, do we have a dozen Black-chinneds or do we have one Black-chinned coming to a feeder twelve times? We'll never get an accurate count, but we can get some idea."

After being banded the bird was put into a netted box, about a twenty-inch cube, where it was fed and allowed to regain a normal heartbeat before being released.

Soon Mack was assisting with the postoperative TLC,

holding the netted enclosure and talking soothingly to a Rufous or Black-chinned or Broad-billed.

"Keep up the good work," I said. "I'm going back to the RV for the tripod, flash, and more film."

When I returned, she was nursing a violet-throated bird no bigger than my thumb. "What's that?" I asked.

"It's a male Lucifer, the only violet-throated hummingbird with a green crown. It has a forked tail and is a very rare breeder around here."

"My, my. How'd you get so smart?"

"It pays to know the right people."

"And it pays to get this close to a hummingbird in captivity," I replied, taking pictures of the Lucifer, some of them capturing clearly his violet throat.

We stayed around the lodge all morning, nursing the banded and talking with other birders, most of whom were staying at the lodge. A Black-headed Grosbeak ate at a larger feeder. A White-breasted Nuthatch hopped headfirst down a nearby oak. A woman asked whether I had seen the Elegant Trogan yet.

"Elegant Trogan?" I repeated slowly, trying to think whether it was a species of hummingbird. "Uhhh, no . . . no, I haven't."

"Nor have I," she confessed.

A man sitting on the stone wall, watching a feeder asked, "You talkin' 'bout the Elegant Trogan? I saw it this morning about five-thirty. You haf'ta git up early to find that one." His tone suggested a major coup.

"Where d'ya find it?" I asked, trying to get a clue to what we were talking about.

"Farther up the trail. A good mile beyond the parking area."

Ho-ho, said I to myself, *so there is a parking area somewhere.* During a pause in the conversation, I pulled out my bird book and surreptitiously looked up Elegant Trogan. At first glance I might have called the eleven-inch bird a parrot. That is to say it is, first of all, colorful. The book described it as a "rare summer resident in mountains of southeast Arizona" and went on to say the "iridescent male is unmistakable." Well, maybe. I was still making plenty of mistakes identifying "unmistakable characteristics" of hummingbirds. But I was having a wonderfully good time doing it.

Hunger at last persuaded Mack to relinquish her position in the recovery room. We made our way down the road to Heidi and lunch. Heidi was happy to get outside and chase the Acorn Woodpeckers that she'd been watching through the window. James Lane warned us in his guide to birding southeast Arizona that we'd have to share our lunch with these clowns if we chose to eat at this particular picnic spot. That seemed only fair in exchange for sitting under the live oaks beside a rushing mountain stream with a chance of seeing a Bridled Titmouse, Cassin's Kingbird, or a Hepatic Tanager. As we munched our lunch, scanned the trees, and reviewed the morning, raindrops began to fall. Thunder rumbled.

"Now aren't we glad we're not huffing up that hill to the campground?" I commented, grabbing the remnants of lunch and dashing for the motor home. Thunder reverberated against the canyon walls. Rain riveted the RV roof. It was still raining when we finished our fruit and Oreos.

"What now?" Mack asked as the storm subsided.

"Do you want to stay around another day and look for the Elegant Trogan at five tomorrow morning?"

"Not especially."

Five years later we would return to southeastern Arizona and spend two weeks tramping these streams, poking around sewage ponds, trudging through washes and lanes and canyons, mining the rich mother lode. But now, novices that we were, we'd seen the hummingbirds, a Mountain Chickadee, an Acorn Woodpecker, and a half a dozen other birds. How much more excitement could we stand? We were ready to move on.

That night in Picacho (pee-CHAH-cho) State Park fifty miles north of Phoenix, we were again the only ones in the campground. Another camper did come in, but without air conditioning, decided not to stay the night. The electrical storm that evening was pure Wagner.

Despite the blistering heat, I snapped the best picture of the trip that afternoon when a Harris Hawk lit on the twenty-foot saguaro at the foot of our rig. So intent was he on the prairie dogs scurrying in and out of their underground passages that he completely ignored my tripod and camera only partially hidden around the corner of the RV. With a three-hundred-millimeter lens, I picked up the black tip of his wickedly hooked beak, the yellow nostril in his white lores, his chestnut shoulder. The chestnut thighs look like pantalets below the richly black body. Ebony talons in contrast to his pale yellow feet and legs grasp the bulbous pink blossoms of the cactus. A single blossom of the saguaro complements the large white patch at the base of his tail.

Another lucky shot that afternoon caught a Chihuahuan Raven posed among five pink blossoms atop another saguaro. The light, or the breeze, at that moment revealed a patch of white neck-feathers. The white rarely shows on this bird, formerly called White-necked Raven.

Mack found the nest of a Cactus Wren in a jumping cholla. The rumor that the spines of the jumping cholla can actually jump out and attach themselves to passersby has been flatly denied by those who should know. However, when Mack removed her shirt a few hours after peering into the nest, she found a spine firmly embedded in her flesh. Try to tell her that spine didn't jump.

We continued to look for birds as we traveled through

Idaho into Wyoming and Yellowstone, where we saw White Pelicans, a Caspian Tern, and a pair of Trumpeter Swans. We added new species of gulls and sandpipers to the trip list, but essentially this maiden venture into the world of birding was an expedition to the hummingbirds of Ramsey and Madera Canyons. Eight of our forty-eight lifers were hummingbirds. The trip list was short compared to some three times as long that we'd tally on later trips West. But those seventy-five were challenging enough when I tried in review to sort out the varied color schemes—Yellow-billed, Rufous-backed, Red-eyed, White-necked, Brown-headed, Sulphur-bellied, Green-winged, Blue-throated, and Orange-crowned. In time, I believed, I would be able to match color, anatomy, and bird correctly.

The trip taught us many things, but nothing more obvious, perhaps, than "for everything there is a season" and the heat of July is not the season of choice for veteran birders in southeast Arizona. But, oh my, we did have a wonderful time, and it was kind of fun to have all those campgrounds, trails, and birds to ourselves.

Magic Birds in a Mystic Marsh

I looked in my heart when the wild swans went over—
And what did I see I had not seen before?
Only a question less or a question more;
Nothing to match the flight of wild birds flying.
                                        — Edna St. Vincent Millay

In *The Yearling*, Marjorie Kinnan Rawlings describes Jody and Pa Baxter's coming unexpectedly upon sixteen cranes dancing "a cotillion as surely as it was danced in Volusia." Two cranes stood alone, making a music that she describes as "part cry and part singing." Of the rest, an outer circle shuffled around a small group whose heads rose and fell, whose wings fluttered as they worked themselves into a frenzy. While Jody and his pa crouched, watching, two from the circle exchanged positions with the musicians. And the dance resumed.

Rawlings in 1938 was probably writing not from personal experience but from some old fisherman's tale, for by then the total population of Whooping Cranes in the whole country was fewer than fifty. By 1981 it had increased over seventy percent to eighty-one. Or eighty-seven, depending upon which bird book you read. None was in Florida. *Sandhill* cranes, yes. Thousands of Sandhills winter on Paynes Prairie. More are scattered throughout the state, but not the majestic white crane, which stands over four feet tall with a wingspan exceeding seven feet.

When Mack and I discussed a second birding adventure, I suggested Whooping Cranes near Rockport, Texas, a good choice for novice birders because they are so findable. After breeding in the freshwater marshes of Wood Buffalo National Park in Alberta, they migrate to Arkansas National Wildlife Refuge on the coast of Texas for the winter.

Off we went one February morning—Mack, Heidi, and I. Through Tallahassee, across the Apalachacola River into the central time zone, the motor home rattled. Probably Lake Pontchartrain was teeming with birds, but we charged on single-mindedly toward Rockport, camping the second night just short of Baton Rouge. The next morning we crossed the Mississippi and vagabonded along the elevated road over the bayous. The miles rolled by. Occasional raindrops splashed on the windshield. The air turned chilly.

"When's lunch?" Mack asked. "Heidi's getting hungry."

"*Who's* getting hungry?"

"Heidi."

"Well, tell Heidi she has a choice," I reported after checking the trip-tic. "A rest area is coming up shortly, just this side of Atchafalaya River. The next chance for a doggie biscuit is sixty miles beyond, about forty miles west of Lafayette."

"Heidi chooses the first one."

Rain was beating a light tattoo on the roof as we pulled into the roadside park.

"Heidi won't want to walk in this weather," Mack commented as I started to make our peanut butter and butter sandwiches.

"Maybe it will let up after lunch."

A sense of well-being prevailed as we ate and watched the raindrops fall. We were halfway to the Whooping Cranes. We'd stay around Houston tonight and reach Rockport tomorrow afternoon.

I watched the raindrops, very large now, plop against the windshield. Then I noticed slush accumulating on the wipers.

"Hey!" I said. "It's almost snowing. What are you going to do about that, Heidi?"

"Search me," she shrugged disconsolately.

Soon it *was* snowing. My first reaction was glee. I hadn't seen a snowflake in four years. I thought of the first year that I taught school. Upstairs in a four-room schoolhouse at the end of the village green in Amherst, New Hampshire, I was searching for relevance in an excerpt from Milton's *L'Allegro* in the only text the school board had provided for my combined junior-senior English class, Long's *History of English Literature*. This was the year to *do* English literature. We had scarcely got beyond

> Hence, loathed Melancholy,
> Of Cerberus and blackest Midnight born . . .

It defied translation. "Sadness born of a three-headed dog?" What had this to say to these farm youngsters?

> Haste thee, Nymph, and bring with thee
> Jest and youthful Jollity,
> Quips and Cranks and wanton Wiles,
> Nods and Becks and wreathed Smiles.

Teacher Ed had not prepared me for this. Had I chosen the wrong profession? As we struggled on to

> Then to the well-trod stage anon,
> If Jonson's learned sock be on . . .

something drew my attention to the window. A longing to escape? There, fluttering in the November air was a flurry of snowflakes.

"It's snowing!" I exclaimed with considerable verve. For

a moment "jest and youthful jollity" filled the room, and one young man *quipped*, "You're the first old person I ever knew who likes snow."

"It's enough to make you homesick, isn't it?" Mack said, noting my distraction.

"Well, who'da thunk it? Way down here near Ol' New Orleans!"

By the time we'd eaten our Oreos and tidied up, the ground was white.

"Where's the next campground?" Mack asked. "We don't have to drive in this."

"There's one in Lafayette, 'bout twenty miles."

"Let's stop there."

We continued circumspectly, happy a half hour later to put in at a well-appointed campground, and happy, too, to have chosen our own exit because the highway patrol closed Route 10 shortly after that. That's the Southern response to a once-in-every-two-or-three-years snowstorm. Next morning the snow was gone, the roads clear, but the cold persisted.

"If this keeps up, I'm going to need warmer clothes than anything I've brought," Mack said.

"Born to shop, you never miss an opportunity, do you?" I chided her. That's how we came to explore Victoria and buy two down-filled jackets that we'll have little call for back in Florida. But for which we were extremely grateful a couple of mornings later on Ted Appell's *Skimmer*. From November 1 to April 1, Captain Ted makes a four-hour, sixty-mile trip twice daily to view the cranes. He confidently offers a total refund if he doesn't find Whoopers.

But before the cranes and even before a campground, we came upon a bay full of ducks beside the highway almost in the center of Rockport. Until then I had never paid much attention to ducks. If it weren't a Muscovy, it must be a Mallard. This milling sea of duck, however, did get my attention.

The most distinctive ones had long, narrow, pointed tails extending at a forty-five-degree angle ten or twelve inches beyond the body—like old-fashioned hat pins. They were Northern Pintails. Some others had green heads like Mallards, but the colors on the breast and side were reversed. Smaller than Mallards, they had long, wide, flat bills, longer than the head itself. These were Northern Shovelers, their spatula-shaped bills well adapted for shoveling. Both Pintails and Shovelers feed without diving.

"They must be dabblers," I commented, trying to master the vocabulary. "But some others with white sides and gray backs are diving."

While Mack and I tried to decide whether *they* were Canvasbacks or scaups, a bystander who had been watching us pore over our bird guides said, "Check the bills. The scaups—both Lesser and Greater—have blue bills coming out at an angle from the head. The Canvasback's bill comes straight off the head like a ski slope." He pointed out Green-winged Teals, Redheads, and more, faster than I could locate them.

As we parted, I said, "Oh, what are those white-breasted ones standing up in the water?"

He looked perplexed and then asked with a smile, "All those white ones? They're the butts of the Pintails. Their heads are in the water."

A tall, long-legged bird with an incredibly long, curved bill fed at the edge of the water. I mean a bill as long as its legs. How could it eat with a beak like that? But it managed, driving that scythelike bill nine, ten inches into the sand again and again. I watched, fascinated by its agility in coping with such an appendage. It was our first encounter with a Long-billed Curlew, a lifer, as were most of the ducks we'd been studying.

Mack's niece Jean flew into Corpus Christi after work that evening, rented a car, and joined us at the Sandollar Campground in Falmouth on the north side of Rockport. Early the next morning, we were headed for Aransas Wildlife Refuge. Although best known as the winter home of the Whooping Cranes, this 54,289-acre sanctuary has most of the waders and shorebirds to be found anywhere in Texas, and many other species, too. Two on our wish list after the cranes were Crested Caracara and White-tailed Hawk.

But first the cranes. The isolated area that they inhabit on the far side of the refuge is closed to the public, but a short way along the motor road, an observation tower provides an overview of the refuge. We scaled the tower. I scanned the grassy salt marshes through the scopes. A park ranger assured me that the white specks were Whooping Cranes.

"Are you sure they're not White Pelicans?" this doubting Thomas asked.

"I promise," she said.

The joy of the long-anticipated moment was diluted with frustration.

"I've come a thousand miles to look at specks?"

"To get a good view, you must go out by boat," she told me.

"How good a view?"

"That depends on how lucky you are."

"We'll know tomorrow. We're going out with Captain Ted."

"He's the best," she said.

"Let's continue around the motor loop," Jean suggested, "and see what we find."

The road winds through a variety of habitats. A thick stand of Virginia live oaks might have produced Wild Turkeys, but it didn't. We found instead a Black-crested Titmouse and an Eastern Phoebe. Twelve more miles turned up neither a Crested Caracara nor a White-tailed Hawk. Several Collared Peccaries (Javalinas) crossed our path. One little one padding along beside its mom cried, "Wait up! What's the hurry?" A Sora Rail paddled in a marshy slough, unaware it was our first lifer of the day. A lone Eared Grebe swam in a roadside pond. Its upturned bill gave it an aristocratic air.

"Keep looking for the White-tailed Hawk," Jean reminded us, but not until after we left the refuge and were nearly back to the main road did Mack cry, "There's a hawk."

"Where?"

"Ahead on the left. It's soaring in circles."

It disappeared behind some trees.

"Drat!" I said. "We've lost it."

"No, it's coming up again on the left."

All binoculars homed in on it. It crossed the road in front of us, flying low.

I said, "It's too dark. It has rusty shoulders. I think it's a Harris Hawk."

"The White-tailed Hawk *is* dark and it *does* have rusty shoulders," Jean said, checking the book. "We need to see the tail. Where is it now?"

"Back on the left, headed for the refuge."

"I've got it," Mack called excitedly, "and it does have a distinct, black line across a white tail."

It circled once more obligingly. Both Jean and I confirmed the diagnostic marking. That was a real prize because although it is common from the Mexico border to Argentia, it is rare north of the border.

"What now?" Jean asked.

"Lunch, maybe?" Mack suggested hopefully. "Heidi must be wondering where her biscuits are."

We hadn't gone half a mile before we came upon a field carpeted with Snow Geese taking a siesta. It was too great a sight not to film. They must have had a watchgoose, though. No sooner did Jean stop the car than the field burst into a squawking cloud of beating wings. What a picture!

After lunch a great Blue Heron stalked the parking lot at Sun-Gun Resort in Capano Bay as though he were in charge of valet parking.

"Photo opportunity!" Jean cried. The heron had other ideas when he saw our cameras. White Pelicans rocked gently in the water at the edge of the parking lot. A lone sandpiper, bobbing and teetering as though it were losing its balance, pecked in the sand.

"It has a nervous tic," I commented.

"An unmistakable characteristic of the Spotted Sandpiper, according to the book," Jean said.

"A Spotted Sandpiper without spots? How come?" I wanted to know.

"It's in its winter plumage," Mack explained.

"I wonder whether it bobs in its sleep," I mused.

Another lifer presented itself before we left the beach, a Wilson's Plover with a wide, black neck-band, pinkish legs, and a heavy black bill. With those two notches in our belts, we drove on to Goose Island and Big Tree, the national champion Virginia Live Oak. A chain-link fence protects the mammoth tree from souvenir chippers. With a circumference of over a hundred feet, its sturdy branches grow almost horizontally, each one as big as a tree itself.

At the beach just beyond Big Tree, identifying several new birds was not child's play. Fortunately we had three opinions to work with so that ultimately disagreements and doubts led to a consensus about American Wigeons, Marbled Godwits, and Willets, which were sharing the beach with more familiar Black Skimmers, Brown Pelicans, and Little Blue Herons.

I was dividing my attention between three Roseate Spoonbills spooning at the water's edge and the Green Kingfisher that we had finally definitively identified when a strange-acting bird appeared a few feet out in the surf. First it tiptoed like a New York debutante through the puddles of a spring shower and then suddenly dashed a few feet head down like a football tackle before changing the tempo to some graceful ballet steps accompanied by the fluttering of wings, only to stop midpirouette and with the deliberation of a chess player about to say "check" snatched something from the water with its pink, black-tipped beak. Its legs were as cobalt blue as the body itself.

"Is that for real?" I asked in puzzlement.

"A Little Blue Heron with Saint Vitus' dance?" Jean proposed. It continued its jaunty performance while we perused our field guides. Consensus was easy. It was a Reddish Egret, which raises its wings to shade the water, the better to see the fish. Clever bird. Once seen, never forgotten. All species are inimitable, but the Reddish Egret strikes me as being more inimitable than others.

At a bend in the beach, Mack set up the scope to scan for Whooping Cranes and did find a pair slightly larger than the previous spots. Intellectually exciting, but nothing to set my pulse racing yet. As we scanned for more, a flock of thirty or forty Whistling Black-bellied Ducks flew into an adjacent field. Their white wings, edged with a band of black, spread three feet tip to tip. To see that flock drop from the sky and drift in for a landing did quicken my pulse. Poetry in motion! Not for the first time that day, I wished Marjory and Eleanor from Connecticut could have shared the moment.

The next morning, bundled in down-filled jackets, wound in scarves, laden with binoculars and cameras, we set out with Captain Ted and forty-three other birders for the salt marshes on the outer edge of Aransas Refuge. The weather was clear and cold. All but the most stalwart stayed in the sheltered enclosure on the main deck, content to watch through glass the three families of Great Blue Herons on nests atop oil riggings in the harbor.

Herons were only the beginning. Captain Ted spotted

others faster than I could raise my binoculars. Hooded Merganser, Blue-winged Teal, Snowy Egret . . .

"Tri-colored Heron at ten o'clock." He explained the system of locating birds for others. Straight ahead would be twelve o'clock. Directly to our right, three o'clock, right behind, six, and so on. Without binoculars he identified Black-crowned Night Heron, Sandwich Tern, Bonaparte's Gull.

"Common Loon, two o'clock."

The *Skimmer,* specially built to cruise in shallow water, approached the grassy edges of several islands, with Ted calling out "Long-billed Dowitcher, Common Goldeneye, Bufflehead, Black-bellied Plover." But not *black-bellied* in the winter, I noted.

"Peregrine Flacon at nine o'clock," he reported. That took some of us scrambling to the upper deck.

"Uncommon to rare in winter," the *National Geographic Field Guide* says of the Peregrine Falcon. I was too slow. All I saw was a speck in the sky, too indistinct to identify.

We idled near a sandbar. Masses of gulls—Herring, Laughing, Bonaparte's—scrounched in the sun. Sanderlings scurried along the sand. Ruddy Turnstones frenetically lived up to their name.

Someone pointed out Willets in their somber, gray winter plumage. *What a nondescript bird,* I thought. Then one raised its wings, revealing striking broad bands of black, white, black. "My apologies," I said. " I didn't know you had that ace up your sleeves."

"Oystercatchers, American Oystercatchers," Ted called out. I finally managed to get my binoculars on them. They were probing the sand with the largest, thickest, vivid red-orange beaks I've ever seen.

"What are they finding?" I asked the man next to me at the rail.

"Shellfish," he said.

"Everybody see the American Avocets?" came over the loudspeaker. "Beyond the oystercatchers at about two-thirty." They were sweeping the water with long, thin, needlelike bills. Even in winter gray, they outdo the Willets because their striking black-white-black wings show whether they are flying or at rest.

Off we went again, the excitement mounting. I stayed on the upper deck, straining for the first crane. Soon came the word that we'd been waiting for: "Family of Whoopers at eleven o'clock." Anyone who had not already staked a claim on the upper deck scrambled up the stairs. "We'll get closer," Ted promised.

He cut the motor, and we drifted toward the tall grasses where the cranes were feeding. "We'll find more in various isolated areas. They are extremely territorial. One pair and one chick, rarely two, may claim as much as twenty acres, returning to it year after year. No other crane dares trespass."

Approximately a hundred breeding cranes with their young have returned to the refuge this winter. Under no circumstances will Ted go close enough to disturb his birds, but with binoculars, I can see the red facial skin of the adults. I'm excited now. This is what I came to Rockport to see. We came upon another family, farther away but easily discernible. Occasionally one fed alone. "Teenagers," Ted explained. We marvel that the young, hatched last spring in Alberta, have survived the long migration.

"Most of them do," he said. He pointed out a family of four: a second-year juvenile and one fledged last spring. Obviously Ted has a close and special relationship with his birds. He calls many of them by name, can tell you how old each one is, how many offspring a pair has had, what misfortunes some have encountered. He speaks of each one as he would a member of his family. In fact, they are his extended family. Again I thought *Eleanor and Marjory should be here.*

On the return trip, we cruised by some of the shell islands where from April to July (after the Whooping Cranes migrate north) Captain Ted takes birders to see the rookeries of Snowy and Cattle Egrets, Tricolored and Blue Herons, Roseate Spoonbills, White Ibis, gulls galore, and the largest Reddish Egret rookery in the world. He continued to identify birds, but most of us had settled back into the protection of the lower lounge to talk about the cranes and wonder how our pictures would come out.

That evening I asked Mack whether she thought we could persuade Marge and Eleanor to join us on a repeat weekend next year.

"Bet we could. They could fly into Corpus Christi and we'd fetch them from there."

They didn't require any persuading. It was arranged, and the next February, Mack and I set out again to see those magic birds. This time, alas, without Heidi, who had left us after fifteen and a half years to chase squirrels in doggie heaven. Actually she had always thought squirrels more fun than birds. Except for robins. In five days we would meet our friends in Corpus Christi.

We crossed the Atchafalaya River without a sign of last year's snowflakes. But word passed along the CB suggested we might run into freezing rain a hundred miles farther ahead.

Late afternoon we were nearing Lake Charles. The temperature had dropped into the thirties, and rain had started. Two truck drivers were chatting on CB.

"How'd ya do on ol' Charley?"

"Crept down the bugger. You?"

"Skated 'n' slipped."

We knew well the bridge they were talking about. It rises like a ski lift and appears to end abruptly in the sky. We'd be there ourselves in another half hour.

"Goin' far tonight?" one asked.

"Short o' Houston. Heard everything's a snarl there."

"Yeah, frozen solid."

Mack turned and asked me whether there was a campground between us and Lake Charles.

"No, nothing 'til we get the other side of the bridge."

We were already approaching the outskirts of the heavily industrialized city. Lumber, oil, chemicals, rubber . . . you name it. They had all been attracted to the city's deep-water port, as we at the moment were being unattracted. Three lanes of traffic churned west, splashing rain and muck in all directions.

"What do you think?" Mack asked. I was selfishly glad it was her turn to drive.

"I don't think we have much choice at this moment. Stay in the right lane, go as slowly as you want, and keep going." Rush-hour traffic was beginning to build. A sand truck passed, spewing sand. Mack had no problem climbing the bridge and cautiously maneuvered down the other side. Twenty-three miles later, we pulled into a five-star campground. Several campers lounged in the office, playing cards and yakking. Five or six heads snapped up the moment I opened the door.

"Which way d'ya come?" a chorus of voices asked.

"From the east."

"Oh," they groaned. "Nobody's coming from the west."

We hastened to hook up. Dark was deepening. Mack then scouted the campground to size up the situation. Returning, she said, "I don't think we're going anywhere tomorrow. Some campers have been here two nights waiting to continue west, and the temperature is still going down."

"What about Eleanor and Marge? We're supposed to pick them up day after tomorrow."

"Can we make it from here in a day?"

"It's possible. Let's see what tomorrow brings. We can phone them if necessary either at home or at the airport."

35

We turned our attention to the matter at hand, how to keep the lines from freezing tonight. The temperature was already in the twenties. Campers conferred with each other, waterlines were left dripping, furnaces ran throughout the night. For the most part, everyone survived unscathed albeit a little chilly around the edges.

The usual campground exodus did not start at dawn. Some waterlines had to be thawed. Hairdryers were handy for that task. Word was passed along from a trucker: the road to Houston is open. By nine o'clock some who had been ice-bound two days and were suffering from cabin fever staunchly set out for the west. Gradually the campground began to empty. Shortly after ten Mack and I followed.

The sun was brilliant. The temperature hung around freezing. In Houston our route turned south toward Victoria and Rockport. For miles we drove through a world of frosty white. Unlike New England ice storms I had known, with ice-laden branches shimmering and tinkling in the aftermath of the storm, the Texas version was only knee-high. Every blade of roadside grass, every sprig of stubble was an upside-down icicle. As far as eye reached, the un-treed plains sparkled in the sunshine.

We camped that night in Edna, reached the Sandollar campground the next morning, rented a car, and met our friends on schedule.

Returning from the airport, Mack suddenly exclaimed, "What were *those*? In the field? On the left? I'm going to bang a U-y and go back." They were geese, but what kind? Not Canada or Snow and too large for Brant. What else could be on the Texas coast?

"Greater White-fronted," Marjory was the first to conclude as we studied our field guides.

"That's trip bird number two," Eleanor said. "We saw a Great-tailed Grackle in Corpus Christi."

Since we pass the Connie Hagar Refuge, where Mack and I saw pintails, wigeons, scaup, and more last year, we planned to stop. But did we have a choice? Once Marge spotted the bay full of ducks, she was almost out of the car before it stopped.

"When do we see the Whooping Cranes?" Eleanor wanted to know as we drove on.

"I'm proposing we wait 'til Sunday not only to save the best for last but mainly because Becky, who will join us this evening, has to leave Sunday morning and she doesn't mind missing the Whooping Crane trip."

"Who's Becky?"

"She's a friend and science teacher from Austin, who includes birding in her science courses. She brings students here on field trips and knows where to find everything we want to see."

"Sounds good."

"And my niece is coming from Dallas tomorrow night," Mack added. "She was here last year and can't wait to get back."

With the agenda established and Eleanor and Marge settled in their motel at the end of the campground, we drove to Goose Island beach with a stop at Big Tree. After ohs and ahs and photographs of the national Virginia Live Oak, we went in search of Roseate Spoonbills, Tricolored Herons, ducks, and, I hoped, a Reddish Egret. Marjory and Eleanor know shorebirds better than Mack and I. They helped us distinguish between Dunlins and Sanderlings and various sandpipers. We scoped unsuccessfully for Whooping Cranes. Three Black-shouldered Kites flew overhead. A Northern Harrier hunted in the marsh. I was about to give up on the Reddish Egret when one flew in and started its antics.

"What a Nervous Nellie," Eleanor said, "but 'twill do for a lifer."

"Don't you have to teach on Friday?" Marjory asked Becky that evening.

"Ordinarily, yes, but Ev wrote my superintendent, extolling my birding skills and asking whether I could be released tomorrow to guide a birding group from Florida and New England. And *voila,* here I am, at your service."

The next morning Becky said, "Okay, ladies, what is your desire?"

"Sandhill Cranes," Marge was quick to reply.

"Crested Caracara, White-tailed Hawk, Peregrine Falcon," Mack, Eleanor, and I said simultaneously.

"Sandhills and Crested Caracara won't be difficult. We'll need a little more luck for the raptors. Let's start out west of town. We'll get into the country, look for some farmland."

Within five miles Marjory spotted three Sandhill Cranes beside the road. She was so excited that she stammered, "Sa-sa-sand. There. Ohhh!"

"We'll spook 'em if I stop," Becky said, "so I'll drive by very slowly. We'll see more. I promise." The cranes went right on eating.

"Lifer," whispered Eleanor.

"So close," Marjory murmured. "Thank you, Becky."

"You're welcome. You know I got up before daylight and planted them there."

A little farther along, Becky stopped beside a pasture with a congregation of vultures. "Okay, ladies, let's look these vultures over carefully because caracaras sometimes hang out with vultures. Look for a white throat and orange-red facial skin at the base of the beak, but not as much red as the Turkey Vulture. It's a little smaller than a Turkey Vulture, too." We scrutinized every bird without finding a caracara.

"Don't despair. The day's hardly started," Becky consoled us. "Keep alert. We're in Crested Caracara country—habitat at least. Of course we can always go to Mexico. That's really their country. It's the national bird of Mexico, the Mexican eagle."

We poked along until Marjory called out again, "Sandhills! At the back of that field. I think. Aren't they?" They were. Out we all piled. They were too far away to be disturbed, but oh, what a picture through binoculars. We counted twenty-five.

"You have a birder's eye, Marjory," Becky commented as we rode on.

A few more miles into the country, Becky slammed the brakes. "There's your caracara on the right. About one o'clock. I'll drive a little closer." But Mack was already out of the car. She doesn't take a lifer sitting down. Next to the Whooping Crane, this was the most important bird on her wish list.

The day produced neither a White-tailed Hawk for Eleanor nor a Peregrine Falcon for me. After lunch, though, we came upon some Common Snipe feeding at the edge of a marsh. They lived up to their reputation of being skittish. At the first alert, off they flew in a zigzag pattern, exposing their brown rumps and orange tails.

Jean arrived that evening in time for dinner at the Sandollar pavilion. We dined on the catch of the day and toasted Sandhill Cranes, Crested Caracaras, and Common Snipe. And tomorrow the Aransas Wildlife Refuge.

Shortly after the turn onto the refuge road, a White-tailed Hawk was circling in almost the identical spot where we found him last year, a trip bird for all of us and a lifer for Eleanor and Marjory.

The only new bird in the refuge for any of us was an Olive-sided Flycatcher unless our friends wanted to count the white specks they saw from the observation tower. Most of the birds that Mack and I found last year were there plus a covey of Bob Whites. The Javalinas performed better for us this time.

A herd of nearly twenty—old ones, young ones, and in between—was grazing or snoozing on the lawn around the visitors center. Deer munched tender leaves not far from the gazebo where we ate our sandwiches du jour. Later on the motor route, armadillos rooted along the roadside oblivious to the passing traffic. But more and more, our thoughts turned to the Whooping Crane ride the next day.

"I wish the crane excursion were only two hours," Eleanor said. I had stressed how cold the offshore wind could be and that they should be sure to bundle up. She repeated her wish the next morning when we woke to cold, wind, and thick fog. "Or maybe one hour," she said laughing.

"Do you want to skip the trip?" I asked. "You don't have to go."

"Well, I do want to see a Whooping Crane."

"Will he go out in this fog?" Marjory wondered. As did I. Visibility was almost ground zero.

When eight o'clock arrived, so did all of us in heavy jackets, woolen scarves, earmuffs, and stocking caps. Jean and I were weighed down with cameras. Last-minute count assured no one had forgotten her binoculars. Cautiously Captain Ted maneuvered through the fog. The herons on the oil riggings were scarcely discernible. I was feeling terribly responsible for getting my friends to this point. We'd promised them Whoopers. If the fog didn't lift, could we see them? For obvious reasons Ted was not identifying many birds.

Twenty minutes into the bay, the fog dissipated as if by the waving of a magic wand. "How'd he do that?" folks asked each other.

"Bufflehead, American Wigeon, Hooded Merganser, Greater Yellowlegs, Black-crowned Night Heron, Black Skimmers, Eared Grebe, Royal Tern . . ." Ted called out. He identified over thirty-five species before we reached the cranes.

"Someone wanted Crested Caracaras?" he asked over the

loudspeaker. "I'll find you caracaras. Stand by." At least two minutes elapsed before he said, "Caracaras at two o'clock. Look in the brush at the edge of the water." As we came alongside, a pair flushed. All my camera caught were streaked rears and some yellow feet.

How did he know they were there? I wondered. He has remarkable eyesight. But *that* far away? When I asked him, he just smiled mysteriously.

As we approached the cranes, I was as excited as I'd been the year before. I knew we'd see a few families at fairly close range. What I didn't know was that six cranes were going to fly low right over the *Skimmer*. I was on the upper deck ready for them. ZZZst, zzzst, zzzst went the cameras. Brillig!

"How are you going to beat that?" Marge asked after she caught her breath. I knew she and Eleanor were happy to be nowhere else in the world at that moment.

We saw several more families of cranes. Ted called them by name and told their stories. Back at the pavilion after four and a half hours on the bay, I heard Eleanor tell someone as she disembarked, "I wish we could have stayed two more hours."

Efforts have been made to establish a Whooping Crane colony in Idaho, but so far without success. Another plan is underway to reintroduce the Whoopers into Florida. But as of this writing, the best spot to view the "magic birds in a mystic marsh" is from Ted Appell's *Skimmer.*

Thief River Falls

The flowers appear on the earth;
the time of the singing of
birds is come.

—Song of Solomon

I must have been dreaming about Alaska when I lost my way in the northwest corner of Michigan's Upper Peninsula. Or maybe the purr of the motor home had lulled me into irresponsibility. "I think I've gone astray," I said to Mack, who was trying to take twenty winks after lunch. "Can you find Baraga on the trip-tic? In five more miles, we'll be in Baraga."

"I don't find it anywhere," she said after a minute. "What did we go through last?"

"Michigamme, but that was back thirty miles or more."

"Have we been through Covington?"

"Not that I know of."

"Do you know what route we're on?"

"Forty-one."

"Well," after another pause, "you need to bang a U-y and go back to where forty-one and twenty-eight split. We should be on twenty-eight."

As I pulled onto the shoulder to make the U-y, Mack cried, "Hold it! Look on the lake." I pulled farther off the road and parked. We got out for a closer look at two male swans that were wasting no love on each other. Talk about defending your territory! With hissing and great flapping of wings, one was

42

driving the other from the lake or at least this corner of the lake.

A passerby with two little children in hand said the *persona non grata* was a widower. Since Mute Swans mate for life, my sympathies immediately went out to the harassed one, now retreating from the onslaught. The attacker, after assuring he had made his point, smoothed his feathers and sedately swam off to his mate on the other side of the lake. Mack and I walked down the path with the woman and her children. They had brought bread to feed the swans. At the prospect of a handout, the cob and his mate glided effortlessly toward us, their necks gracefully curved, their wing feathers raised. They looked like the swan boats on the Boston Common. As they drew closer, we saw three downy yellow cygnets snuggled between Mama's raised wings, as sweet as cherubs on a float in the Rose Bowl Parade. One slid into the water to try its luck with a piece of soaked bread, but the other two contentedly surveyed the world from the coziness of Mama's back while Mom and Pop, momentarily losing their dignity, gobbled up all the bread the children had brought and hissed for more.

A roll of film later, we were on the road again.

"At least the fifteen-mile detour was not in vain," Mack commented as we headed south. At the junction of routes forty-one and twenty-eight, I turned west toward Wisconsin.

We camped that night not far from a school named Chief-Big-Bug-O-Gi-Shig. I suppose a child could learn to spell that. But how does it sound in a basketball cheer? A pair of orioles fed their young in a nest near our rig. The next morning their flutelike calls piped us on our way.

Not five miles out of town, a doe leaped across the road ahead of us. Bambi, a miniature of Mama, bounded like a rubber ball behind her. We followed the shores of Lake Superior in its fog most of the morning. Wisconsin, famous for its cheeses, deserves mention, too, of its wayside flowers.

Streams of lupine lined the highways, blends of reds (mostly Indian paintbrush) and yellows, whites and blues, sometimes solid carpets of varied wild flowers.

The ultimate goal of this present expedition was Alaska. In Edmonton, Alberta, we would join other birding campers for an Alaskan adventure. Our immediate goal, however, was to bird around Thief River falls, Minnesota. Becky Huffman, a friend dedicated enough to birding to drive from Austin, Texas, would join us there for two or three days.

Thief River Falls has within a radius of sixty miles five large, managed wildlife areas. We were going to sample as many as time allowed, starting the first afternoon with the Wetlands, Pines and Prairie Audubon Sanctuary. En route to it, we came upon a stand of trees chock 'o block full of Black-billed Magpies. During the brief photo stop, I learned what "to chatter like a magpie" means.

Penny, a German shepherd, and her master met us at the edge of the sanctuary, where they live. As we talked Mr. Sparkman said, "Penny, go find Rosie." Penny disappeared inside a shed and soon returned with Rosie, an eight-week-old raccoon, scampering behind her. Rosie was quite agreeable to being held and photographed. Shortly after Penny returned her to the shed, Mr. Sparkman offered to walk with us through some of the sanctuary trails. And where he goes Penny goes. I've had more knowledgeable bird guides than Penny but none happier to be included. What had been a dripping, muddy morning had turned into a gorgeous, warm afternoon. We were happy to be strolling through the wetlands, pines and prairies of Minnesota with someone willing to talk with us about birds.

An hour later, back at the entrance of the sanctuary, the first members of the Audubon Club were appearing with goodies for a potluck supper. "From Florida?" someone asked in a tone that made me wonder whether I had said Mars.

"And Texas! You must stay and join us in our potluck," added another. We protested that we must be on our way.

"To where?" a woman challenged. For which I had no quick reply. We did stay and talk while others gathered, bringing their potato salads, baked bean casseroles, homemade cinnamon buns, and chocolate brownies. Soon the campfire was crackling. We continued to mingle with the growing crowd. Each introduction was acknowledged with an amazed, "from Florida and Texas! My, my!"

"You must stay," I was urged for the third or fourth time. The aroma of fried onions reached my nostrils.

"I'll check with my friends," I said and went in search of Mack.

As I approached, I heard her say, "I'll see what Ev and Becky say." The result, of course, was that we stayed and had a wonderful time there under the pines beside a flower-lined mirror lake, picking up several tips about birding in the area.

"What about moose?" I asked. "I want to get a picture of a moose with a great rack lifting his head against the backdrop of a peachy-coral sunset. A sort of

The stag at eve had drunk his fill
Where danced the moon on Monan's rill."

"I don't know about a huge rack or Monan's rill," a man said, "but you might see a moose around Goose Lake in the Pembine Wildlife Management Area."

Another added, "It's not far from here. I can give you directions. This is about the time of evening they come to the lake to drink."

Warmly entertained and amply fed, Becky, Mack, and I said our thank yous, urged our hosts to look us up in Florida or Texas, and set out to find Goose Lake. Whether it was Goose Lake or not, we did find a small, marshy pond on the "Historic

Pembine Trail." Among the watery grasses swam a Red-necked Grebe with babies, a lifer for both Mack and me. A deer bounced through the field and crossed the road. But as far as moose were concerned, it was, as Becky said, a wild moose chase. A faint light still filled the sky when we returned to camp in the city park at ten o'clock. We were being gradually introduced to the long days we'd find in Alaska.

The next evening we were back at Goose Lake. Becky recognized a hollow, croaking **conck-a-taconck** as the call of an American Bittern on its breeding ground. I would have dismissed it as a frog. Though we might have been staring straight at it, none of us could see it. A Veery called from a nearby bush, its clear, flutelike notes rolling down the scale. But we couldn't find it either. 'Twould be two more years before Mack and I would see our first Veery on the Dry Tortugas in migration, not here in its natural habitat.

On one side of the road, a flock of Yellow-headed Blackbirds fed in a field. On the other Black Terns wheeled in a frenzy of whirls like Fourth of July sparklers in their erratic pursuit of insects over the marsh. They are a striking bird in flight, with black head and body and with black underwing coverts all in sharp contrast to the white of the rest of the wing. They would have stolen the show that evening even if they had not been lifers.

Grasses glistened in the soft light of sunset. Fence posts marched silently into infinity along the sandy track. Reluctant to disturb the peace, we loitered beside the car. As we stood, a Ruffed Grouse appeared in the field and moved toward us, the third lifer Goose Lake had produced in two evenings. It was a friendly sort, following us for some distance along the road's edge as we drove slowly away.

The next day at the Agassiz National Wildlife Refuge, I asked about moose. "Oh, you and your moose," Becky spoofed.

"You might see one—or more," the woman at the desk told me, "but the best time is either early morning or dusk. The refuge has about 250. So they are out there. You'll be more likely to see white-tailed deer. Be quiet, patient, and alert, and there's no telling what you'll see."

"Foxes?"

"Maybe."

"Or loons?"

"Common loons, yes. but I'll tell you what you won't see. We have the only resident pack of eastern grey wolves in any of the national refuges of the lower forty-eight states. They travel the entire range in winter but stay in the uplands to the east the rest of the year." She handed us a key, giving access to the auto trails. "The roads cover only a dot of this huge refuge," she said. "Four or five miles are well maintained. Use your judgment about any of the others. They can be wet and slippery. Some are impassable. It could be a long walk back." We thanked her, said we'd be careful, and went on our way.

Most of the songbirds had migrated. Tree Swallows, blue-birds, and some woodpeckers were still around. Becky identified a flash of yellow with a black mask as a Common Yellowthroat. That was a first. Mack saw a female American Redstart; Becky saw a male. I was still looking when we left Thief River two days later. Somewhere in the refuge was a flock of White Pelicans. However, I saw only one—skimming along a stream. The orange knob on its yellow bill was a mark of breeding. For the most part, the birds that day were gulls and water fowl. For the most part, that is, except for one owl.

"What's that in the tree up ahead on the right?" I asked.

"Looks like an owl," Mack said.

"In the daytime?"

"Could be," Becky replied. "Some are diurnal."

It was an owl, a Great Horned Owl, a big fellow nearly two

47

feet from ear tip to tail tip. Becky slowed the car to a crawl. I brought the camera to my eye.

"Shoot," Mack said just as the owl flew. At the next tree, it settled again. Becky drew closer. I had it in the viewfinder.

"Now!" Mack directed as it flew. In this fashion we proceeded from tree to tree until I finally thought *enough of this* and shot a picture that was identifiably an owl but not recognizably a Great Horned Owl.

"Let's do gulls," Becky suggested. "Do you have a Franklin's Gull on your life list?"

"Not yet."

"Well, you do now. Many of these catching insects over the marshes are Franklin's. They have a black head like the summer Laughing Gull, but they are a little smaller and most easily distinguished from the Laughing Gull by the white spots on their wing tips."

"According to this brochure the woman gave us, Franklin's Gulls breed here in a colony of up to 25,000 birds," I added.

"But they're not all Franklin's squawking out there," Mack observed. "Some are terns."

"Right," Becky said.

Under her tutelage I learned that Common and Forester's terns are almost identical except for their tails. "Check the tails," Becky told us. "The Common are dark on the outside and white in the middle. The Forester's are light on the outer edge and white in the middle. It's that easy." But when they sped by me with those gorgeous forked tails, I could have caught a shooting star in my bare hands as easily as tell what color edged the tail. I was satisfied to say a tern in flight is a beauteous thing.

For the most part, as I started to say, the day was spent among the water birds—Ruddy Ducks, Mallards, Northern Shovelers, Gadwalls, American Coots. One family of coots had reached the rusty feather stage; another looked like fuzzy tennis balls with beaks. The latter bounced on the surface, trying to get the hang of that funny little jump their parents do as they dive for yummy vegetation floating below the surface. A Sora Rail pecked nervously in the weeds at the edge of the marsh. A Black-crowned Night Heron stood glumly staring into space. Redheads and Ring-necked Ducks, Blue-winged teals, Wood Ducks (those most handsome of all ducks) and Pied-billed Grebes foraged among the duckweed, contail, and spikerush, ignoring us as we compared and identified the various species. On a log mid-marsh, three Double-crested Cormorants perched meditatively. A lone Red-tailed Hawk flew overhead, screaming a harsh **keeeer, keeeeer, keeeer**. No moose wandered into view.

'Twas late afternoon before we headed back to Friendship Garden Campground. On the way we passed a newly plowed field dotted with Yellow-headed Blackbirds. Only their yellow heads stood out against the dark soil.

"Looks like a field of egg yolks," I commented. They are a very showy bird in flight—those dark brown bodies, yellow heads, and two white spots on their wings.

We were too tired after our homemade spaghetti supper to go back to Goose Lake to look for moose. Becky and Mack took their twenty-five-cent metered showers and I my in-house free one and called it a good day. In the cool of evening, we sat beside the motor home, enjoying the birds in the city park—robins, swallows, a Yellow Warbler (a lifer), goldfinches, Cedar Waxwings, and a family of orioles in an elm tree by the river.

"Where to today?" Becky asked at breakfast the next morning.

"We have several choices," I said, browsing through the brochures. "Thief River Wildlife Management area thirty-five miles from here has Golden and Bald eagles and Black-billed

Magpies. Hayes Lake features Bald Eagle, Gray Jays, Spruce Grouse, and fall migration."

"Forget that. This is spring."

"What about Beltrami Island State Forest? It has Great Gray Owl, Spruce Grouse, Black-backed and Three-toed woodpeckers, Connecticut and sixteen other breeding species of warblers."

"That's it," cried Mack. "A Connecticut Warbler could make me very happy."

"Becky?"

"Sounds fine to me."

'Twas a good choice. Becky was a big help in identifying warblers. We had three lifers before lunch—Tennessee, Mourning, and Nashville. Plus a Black-billed Cuckoo. Like the Agassiz refuge yesterday, Beltrami Island State Forest was once covered by the glacial waters of Lake Agassiz. The sandy ridges created by that ancient lake are covered today with pines and surrounded by large expanses of lowlands and peat bogs.

The weather was ideal for birding, the temperature having risen from fifty-two at six o'clock to eighty degrees Fahrenheit by noon. However, 90 percent of today's birding was done from the car because huge flies swarmed around us like bees in a hive. The car drew them like a magnet. I've never seen so many, so big, so loud, so persistent. Fortunately they didn't bite. Unfortunately the mosquitoes did. Not deterred by these realities of wetlands, we spent five hours along the fifteen miles of the Red Lake section of the forest.

Unlike yesterday, today's birding was mostly among trees. In addition to the four lifers, we saw Yellow-billed Sapsuckers, Rose-breasted Grosbeak, Ruby-crowned Kinglets, a Pileated Woodpecker and more—fifteen additions in all to our Thief River bird list. Plus we heard both a Veery and an American Bittern, but saw neither one.

On the way back to camp, I asked, "Not counting life birds, what was the most memorable moment of the day?"

"The Common Snipe," Mack said without hesitation. "Wasn't she *darling?*" We had come upon a snipe standing in the middle of the road. Now snipes are generally very flighty. Well, of course, most birds are, but snipes are extra shy. However, this one stood her ground, doing a funny little bobbing up and down with her whole body.

"She looks as though she's going to upchuck," I commented.

After what seemed at least a full minute, she turned and with dignity in every deliberate step she took returned to the side of the road from which she had come. Then instead of disappearing, she reversed once more and recrossed the road, this time with two tiny chicks in single line behind her.

"*Darling! Aren't they darling!*" Mack kept repeating.

"What was your memorable moment?" I asked Becky.

"The showy lady slippers," she said. "Need you ask?"

"When you slammed those brakes, crying 'Oh, my God!' I thought you must have seen either a two-headed Pileated Woodpecker or a moose calfing."

"First of all," she explained, "I'd never seen a *showy* lady slipper. It was a lifer for me. Secondly, this is the only place in the country where they grow and I was told back in town they'd finished blooming for the year. But they were at their peak!" She and I had risked flies, ticks, and mosquitoes, squatting around those posies taking pictures from every angle.

"What was your memorable moment, Ev?" Mack asked.

"The Bobolink you spotted on the utility line this morning. Boblinks and Baltimore (what they now call Northern) Orioles were part of my life when I was a kid on the farm in Connecticut. They and summer went together. But with the exception of one I saw five years ago in Canada, this was the first one I've seen in fifty years."

51

Back at camp, Becky said, "I hate to pull the curtain on all this good birding. We've only started to sample the area, but I have to get back to Austin."

"And we to Edmonton."

Becky left at six the next morning. Mack and I were not far behind after saying good-bye to the oriole babies. The parents were ferrying food to four mouths gaping at the nest's edge. A few days more and they would be on their own.

"How many birds, total, did we see around Thief River Falls?" Mack asked as she pulled the RV onto the highway.

"Seventy-five."

"How many lifers."

"Ten."

North Dakota: Route 2

The bird her punctual music brings
And lays it in its place.
Its place is in the human heart
And in the heavenly Grace.

—Emily Dickinson

We had built a couple of extra days into our Alaska itinerary for birding in North Dakota. Kevin Zimmer's *A Birder's Guide to North Dakota* offers a large menu. From it we had selected first J. Clark Salyer National Wildlife Refuge and three target birds: LeConte's Sparrow, Baird's Sparrow, and Chestnut-collared Longspur.

We camped in Rugby, not because it is the geographical center of North America, but because it is big enough to have rental cars. We were off early the next morning, a beautiful blue-sky day that was going to be hot but with a breeze. Finding a lifer we weren't even looking for before we reached the refuge boded well for the day. Unlike the sandpipers I had known, this Upland Sandpiper lives in grass country. It's a twelve-inch bird that characteristically stands on fence posts. There it was at seven o'clock that morning, posing on a fence post. We studied it until it flew and watched until it lit on another post, holding its wings erect a moment after landing, a defining characteristic of the Upland Sandpiper.

The Salyer Refuge runs fifty miles along the Souris River from Bantry, North Dakota, to the border of Manitoba. Mack asked at headquarters about our target birds.

"Are you going to take the twenty-two-mile auto tour through the refuge?" the ranger asked.

"We plan to," she said.

"You'll find markers along the trail describing what to look for at various points. You'll be going through several different habitats—marshes, wooded river bottoms, and sandhills. Look for your LeConte in the meadow of tall grass at marker number five. But they'll try your patience. They're there, but they stay hidden among the grasses."

"What about Baird's Sparrow and the Chestnut-collared Longspur?"

"Baird's is less likely. Only because it's farther west. Out around Kenmore."

"The Longspur?"

"Perhaps. Take your time. You'll find short trails where you can leave the car and get closer to the birds, especially the ducks."

The drive was almost aborted before it started. A pair of Killdeer with one baby was in a wheel track. The parents moved to the side, but the baby wouldn't leave the rut. And I could see why. The grasses towered over its wee head. It ran as fast as it could, squeaking "Help! Help! Help!" The parents did their broken-wing act but seemed helpless in persuading the infant to join them.

"A-ha," thought I. "Let me out, Mack. I'll catch it and hold it while you drive by." It was the tiniest and fuzziest little squeak imaginable, fitting right into the cup of my hand. It pooped (I'd have been nervous myself in its place) enough to almost cover the head of a pin. Placing it safely back in the track with nary a *thank you* from the frantic parents, I refrained from giving a lecture about other cars that might be coming this way.

As it turned out, we might have let the chick lead the way. We spent seven and a half hours on the twenty-two-mile drive, and the baby was probably going at least three miles an hour. During those seven and a half hours, we saw hundreds, probably thousands, of ducks. The refuge bands four thousand ducks a year, many of them later identified in South America, Mexico, and all over the United States.

We searched the grasses unsuccessfully at marker No. 5 for LeConte's Sparrow. Although Mack and I have identified nineteen species of sparrows in the past three years, we have at least ten more to go. But we didn't find them at Salyer's. Although we emerged from the birdland trail with no new birds, we had no regrets either. It had been a beautiful, scenic, photographing day.

"There's a grassland trail farther north," I reminded Mack.

"How far north?"

"'Bout seventeen miles."

"How long is the trail?"

"Five miles. We could walk it if it were earlier in the day."

"Can we drive it?"

"The guide says it's passable by car if it hasn't rained lately."

"I don't think it's rained here lately. What d'ya say?"

"It doesn't get dark 'til nearly eleven. Let's go for it."

We crept along through a sea of grass as high as the car windows. The tracks were barely discernible. Birds, flushed by our approach, instantly disappeared back into the grass or flew away. Finally one little chap popped up like a kernel of popcorn but dropped back down just ahead of the car.

"I think it was a sparrow," Mack said. It popped up again as though it were as curious as we. "It has a gray cheek."

"I saw a white stripe through the crown," I added.

"What d'ya think?"

"Could be," I said cautiously.

55

"Next time it comes up, notice whether the breast is kind of orangey."

"If there is a next time." There was.

"What d'ya think?" Mack asked again.

"I think it's being wonderfully cooperative." The third time it didn't disappear. Instead it lit on a blade of prairie grass, which arched slightly under the ha'penny weight. Perched not twenty feet from us, it lifted its head to the heavens, opened its little beak, and sang *tickity-tshshshsh-tick, tickity-tshshsh-tick*. From the field guide beside LeConte's Sparrow, I read, "(It) is fairly common but secretive; scurrying through matted grasses like a mouse. Song is a short, high insectlike buzz."

"That's it!" I cried. "Chalk one up for the day."

Not a hundred yards farther on, but we were traveling slowly, Mack said, "How'd you like to chalk up two for the day? Look at the tall clump of grass on the right." Before I could even check for a black triangle on a white tail, I saw a bright chestnut collar. That male in his breeding plumage looked scarfed for skiing.

"That's your Chestnut-collared Longspur. All five and a half inches of it," Mack said.

Near the exit from the grassland trail, some Red-winged Blackbirds were tormenting a Swainson's Hawk. As they flew in front of the car, one blackbird lit momentarily on the hawk's back, a remarkable sight through my binoculars.

"Do things always go as smoothly on your trips as you make them sound?" a friend once asked. "What about flat tires on lonely roads or broken water hoses? Do you ever run out of gas? Get lost?" Or, I might add, set a field of grass on fire with an overheated engine? The thought had gone through my head that afternoon.

To those queries I can relate one incident from North

Dakota that I could have lived without. I had never been so frightened in my life (well, except perhaps when I glissaded onto the Arapahoe Glacier in Colorado, but that was of my own choosing and no one else was endangered). We had rented a car in Minot in anticipation of an early start the next morning to Longspur Pasture still in search of a Baird's Sparrow. Not wanting a rented car to sit idle, we drove into town late afternoon, did a few errands, and found yesterday's *U.S.A. Today* at Albertson's supermarket. So far, so good. Back in the parking lot, the instant Mack shifted the 1985 Volkswagen Quantum into gear, it *shot* into the crowd of shoppers in front of us. Now Mack's a skillful driver, but in no way could she maneuver that missile gone wild through that parking lot without leaving mayhem behind us. In a split impulsive second, we were in reverse, crashing into two lines of empty grocery carts behind us. In the next impulsive second, she cut the ignition. The whole incident lasted probably no more than five or six seconds, only long enough to review a lifetime. A child was screaming, but miraculously no one was hurt. Even the grocery carts escaped serious injury.

Why a 1985 Volkswagen Quantum in 1989? Because between North Dakota's centennial celebration and Fourth of July weekend, it was the only car available. Mack thought perhaps forgetting to say "Rabbit, Rabbit" that morning for the first day of the month might have explained the stuck accelerator, but when Dorothy came from the rental agency, she said somebody must have said, "Rabbit, Rabbit" under her breath to have been so lucky.

"Do you want another car?" she asked.

"No, thank you," Mack and I replied in unison.

Back in camp with normal breathing restored, Mack asked, "What do you say to our just staying around camp tomorrow, do some chores, get caught up on correspondence? What do you say to that?"

"Sounds good to me. Baird's Sparrow can wait." And wait it did until we found it two years later in Oak Hammock Marsh north of Winnipeg.

Taking a break between chores the next day, I was talking with two women in the campground. They were from Saskatchewan and were interested in our upcoming trip to Alaska.

"Just you and your husband?" one finally asked.

"No, no husband," I replied.

"Just two women?" she gasped.

"And you're driving through Edmonton!" the other marveled.

Route 2 through North Dakota is straight. I mean s-t-r-a-i-g-h-t. From the sign "Roadside Picnic Table 2 Miles," I could see the picnic area. As the road humped along, we guessed distances.

"How far to that tower on the horizon?" I asked. Mack guessed three miles; I, two. It was five. Something in a little roadside pond caught Mack's eye, something smaller than the cows cooling their bellies. She banged a U-y for a closer look. It turned out to be a lifer, a Wilson's Phalarope. With it were gulls, Marbled Godwits, and Willets, one of my favorite birds since they first flashed their beautiful black-and-white wings for me on the Texas coast in Rockport.

I watched waves pass over a field of grass as we ate breakfast one morning and thought of Willa Cather, who describes the grasses of Nebraska looking as though buffalo were running under them. Frequently along the road in North Dakota, I was fascinated by the colors of the grasses. In addition to the sweet yellow clover blending with the blue retch beside the road, whole fields were filled with more subtle colors. Tawny grasses mixed with the pinks of sour grass. Pale blues, purples, burgundy, and yellow—so soft, so lush—cried out for a paintbrush or camera. But, on the other hand, "I think that I shall never see . . ."

Within two hours of crossing into Big Sky Country of Montana and mountain time, we had snared two lifers, Lark Buntings and a Ferruginous Hawk. Route 2 was now a single lane in each direction. With narrow shoulders our roadside birding was sharply curtailed. Consequently we missed several chances to look for McGown's Longspur, which inhabit those short, dry prairie grasses. We might have tried harder to make an opportunity had we known four years would pass before we'd find our first McGown's on the Pawnee National Grasslands of Colorado.

In Havre our route turned north through Calgary to Edmonton. We'd scarcely hooked up at camp before raindrops began to fall. Soon hail was dancing like Mexican jumping beans, sounding like a hundred woodpeckers on the RV roof. Never mind. 'Twas only a shower. Tomorrow we could do laundry and visit the famous Edmonton Mall. The next day we'd be on our way to Alaska.

Wandering Tattlers

I'll walk where my own nature would be leading—
It vexes me to choose another guide—
Where the grey flocks in ferny glens are feeding,
Where the wild wind blows on the mountain side.

—Emily Brontë

The sun was shining brightly as our seven rigs peeled out of the Glowing Embers Campground at 7:03 A.M. Dick had written in his newsletter last winter: "Liz and I are going to bird in Alaska next summer. If anyone wants to tag along, meet us in Edmonton July 8 for departure July 9." So there we were that morning, as unstructured a caravan as you are likely to find, joined only by our love of birding. CBs crackled as we tested our communication system. Within an hour, rain was beating against our windshields. But who cared? We were going birding in Alaska.

Stretched a mile along the highway, we were an assorted string of motor homes, trailers, and fifth wheels. Martha from Arizona was traveling alone. Jenny Kate and Wally had come from Colorado, Jo and Ted from Texas, Mack and I from Florida. The Bjorks from Nebraska and the Gees from Ohio completed the seven. Mary Jean and Fred, eschewing such an early departure, caught up with us that evening.

At first scraggly conifers lined the road, limiting our view. Then the country opened out. Fields of lemon yellow, which for the lack of a better name I had been calling mustard, reached to the horizon. Through the chatter on the CB, I learned it was rape, or canola, the source of canola oil. When I commented on the beauty of the canola fields as I registered at the campground that afternoon, the stern-faced proprietor with all the charm of Madame Defarge snorted, "That's rape! No one around here calls it anything but rrrrape!" Because it grows quickly, it is well suited to the climate of the Peace River Valley that we drove through today. It is indispensable, too, for the world-famous honey industry in the Dawson Creek area.

In contrast to the beauty of the lemon-yellow fields, sometimes patchworked with squares of green or amber grain, we saw carnage. Two crows picked at the carcass of a deer. The body of a moose, apparently a highway casualty, lay in the grass along our way. The showers that tried to rain on our parade gave way to sunshine by midafternoon.

The road was excellent. We cruised into Tubby's Tent and Trailer Camp in Dawson Creek at Mile One on the Alaska Highway at four o'clock. The 385 miles, which had seemed such a challenge before we left Edmonton, evaporated in the excitement of the adventure as quickly as the rain between showers.

I don't know what I had expected of Dawson Creek. Something Jack Londonish? Probably not dog sleds, ice, and snow, but reality did temper imagination when I found myself in a busy city with a museum, a nine-hole golf course, tennis courts, ice arenas, a curling rink, an outdoor pool, and enough traffic to justify a traffic circle. The temperature at four o'clock was in the high seventies Fahrenheit.

Travel did not allow time for birding that first day, but the Alder Flycatcher where we stopped for lunch in Valleyview was a lifer for me. Magpies were chattering down by the trash cans as I made my diary notes at 10:45 without the aid of electric lights. The sun had just dipped below the horizon. A mauve and coral sunset spread its glow as quiet settled over Tubby's Tent and Trailer Camp.

61

Our caravan departed eagerly and promptly the next morning at 7:00 A.M. Neither the Honey Place with the largest glass beehive in the world nor the 150-foot oil drill in front of St. John's tourist center tempted anyone to stop. But by the time we reached Taylor, with its population of 912, the urge to bird overcame us. Like kids with new toys, we wanted to set up our spotting scopes and get on with the real business of the trip. Someone found in *Mileposts,* our indispensable mile-by-mile guide, an access to Peace River up ahead. We caucused by CB. The vote in favor of stopping was unanimous.

Beside a small pond, we trained our binoculars on grass birds and rock birds and finally on a little family of Common Goldeneyes. The babies followed Mama in single file as she putt-putted around the pond. They must have had CBs, too. We set up our scopes, more to compare than to use them. We admired the blue sky and started to get acquainted. A half hour later, a string of rigs was again heading up the Alaska Highway.

Mack stopped at a post office. It was then nearly ten o'clock. "When will the mail go out?" she asked.

"Oh, 'bout suppertime," the postman replied. She didn't think to ask which day.

We reached Wonowon at milepost One-O-One, population 150, unincorporated, before noon. The town was called Blueberry until it became an official control gate on the first *highway* during World War II. We heard some pretty impressive stories about this fourteen-hundred-mile highway that ten thousand soldiers hacked out of rock, mountains, forests, streams, and permafrost in eight months.

Rape fields and oil rigs soon gave way to stunted spruce and raw wilderness. I caught glimpses of snowcapped vistas, but only teasers. A Yellow Warbler dive-bombed our RV and lived to tell his spouse. I don't know which suffered the greater trauma, the warbler or Mack. Word passed along the CB from Dick in the lead, "Watch for eagle on the right."

Some of us camped at Fort Nelson's West End Campground, enjoying the amenities of electric, sewer, and water hookups and coin-operated showers. The rest boondocked, a new verb in my vocabulary.

BOONDOCK, v. (intransitive) to camp beside a babbling brook, at a roadside pulloff, in a mall or shopping center parking lot, or a rustic campground without hookups
MOTIVE, to smell the flowers, to escape the madding crowd, to save money or all of the above

Nor did the boondockers all boondock in the same place. One rig stopped short of Fort Nelson, two went sixty miles beyond. Wally and Jenny Kate chose the parking lot in the center of town so they could "bike and get the sense of the place." In fact they biked out to the West End Campground to get a sense of the rest of us. Such is the rugged independence of birders.

As we queued the next morning for departure, Wally came to Mack and me and said, "Jenny Kate and I are going to bird first today and travel later. Want to join us?"

"Sounds good to me," I said.

"Mack?"

"Just my cuppa tea."

"I'll tell Dick we'll catch up with him tonight. Then let's head for the dump."

Within an hour we had found two life birds at the town dump, a Boreal Chickadee and a Bank Swallow. A Mourning Warbler teased us until we found its nest in a patch of wild raspberries. The sky was blue, the sun was shining, the wind was brisk. The excitement and the feeling of well being were as keen as when we pulled out of Glowing Embers three days before. Nibbling wild raspberries, hearing bird calls, feeling the wind, and studying the infinite variety of grasses are all perks inherent to birding

Leaving Fort Nelson at last, we dawdled along the highway. Found a Western Wood-Pewee, a lifer for me. The road hugged the banks of Muncho Lake, snaking between sheer cliffs on the right and green glacial waters on the left. We pulled off, awed by the beauty. Across the lake the land rose sharply. Short, thin, dark green spruces marched in disorderly array up the banks. For a moment I thought Birnam Wood was moving. I lapsed into daydreaming until Jenny Kate called from where she was picking flowers, "What's that white bird?"

Up went the binoculars. Quick! Check the books.

"It's a gull—a gull with, with . . . yellow legs," Wally said.

"And uh, and uh, yellow bill," Mack added. "With, wait a minute, with no markings on the bill."

"Black wing tips . . . with a spot of white on the black." That from Wally.

"It has to be either a California or a Mew Gull," I concluded, flipping through the gulls in the field guide. Then it called, a call like a mew of a cat.

"A Mew Gull," we all exclaimed at once, the first Mew Gull for all of us.

Elated we turned our attention to the cliffs on the right. Swallows were flying in and out of the crevices of the rocks. Mack studied her book. Wally squinted and puzzled. "How about a Violet Green?" Mack asked. "See how little they glide and how rapidly they flap their wings?"

"Note also," Wally added, "the white flank patches that almost meet over the tail."

"Am I ever glad I have you two along," I said. "I can't count wing flaps or see whether white patches meet or only *almost* meet over the tail."

"Me either," admitted Jenny Kate.

"Take our word for it. We have ourselves a Violet-green Swallow."

"Six lifers before lunch," Jenny Kate said. "I'll be score-keeper."

It may have been before lunch, but by then it was three o'clock. We munched granola bars and tallied our mileage. We were 220 miles from the night's designated campground in Watson Lake. We must press on. But how do we press on through those Canadian rockies crying out on all sides to be savored? *Mileposts* says, "Pick blueberries by the roadside but beware of bears. They like berries, too."

On we drove, poking along riverbanks, slowing for "dangerous curves," and stretching to see mountaintops. At the same time, we had to look, we were warned, for moose and stone sheep on the highway. Shortly beyond Stone Mountain, we did find Dall sheep in the road, first one and then a family. At six o'clock we conferred. We still had ninety miles to go. The highway was deteriorating. Stretches of washboard shook us like a rag doll in the jaws of a grizzly. Wally and Jenny Kate decided to keep going, hoping "the road will get better." Mack and I were hungry. We chose to pull off by a little stream and raid our fridge. The sun was still high. Birds flitted among the branches overhanging the stream. Fish darted in the sunlight. Our stomachs finally satisfied, we persuaded ourselves to move on.

Forty-five miles short of Watson Lake (the road did not get better), we entered the Yukon Territory at Contact Bridge, so named because construction crews working from the west and from the east met there on September 25, 1942. We stopped at Contact Creek Lodge for gas. I gulped when the register ticked past one hundred dollars. The light was fading when Mack and I drove into the campground, where an hour earlier Jenny Kate had reserved for us the last available campsite.

While Mack hooked up to electricity and water before the light faded further, I went to tell Dick that the last of his chickens had found their roost. He was welcoming Anni and Bill, newcomers to our group. They are full-time campers, vagabonds of the road, Anni said. Their fifth wheel made the ninth rig when we pulled away from Watson Lake the next morning.

The road continued to be spine-shatteringly rough well past Rancheria, fifty miles beyond Watson Lake. It reminded me of a postcard that I picked up recently. Beside a picture of a road with sharp curves following a winding white-water river were these lines:

Winding in and winding out
fills my mind with serious doubt
as to whether "the lout"
who planned this route
was going to hell or coming out.

I didn't mind the curves and the bends, but even where the highway was well paved, as much of it was, we had to be constantly alert for the frost heaves, which threaten the strongest of springs.

At Morley Lake Rest Area, the caravan stopped for lunch. The snowcapped Cassier Mountains, stretching into the distant clouds, dwarfed our little band of birders. Brilliant fireweed, which lines the highway, grew in lush clusters around the rest area. With the temperature in the eighties, we rolled up our sleeves and loitered in the sunshine. I got some good pictures of Gray Jays and fireweed.

Lunch break over, we followed Dick back onto the highway. We discussed by CB the smoke rising from several fires in the mountains. Because moose and other wildlife thrive on the tender young plants and aspens that spring up in the clearings after a fire, these fires are allowed to burn. I learned that fireweed gets its name not from its color but because it is the first vegetation to reappear after a fire.

We camped for a couple of nights in Whitehorse, the biggest city on the Alaska Highway. Twenty thousand, two-thirds of the Yukon Territory population, live in Whitehorse. Years ago when I was tent camping, I inquired about a camp-site in Cody, Wyoming. "You'll find a place at the end of the parking lot across from the rodeo," a passerby told me.

"Is that the only place?" I asked, not being one to buy the first pair of shoes I try on no matter how much I like them.

"Wal, no, ma'm," the sidewalk chamber of commerce replied. "Wyoming has a population of two persons per acre. Y'kin put yer li'l ol' tent up jist about innywhere ya want 'n' never crowd a body ner uh bear."

I figured the Yukon Territory could be equally accommo-dating to anyone inclined to boondock.

The Yukon River, 1,984 miles long, runs through White-horse. Several of us crossed it in Miles Canyon, where we went to look for—what else—birds. We found a Dark-eyed Junco and a Spotted Sandpiper with three babies, but the scenery more than the birds rewarded our early morning reveille.

At a private game farm that afternoon, I saw my first herd of muskox. Now that's an animal only a mother could love, though I understand their hair makes wonderfully warm, soft sweaters. In our walk around the extensive grounds, we found eight new trip birds, including a Bohemian Waxwing, which was a lifer for many of us. It posed obligingly for a generous sighting.

Then scrubbed and fed, we were off for an evening at the opera. *Frantic Follies* was a feast of frontier frolics, with gener-ous portions of Robert Service, whose poetry is much cher-ished around there.

We caught our first glimpse of the Kluane Range before

reaching Haines Junction the next day. After cinnamon rolls and brochures at the Visitors Center, our laissez-faire group split. Those who chose the birding detour would rejoin the rest of us at our layover in Tok in two or three days. Mack and I went with the detail headed for Kluane Wilderness Village. For the rest of the day, we traveled parallel to the Kluane Range, Canada's highest and the world's largest Alpine icefields. Looking out at eight-thousand-foot peaks, I tried to visualize the two sixteen-thousand-foot mountains out there obscured by the clouds. *Am I in the Yukon or the Alps?* I wondered.

A campground on the left with a woodcraft shop next door and a motel with restaurant across the street pretty much sums up the human encroachment upon the Wilderness Village. The chief denizens were friendly ground squirrels all too willing to run up my pants leg. Though ordinarily Mack and I took our meals in house, we joined Liz and Dick in sampling the salmon in the restaurant across the street. As we ate, sitting at tables made from the boles of local trees, we looked out upon the Kluane icefields to the west and a meandering stream to the east.

Strolling along the river's edge after dinner, we came upon a lone sandpiper-like bird. The river was wide and rocky, but the water, shallow. The bird bobbed its tail as it pecked among the gravel. It was too large for a Spotted Sandpiper, which also bobs its butt. And the bill was too long. It stood too erect. Could it be a Wandering Tattler? They nest along mountain streams. They are two inches longer than a Spotted Sandpiper, and the bird book said they do sometimes "teeter and bob."

Not letting wishful thinking mislead us, we made no decision on first sight but were back at the river's edge before breakfast. The temperature was forty-four degrees Fahrenheit, the time 6:45. The bird was still working the river's edge.

Doesn't it sleep? Its body bobbed with a hicuppy rhythm. In the cold reality of dawn, we agreed it was a Wandering Tattler.

"Wandering Tattler," Liz mused, "just like us."

As we surveyed the loveliness and the loneliness about us, an Arctic Tern flew overhead. Two firsts before breakfast!

Sunshine flooded the Kluane Range and the little wilderness village in the valley as we took to the road again. We reached the Alaska border shortly before noon—1,579 miles and six days from Edmonton. Mack spotted some Northern Shovelers and a loon on a lake in the pines across the road. Out came the scopes. We sat at the border, ate lunch, took pictures, and turned our watches back an hour to Alaska time.

The Alaska Highway is not without its hazards. Flat tires and broken windshields are common, but we had been lucky. Dick had had a flat tire on his trailer; Anni and Bill had broken a leaf of a spring before they met us in Watson Lake. But this afternoon we saw a sadder sight as we wound our way up a mountain road. In the ditch by a sharp turn lay the burned-out skeleton of a motor home. Who knows the plot of that mute story?

We camped in Tok, the first town in Alaska, and indulged in our first Alaskan salmon bake. Given a choice of salmon, halibut, or reindeer sausage, I chose salmon. A memorable treat from the first whiff of the open fires to the last morsel of salmon, baked beans, and slaw in the open-air pavilion.

"Remind us to stop here on our way back," Mack said, licking her lips and siphoning up the last shred of her salmon.

In Tok we were reunited with the boondockers who digressed back at Haines Junction and joined by Betty and George, who had come up the Inside Passage. Our caravan of ten was now complete. For the next few weeks, we would be traveling less and birding more. Lady Luck willing!

Denali, the Big One

There's a land where
the mountains are nameless
and the rivers run
God knows where.

—Robert Service

En route to Fairbanks, we stopped at Moon Lake to look for a pair of Tundra Swans. The road into the lake was narrow, steep, and rocky, but the prize was going to be worth the jolts and bumps. About a half mile off the highway, I sensed confusion up ahead. Dick in the lead, with his fifty-two feet of van and trailer, followed closely by fifth wheels and thirty-six-foot motor homes, was the first to discover the cul-de-sac had no turnabout for the likes of us. How the swans must have laughed as they peered through the reeds at these humongous machines inching and squeezing themselves around. How unlike the agility and elegance with which swans glide. Once realigned we just kept on jolting and bumping back to the highway. Surely other Tundra Swans must be waiting for us somewhere. As the last vehicle pulled away, the cob chortled, "Serves them right for disturbing our peace."

A few hours later, we were camped on the outskirts of Fairbanks ready to bird. Seventeen pairs of eyes were none too many to search out a Three-toed Woodpecker in a burn a dozen miles outside the city. A forest fire three years earlier had made this an ideal habitat for the Three-toed Wood-pecker and Northern Hawk Owls. An hour passed, but once we found it, the Three-toed was easy to identify. It is the only woodpecker that has a yellow crown and black-and-white bars down the back.

The Boreal Owl was tougher, so tough we gave up on it. And we had almost given up on the Northern Hawk Owl. We were leaving the forest when Martha's voice came over the CB, "There it is!" About thirty yards into the woods, it sat high in a pine tree, calm and cooperative, blasély turning its head as a line of scopes mushroomed along the roadside.

"How did you ever spot that?" I asked Martha later.

"Just luck," she said modestly. But I suspect she is one of those who are born to bird. Keen eyesight is one of the prerequisites.

We climbed Murphy Dome Road to a height of three thousand feet, looking for grouse and ptarmigan, but found only feathers and bones. Creamer Dairy Nature Trail produced a Solitary Sandpiper, one Green-winged Teal, and some Northern Pintails. Three Sandhill Cranes flew overhead. A return visit another day offered nothing more.

"Summer doldrums," Wally said. He's an eager birder and a good spotter.

The Tanana River was flowing too fast for ducks, but Liz spotted an owl as we drove along the dike. Great Gray Owl? Or only Great Horned? We couldn't agree, but the holdouts finally admitted it was *only* a Great Horned.

Wally knew a place by Smith Lake where we found some American Wigeons, a Horned Grebe, Buffleheads, and had an excellent sighting of a Red-necked Grebe. Another day we abandoned our wheels at the end of a no-outlet street off Seese Highway and struggled through wet bogs hidden by beautiful shoulder-high pink grasses to some wetlands but no birds. Summer doldrums, indeed! The campground offered more. It had lots of Black-capped Chickadees, some Water Pipits, and at least one Arctic Warbler, a lifer for me. The group never

71

did agree upon the identification of one little yellow bird that defied all of our attempts.

On our last day in Fairbanks, Anni and Bill joined Fred and Mary Jean in a seventeen-hour bus trip up the unpaved Dalton Highway to the Arctic Circle. They left, assuring us they would be back before dark. We amused ourselves with things we would do before dark, for even though we were a month past the summer solstice, the sun scarcely dipped below the horizon before starting its ascent for the new day. It was never really dark. But each day was losing six or seven minutes of light. That translated into an hour of light now being lost every nine or ten days.

As we sat around the campfire circle evenings, munching Ted's Texas peanuts and discussing everything from birds to cabbages and kings and the price of salmon back home, we knew finding the bird—or naming the bird—was only one component of this birding game. Companionship and the search itself, even when unfulfilled, were important, too. Four days in Fairbanks had further whetted our eagerness to bird. The time had come to move on to Denali Park.

The Visitors Center at Riley Creek was overcrowded, the campground overactive, and the shuttle service into the park fully booked for the rest of the day. Rising above all the confusion, our brave little band of eighteen (Wally's sister from Boston had joined us for the weekend, and the Gees had fallen behind because of transmission problems) pooled cars and drove the first twelve miles into Denali Park, as far as we were allowed to go in private cars. We hiked around the headquarters at mile three, checked out the malamute sled dogs at the kennels, and strained in vain through the distant mists for a glimpse of Mount McKinley.

"I think I can almost see it," Anni said.

"Sure you can *almost* see it," Fred replied, "and I can *almost* see a herd of elk in a quadrille on the highest pinnacle."

A magnificent caribou crossed our path. Slam the brakes! Grab the cameras! Those racks can weigh forty pounds. I tried to imagine a forty-pound knapsack on my head.

A little farther along, Willow Ptarmigan, which had eluded us in Fairbanks, were huddled beside the road. Wally spotted them first, two females and several chicks so well camouflaged that I began to suspect Wally of an overactive imagination until they scuttled to a nearby bush. This was all prelude to a full day in the park the next day.

Although our birding caravan did not always move in unison, we were 100 percent, eighteen-person strong when we clambered aboard the school bus at Riley Camp the next morning for a fifty-mile peek into a park as large as the state of Rhode Island. The thirty-six passengers were evenly divided between birders and *the others*. Ernie, our genial guide and driver, reminded us the park's purpose is to protect wildlife. Human beings are privileged to observe as long as they do not interfere with the natural life of the animals or plants. He told us of visitors who only yesterday had witnessed a wolf killing a bear cub. Because wolves came so close to extinction in the park, their comeback is of special interest to the park management. Ernie could not promise wolves, but he hoped we would see some as well as the four other magic animals of the park.

"When you see something, shout STOP," he instructed us. "Then tell everyone what you see and where it is."

We were scarcely past the malamute kennels when George shouted, "STOP! Grouse on the left." The bus tilted precariously to port as eighteen birders stormed the windows.

"Grouse? Or ptarmigan?"

"Ptarmigan. But is it Rock or Willow?"

"It's too big for Rock." Ernie waited patiently while we identified and photographed a Willow Ptarmigan with eight chicks. The non-birders, who were straining to see bear or moose, were not sure what to make of all this to-do over a bird.

By the time we reached Savage River and someone called, "STOP! Harlequin Ducks on the right," they were as amused as puzzled by our antics.

Then the shout came, "STOP! Bear on the left." A bear with two cubs grazed on the rise of land across the gully. The bus rocked again, this time with all thirty-six crowding the windows. Cameras clicked. Mother bear stretched on her hind legs to assure no danger threatened her babies. She was very light, a tawny cinnamon. The cubs, romping like kittens, were darker.

"She's a Toklat grizzly," Ernie told us, "very shaggy and unkempt if you could see her closer. Anyone want to get out?"

"How fast can she run?" Fred asked.

"'Twouldn't take long to find out," Ernie replied. "Any takers?" Thank you, Ernie, but no thank you. This was quite close enough.

Dall sheep grazed on Igloo Mountain, only white specks on the upper cliffs. A little farther along, high, high in the sky soared a Golden Eagle. At the Toklat turnaround (Toklat means *fresh water*), several caribou swatted insects and scrounged for food in a dry riverbed. The weather was beautiful. Ernie allowed us plenty of time to wander around, examine the gravelly terrain, converse, and take pictures. The mountains, stark in their remoteness, were magnificent. A Long-tailed Jaeger flew overhead, close enough for an easy identification.

We had scarcely started to retrace our route when a big bull caribou stepped into the road in front of us, close enough to make the photographers in the group very happy. The scenery seemed even more spectacular on the return than on our approach. The narrow road, sometimes single-laned, wound in and out along streams and around mountains. Like a zoom lens, we went from hairpin turns into openings with distant vistas. The drivers of the school busses had a strict code of the road, who pulled off the road for whom. For instance, the climbing bus had the right of way over one descending. The drivers also had signals to indicate to a passing bus anything special up ahead, such as "bear in the road" or "moose on the left."

"STOP! Caribou running on the right."

"With a wolf stalking it," Ernie added. I sensed he was a little excited himself. "We will watch awhile if you will all be very quiet. We must not disturb or threaten the wolf in any way."

It was downwind. Then a second wolf appeared. The first one made its way onto the road, came upwind, and passed within ten feet of the bus. Ernie explained how carefully, how skillfully, how patiently wolves work, and always as a team. We began to take sides, caribou versus wolf. Ernie left no doubt as to where his sentiments lay. Mack was cheerleader for the caribou. "They almost became extinct," Ernie reiterated, "and they hunt only the old and the weak. That female caribou will not live long even left to herself. The wolves must eat, even as you and I." He would have liked us to share the thrill of the kill, but this pursuit had only started. "As many as ten or a dozen wolves may work this caribou for hours before they attack," he explained. We watched five or ten minutes longer and then reluctantly pulled away from the mounting drama.

A few more miles and photographs down the road, we came upon a moose and calf munching in the undergrowth. They completed the magic five animals of the park—bear, Dall sheep, caribou, wolf, and moose—all in one trip, plus several special birds.

The third day we all started out on the Taklat bus again. As always the driver stopped at the McKinley lookout. Our radar couldn't pierce the clouds. "I haven't seen that mountain more than three times this summer," he told us. "It's too cloudy in the summer."

Some twenty miles into the park, a few of us asked to be let off at Tattler Creek. We wanted to bird the wild. The bus pulled away, leaving us standing in the road surrounded by lush wilderness on every side. The ranger's warning had been specific, "Never turn your back on a bear." The recommended procedure upon meeting a bear is to raise both arms, keep facing the bear, and quietly back away, saying, "Hello, Bear. Hello, Bear." If the bear sees I am passive and unarmed, it may not try to de-arm me. It *may* not. The important thing about a bear is not to surprise it. It is also advisable not to carry a ham sandwich.

By now long-legged Dick, who travels like a deer, was down the bank and across the creek in search of ducks or whatever the willows and the alders concealed. Mack, following Dick's leaps from shifting stone to wobbly rock, lost her balance and plunged unceremoniously into the icy stream—field guide, binoculars, dignity, and all. The air at this height was in the fifties that afternoon as we flagged a bus returning to the base and put Mack on it.

With Mack headed for warmth and dry clothes, we proceeded to thrash around Tattler Creek, trying to strike a balance between enough noise to alert a bear but not enough commotion to disturb a Harlequin Duck. Not far up the rocky creek, a female Harlequin with three babies was riding down the rapidly moving stream. Her yellow chicks, not more than four or five inches long, bounced like ping-pong balls down the tumbling water. Mother was feeding but the babies were just along for the ride. Thirty or forty feet downstream, Mother turned and swam upstream with as much ease as she had ridden down, the babies right behind her.

We watched several round trips before moving farther up stream, making frequent precautionary "Hello, Bear" calls. Finding neither bears nor more birds, we worked our way back to the road. Arctic Warblers flitted among the willows. The weather was cold and windy, with occasional sprinkles of icy rain. After a couple of hours, we flagged a bus and returned to camp. There we found that Mack had ingeniously gone through the woods to the hotel and dried herself out under the hand driers in the women's room. What's more, she had picked up a lifer, a Varied Thrush, in the woods between the campground and the hotel.

Three rigs did not show up for the eight o'clock departure the next morning. While we waited, the CB crackled, "Wally to Dick. Don't wait for the rest of us. We're going into the park once more as far as the McKinley lookout. Can't bear to leave without giving that mountain one more chance to show its face." The rest of us stoically pulled onto the George Parks Highway and headed south. Why fight fate? Our route traversed some of the grandest and most rugged land that we had yet encountered in Alaska. My head pivoted like an owl's, trying to absorb it all.

About an hour down the road, with a kind of second take, I suddenly gasped, "Mack! What's that . . . that mass . . . that, that wall of white . . . on the right . . . in the sky. Is it . . . ?"

Mack reached for the CB. "Dick! Dick! That's McKinley. We're pulling off." We all pulled off. We stared. We gasped. We congratulated each other. Where had it come from all of a sudden, full-blown, filling the heavens? There in a practically cloudless sky, towering above the snowcapped range below it, stood this 20,320-foot pile of snow shimmering in the sunlight. Edna St. Vincent Millay says, *Euclid alone has looked on beauty bare,* but if this was not *Beauty bare,* I never expect to see it. I would not trade places with Euclid for all the caribou racks in Alaska.

From fifty? Sixty? miles away, it dominated the landscape. Once adjusted to the euphoria, I realized I must take pictures. Clouds were already forming to the east, but the entire slope was still in the clear. Tripods and scopes sprang up like fireweed after a fire. Lenses ranged from a wide angle to telescopic as photographers made their choices, angled for views, and plotted composition, working from a field splashed with fireweed back across miles of rises and dips, black forest, and wilderness to the snowcapped range that forms the footstool for McKinley, or Denali, "the Big One," as the natives call it, maybe sixty miles away.

Forty miles later we stopped again for pictures of the Big One from the bridge over Little Coal River. Off and on for another hour, we caught glimpses, though never as crystally unclouded as that first spectacular, sun-flooded tableau.

Mack and I stopped to shop in Wasilla. We both needed warm coats for launch and ferry rides in the upcoming glacier country. Still ebullient, we could not refrain from telling two clerks of our ecstatic morning. One of them replied, "You were lucky. I've seen it only twice in my lifetime."

The other woman commented indifferently, "I've never seen it."

Anchorage, City of Lakes

A bird in the air
    shall carry the voice
and that that hath wings
    shall tell the matter.

—Ecclesiastes 10:20

Two female moose strolled through the campground in Palmer as though they owned it, and probably they did. We camping birders were the trespassers. Birding along a side road a little later, I met a splendid male. He stepped like the monarch that he is sedately into my path not fifty yards in front of me. We stared at each other, he chewing his cud meditatively and I wishing my binoculars were a camera. Shortly he sauntered off into the bushes across the street.

Camping two nights in Palmer gave us a free day to go our separate ways. George left early to fish. Some took the advice of our Mountain View Campground brochure and drove around the outskirts of Palmer along Fishhook Road and the Bodenburg Loop to admire the colony houses and barns remaining from the Matanuska Valley Colony, one of Roosevelt's New Deal projects in the 1930s when he brought 203 families, victims of the Dust Bowl and the Great Depression, here to cultivate this potentially rich valley. Some descendants of those families still live and farm there.

The famous Matanuska Valley vegetables were in season, and so Mack and I chose to visit a U-Pick farm. The weather was gorgeous, the temperature in the mid-seventies. The farm we selected provided everything needed for the task—baskets, wheelbarrows, potato forks, knives, and great sinks for washing our diggings and our pickings. Wandering through the lush acres, we made our selections, gathering all we thought we could reasonably eat or store—peas, beets, lettuce, broccoli, turnips, rhubarb, and potatoes. The bill? Three dollars and fifty-seven cents. A woman with three little children in tow was picking her third wheelbarrow full of broccoli. She told us that she bottles it. It was her second trip to the farm for broccoli that week.

When George left camp to go fishing that morning, he said to Betty, "If you start a fire in the grill around five-thirty, I'll show this crowd what grilled salmon really tastes like."

In the soft light of early evening, figures began to wander by twos and threes across the campground to the picnic shelter where George was tenderly tending his day's catch over the coals. The rest of us came, bearing the results of our labor, too—salads, baked beans, macaroni and cheese, brownies, and fruit compote. Strictly gourmet all the way. We sipped wine and exchanged stories of our day's adventures until George gave the signal that his three beautiful salmon were ready.

We were just a tiny band of birders, a dot of humanity dwarfed by the mountains rising sharply to the east, but that was no measure of the enjoyment of the evening. As the light faded (as much as it was going to fade in this northern summer sky), we returned to our various campsites, each carrying as much leftover salmon as George could persuade us our fridges would hold.

Our birding group gradually became more of a network than a caravan. With Dick and George each maintaining a message service, we could cater to our individual priorities, personal time schedules, or mechanical breakdowns and still have a support group in the environs. Leaving Palmer, Dick,

Liz, Mack, and I moved on to Anchorage where we camped for a week at Golden Nugget Campground a few blocks from downtown.

Anchorage abounds with birding opportunities. That Lake Hood on the edge of the city is the largest and busiest seaplane base in the world does not bother the birds in the least. Grebes and Arctic Loons nest there. Along the banks of the lake, I saw parent gulls feeding Mew babies barely out of their nests, oblivious to the constant roar of seaplanes departing and arriving. Wigeons, Arctic Terns, Green-winged Teals, Spotted and Least sandpipers all went about their daily duties undisturbed by human traffic. Canada Geese, a parent at each end of the line, paddled their families along the banks looking for handouts.

Lake Spenard, Westchester Lake, Goose Lake, Connors Lake, Sand Lake—Anchorage could have been called Lake City. Judy, our guide for a day, recommended DeLong Lake for loons. "If you just sit there, you'll see a pair of Pacific Loons," she told us.

Oh, sure, I thought. Actually we didn't even have to sit. We stepped out of Dick's van, approached the little lake, and there was a loon, a Pacific Loon. Before I could even say *lifer three hundred and eighty-seven,* the submerged mate surfaced. The resident pair.

But it was not that way with grouse. I dearly wanted to find a Spruce, Sharp-tailed, or Blue grouse—all three or any one. With Judy we tramped the ski trails at Hillcrest Park until the drizzle turned to rain, but found none. In the rain we climbed in Dick's van into Chugach State Park, winding past homes that were mere dots in the mountainsides when seen from below. Two more hairpin turns and we reached the trails that would provide good birding (including grouse) some drier, warmer, less windy day. 'Twas not that we were not rugged birders prepared to face glacial chill and hurricane winds, but

Judy had only a day to give us the overview of the Anchorage area. Though the temperature in town was sixty-three degrees that morning, the wind-chill factor atop the park was closer to thirty-three. Dick and I compared notes on the chemical toilets and agreed both had "strong updrafts."

We birded Potter Marsh, a state game refuge south of the city. The rain let up as we walked along the boardwalk. We would return there more than once in the coming days for the geese in the grass and the ducks in the water. The salmon, were running at Ship Creek where Judy helped identify indisputably a new bird, a Glaucous-winged Gull. Still, without Judy I fear I am going to find Glaucous and Glaucous-winged confusing. "The Glaucous has paler primaries," Judy patiently explained. That's all well and good and may be a little help if the two fly by slowly side by side. "And the Glaucous is larger," she added.

"How much larger? " I asked.

"Twenty-four to twenty-seven for the Glaucous-winged versus twenty-six to thirty-two inches for the Glaucous."

"Umm. Guess I'll stick to the primaries."

In Earthquake Park, Judy recreated in our minds something of the devastation the earthquake of March 27, 1964, brought to Anchorage. Millions of dollars of damage resulted eventually in a tremendous amount of rebuilding, from which a distinctly new city emerged. The park is a memorial to the suffering and the courage that combined to make the new Anchorage. Numerous plaques portray the events of the quake. The destruction was so severe and so extensive that the town of Portage fifty miles south was completely destroyed. It has never been rebuilt. The earthquake occurred on Good Friday, and coincidentally it was Good Friday twenty-five years later when the Exxon oil spill spewed ruin along the coast of Prince William Sound.

"There's lots more," Judy said as we stood among the trees

on the bluff in Earthquake Park, "but I've pointed out enough to keep you busy a few weeks and now I must run. Be sure to do the Coastal Trail," pointing to the path that runs along the mudflats far below. In the midst of our thank yous and good-byes, she pointed to a bird in a tree overhead. "Anyone need a Common Redpoll?" she asked.

"That little fellow with the orangey-red cap and black chin?" Liz asked.

"That's the one."

"It's a lifer!" Mack cried. "What a way to end a day!"

The next morning Westchester Lagoon was teeming with gulls and ducks, plenty to keep us busy while we waited for the rising tide to push the shorebirds in across the mudflats. The Coastal Trail, crossing the lagoon, runs for eleven miles along the Knik Arm. It is paved and wide enough for joggers, amblers, bicyclists, and birders to share amiably. At some hours traffic is heavy: jogging mothers pushing big-wheeled strollers before them, youngsters on roller skates hitchhiking a ride behind Daddy's bicycle, a whole family on bikes of various sizes with a wee one on her tricycle valiantly bringing up the rear. None of this interfered at all with the birds being urged closer by the tide rising out of Cook Inlet. We had excellent sightings of Short-billed Dowitchers, Solitary and Spotted sandpipers, a Red-necked Grebe with babies, many ducks, gulls, and one small sandpiper whose identity remained in dispute through several visits. Could it be a Rock Sandpiper? That would be a new bird. Or was it a Least Sandpiper? Or neither? Eventually consensus declared it a Pectoral Sandpiper, another lifer.

One pleasant morning found us strolling again along the Coastal Trail. The sun was shining. The temperature was in the mid-sixties. Our attention, usually focused on the beach, was drawn to the magnificent view of the mountains to the north. As we admired it, Liz said, "Isn't that Mount McKinley?"

It was. We were looking at the south side of the mountain a hundred and thirty-five miles away. Attracted by the view, we missed whatever a Bald Eagle did to offend some gulls, but offended they were. He was being roundly driven out of the territory by a raucous flurry of gulls. It was not a dignified performance by our national symbol, but he kept going. The gulls saw to that.

Russian Jack Springs was the place for passerines. The bike route branching off from the golf course took us to woods full of twitters and flutters. Two lifers showed up on our first visit, a White-winged Crossbill and Pine Grosbeaks. Even a spate of rainy weather didn't keep us from returning to Russian Jack Springs several times between showers. One spot was especially vibrant with avian activity: flocks of Pine Siskins, flocks of Redpolls, juncos, Yellow-rumped Warblers galore, chickadees, a couple of Western Wood-pewees, robins, and one MacGillivray's Warbler.

Counteracting this rush of good luck, Dick and Liz had the misfortune of having their own van rammed as they were returning from the Elmendorf Air Force Base. Fortunately neither of them was hurt, but the van had to wait for parts to be freighted up from the Lower Forty-eight. While they waited, Mack and I set out solo for Homer. Whatever grouse—Blue or otherwise—roamed the Chugach trails would have to wait another visit.

For some miles the road south of Anchorage hugs the shore of Turnagain Arm, so named for John Cook's remark when he came again to a dead end in his search for the Northwest Passage. We looked for beluga whales and caught our first close-up glimpses of glaciers. Of Portage, forty-seven miles south of Anchorage, *Mileposts* says simply: PORTAGE. No facilities. Town was destroyed in the 1964 earthquake. We knew that from the information at Earthquake Park, but still I was unprepared for the bleakness. True, there was nothing—nothing but stark acres of dead trees, such a contrast to all the beauty that we had seen from the moment we entered Alaska. We would return to this desolation in a couple of weeks, to a town with nothing but a name and a railroad track.

A few miles farther along, we detoured to the Portage Glacier and went out on the new *MV Ptarmigan* through the blue jumbles of icebergs to the chilly edge of the frozen river making its way off the glaciated miles of the Chugach Mountain Range. Later we lunched in the parking lot, gazing out at Portage Glacier on our left and Byron Glacier on our right.

"Not hard to take," Mack commented, helping herself to another Oreo.

"Not hard at all," I agreed. The next stop would be Homer.

Puffins and Glaciers

No ladder needs the Bird but skies
To situate its wings
Nor any leader's grim baton
Arraigns it as it sings . . .

—Emily Dickinson

A slanting ray of sun pierced the V of Grewingk Glacier inching its way through the overlap of two mountain slopes at the east edge of Kachemak Bay. In the foreground, in Mud Bay, low tide lapped the golden sandbar from which a half-buried stump of driftwood tilted skyward. On a scraggly, outstretched root perched a Bald Eagle intent upon the water below. Past Mud Bay the road led to Homer Spit, a gravel ridge extending nearly five miles into the bay.

Small shops, souvenir kiosks, restaurants, and charter services lined the spine of the Spit. Fisherfolk were fishing from the shore for king salmon. Late afternoon tourists strolled the street. Groups gathered to watch the fishermen from the chartered boats weigh in their halibut—28, 45, 56 pounds—and pose for pictures beside their trophies. That these were not the 250 pounders the halibut derby produces did not diminish the thrill of the catch. In the campground beside the small-boat harbor, RVs perched awning to awning at the water's edge. There Mack and I found some of our boondocking buddies whom we hadn't seen for a week.

Together through rising and ebbing tides, in showers and in clearings, we birded Mud Bay and the Spit for several days.

Northern Pintails, American Wigeons, Greater Scaup, and Surfbirds swam busily at the head of the bay. The tide coaxed in Whimbrels, Western Sandpipers, and Black-billed Plovers. One morning as we watched fisherman mend snags in their fifteen-hundred-foot net stretched full length along the beach, some small birds fed at the edge of the turning tide. They were bigger than peeps. About the size of a Dunlin but with a shorter bill. "And darker," Mack observed. Darker than peeps, predominantly black. The little flock flew, banked, and settled again on the rocky shore. But in that short flight, the bold black-and-white pattern of the wings confirmed they were Black Turnstones, a new bird for most of us.

One day Betty suggested having lunch at Land's End, since we were birding at the tip of the Spit anyway. Eating on the deck in brilliant sunshine and brisk breeze, we were able to bird right through spinach salads and halibut Florentine. Arctic and Aleutian Terns screamed overhead. With binoculars we identified a Fork-tailed Storm Petrel far over the waves. Wally spotted a Kittlitz's Murrelet. A Bald Eagle skimmed by with fish in its talons. It circled several times. Was it eyeing my halibut lunch?

Gradually we birded our way from the Spit back toward town. Hundreds of ducks were feeding on Beluga Lake in the park behind McDonald's restaurant. Yellow and Wilson's warblers flitted in and out of the marshy grasses that edged the lake. In the lagoon beyond the airport, thousands of Aleutian Terns swooped and squawked, tending their nursery. We parked at a distance and approached slowly, not wanting to spook either the parents or the babies. In the town beyond the lake and lagoon, we found Alder Flycatchers, Black-billed Magpies, Black-capped Chickadees, Ruby-crowned Kinglets, and Orange-crowned Warblers.

East Hill road climbs out of town to the bluffs on the Skyline Drive, where residents enjoy, as we did, spectacular views, looking across the bay to glaciers spilling down from the Harding Icefields straddling the Kenai Mountains. Paint brush, lupine, and wild rose blanketed the bluffs in a pastel mix, and whole fields were ablaze with fireweed.

Glaciers and snowcapped peaks had been a part of every day since we first glimpsed snow in the Cassier Range over three weeks before, but I still reached for my camera at every turn. A pair of Stellar's Jays pecked in the undergrowth beside the road. We browsed along Diamond Ridge, still looking for grouse or a Northern Goshawk in the heavy spruce and birch forests, but the views outdid the birding that afternoon.

Despite the abundance of birds throughout the town, for me the capstone of birding in Homer was the excursion to Gull Island. With four others Mack and I went out from the Spit into Kachemak Bay in a wee skiff piloted by Skipper Scott, who teased Mack when she asked, "Will we see any Tufted Puffins?"

"We might see one." He paused. "If we're lucky." After another pause he said, "In fact, there's one right now," pointing to a wooden one on the prow of the skiff. Then off we went for a morning in the deep, magnificent waters of the bay.

Almost immediately birds were bobbing all around us—some Common Eiders, but mostly Common Murres and Tufted Puffins. "Help yourself to a puffin," Scott said to Mack. He cruised close enough for us to verify the pale yellow head tufts drooping over the backs of their necks. The Common Murres were indeed common. The bay was full of them. Startled, a Black Scoter flew up in front of us, helicopterlike. Scoters lift themselves from the water more easily than most diving ducks. Puffins, on the other hand, splash along the surface, their stubby wings thwacking the water in a brave but not always successful effort to become airborne. When frightened they are more likely to dive than fly. Those stubby wings propel them like torpedoes. They literally fly under water.

Finally Gull Island loomed before us. Sixty-foot Rock rode beside it like a ship about to dock. The clacking and the kawking and the cree-aking grew vociferous. Eight species breed there, chiefly Glaucous-winged Gulls and Black-legged Kittiwakes. Cormorants—both Pelagic and Red-faced—jostled for positions on the upper ledges, silhouettes against the blue sky. Out of water Common Murres stand erect on feet far back on their bodies, a stance that earns them the name Alaskan Penguin.

Scott cut the motor and drifted between Sixty-foot Rock and the island, close to some young Glaucous-winged Gulls nestling in their little cups of grass and seaweed. The Common Murre makes no nest at all. It just drops its single egg on the bare ledge. But Mother Nature has insured against such casualness by making it a pear-shaped egg that rolls in a circle instead of falling off the ledge. In contrast to no nest, the Black-legged Kittiwakes attach sturdy nests to the ledge with a mixture of seaweed, moss, and mud. The nest, though, is so tiny the incubating parent (they take turns) sits with its breast pressed against the rock and its tail extended over the water. With living quarters this tight, how do the thousands of birds ever find their young when they return from the sea bearing cod, herring, shrimp, squid, or aquatic insects, each catering to its particular taste? But they do go straight as an arrow to their own chicks.

Scott circled the island. It was three hundred and sixty degrees solid with birds. As we watched, a predator approached. Every parent became an instant attack bird. The clamor crescendoed. The sound and flurry were awesome. After the danger passed, the commotion subsided to the normal uproar. I marvel at the amazing chaos, realizing, of course, that *chaos* is my human perception of the situation.

We came upon seals basking on a sandbar in China Poot Bay. I was hoping for an American Dipper in one of the streams tumbling down the mountainsides, but fog overtook us and we had to return to the mainland. The American Dipper, or Water Ouzel, is a common resident on the south side of Kachemak Bay, but it continues to elude me.

I should not complain. I had exceeded my wish list for Homer by three. The time had come to move on. The boon-dockers would detour through Crooked Creek and meet Mack and me in Seward in a couple of days. Before saying good-bye to our little camp overlooking the bay, we took one more walk down the fireweed-lined path to the water. White-winged Crossbills cavorted in the spruces, a Northwestern Crow hunkered down on a windswept cliff, and in the bay a lone Pigeon Guillemot waved fire-engine-red feet as it took off from the water.

We settled in at Bear Creek Campground on the north edge of Seward with full hookups for $13.50. That was reason-able. Plus $2.50 for a five-minute shower. Mack was in shock! Why so much? Because glacial water takes so much electricity to heat, and Mack admitted she preferred it heated. We rented a car and drove to Exit Glacier, which is remarkably approach-able, as early explorers discovered when they found they could walk right off it. We climbed the path until I stood probably not more than thirty or forty feet from that great jagged wall of ice. Raindrops splattered gently on my nor'easter. The ice in the crevasses glowed blue. To the side a hundred feet below, the age-old melting continued, transforming the glacier into a web of meandering streams.

The next morning we were out on the glacier road before six o'clock in search of grouse, which were supposed to be plentiful before the traffic starts. But the traffic must have started. Fishermen and their pup tents were ensconced among the trees here and there along the stream. The grouse were more exclusive. By afternoon two of the boonie rigs had staked their claim on the beach in town. We found them there and went with Wally, Jenny Kate, and the Bjorks in search of Chestnut-backed Chickadees, which Wally had heard live behind the high school. That they may, but we struck out: pleasant walk, interesting school, but no chickadees.

Dick and Liz joined us in Bear Creek Campground the next afternoon, new radiator installed and running smoothly. And when we returned to the campground for dinner, much to our surprise, the Gees had checked in, too. Though we had known each other only a few days before transmission problems had caused them to drop out back on the Alaska Highway, the reunion was joyous. Such is the bonding of those who bird.

'Twas now the second week of August. Many of the songbirds had already started south, but some of us wouldn't give up on the Golden-crowned Sparrow. It should be in Seward. The next afternoon a little expedition set out to search along a winding, wooded trail on the edge of town. The path was moss-lined and so soft to walk on that I found myself imaging what it would be like to be an Indian moving stealthily through the spruce forest. Suddenly I was hushed back into reality. Shhh! On a branch not ten feet off the path sat our Golden-crowned Sparrow, its crown brilliant in the beam of sunlight slanting through the conifers. Though it did not show its face again, through the trees came its plaintive whistle: *oh dear me.*

The songbirds were bonuses because for most of us Seward meant primarily a cruise into the Kenai Fjords. The winds were strong and the water rough when we set out in the seventy-foot yacht *Pacific.* Although mal de mer claimed her share, including one of ours, the cruise steamed on—past the playful little sea otters lying on their backs applauding us, past the eagles on the east bank and the seals and the sea lions before we entered the open waters in search of pelagic birds. For the dozen or more of us who spent at least nine of the nine and a half hours in the bow, wind-blown and spume-sprayed, the day was wonderfully exhilarating. And we did see birds—shearwaters, jaegers, Rhinoceros Auklet, Ancient Murrelet, Black Oystercatchers, Horned Puffins, and more. The Horned Puffins stay far out at sea, not as friendly as their tufted cousins in Kachemak Bay, but we spotted a few. All in all I chalked up eight lifers that trip, almost one an hour.

The day's outing also included some humpbacked whales breaching and a close encounter with the wall of Holgate Glacier, but not so close that we would have been upended had the glacier calfed. The skipper idled beneath the massive wall so high that we looked no bigger than a toy phalarope in the icy sea. The glacier grumbled, cracked, and boomed. Wispy avalanches blew off the surface and dissipated in midair, but no thundering berg broke loose. Our yacht passed numerous huge chunks as it plied its way back to the open sea.

September was breathing down our spotting scopes. Although Jenny Kate wanted to stay in Alaska until December, she and Wally had commitments back in Colorado and must soon start for home. Like a glacier our caravan was calfing. Some were going north to Dawson City—and perhaps even to Inuvit before they headed south. The Gees would go on to Anchorage and start playing catchup after their mechanical problems. Martha had a reservation to return to the Lower Forty-eight via the Inland Waterway. Dick and Liz, Mack and I wanted to explore the Valley of the Eagles. We would leave the Alaska Highway at Haines Junction and follow the Chilkat Valley south to Haines.

In Portage we boarded the train for Whittier. Portage, like Valdez, where we would spend the night, was completely wiped out in the 1964 earthquake. Both towns dropped six feet into the sea in one day, uprooting trees whose roots were then killed by the seawater. Those trees still stand like gray specters in both towns. But unlike Valdez, Portage was never rebuilt. It is a nontown, with one small hut for a railroad station beside lanes marked off on the tarmack where vehicles wait for the train to Whittier.

Boarding the train was a new adventure. Having arrived early, we were the first two rigs in what over the next hour and a half became four lines of RVs, eighteen-wheelers, miscellaneous pickup trucks, and motor cars. Being first in line, we were privileged to drive the full length of flatbeds. I was glad it was Mack's turn to drive. Up the ramp we went, following Dick and his trailer. A flatbed must be more than eight feet wide because our RV is eight feet, and at times I could see three or four spare inches when I looked down from the passenger's seat. That was after I had warned Mack between clinched teeth, "Move over! The hubcaps are scraping the guide wire."

"I can't move over," Mack hissed back. "I'm hanging over the guide line on this side."

As we crept along some twenty flatbeds, keeping close to Dick, I commented, "Who says we can't drive to Whittier?"

Finally the four lanes of waiting vehicles were loaded and the train started. I had just reached for my camera to take some magnificent pictures of Portage Glacier from this unusual angle when we plunged into a tunnel. Riding high in our rig, we pitched and rolled in total darkness. To ease the tension, I commented, "I don't suppose riding white-knuckled is any help to the engineer." Two tunnels and twenty-five minutes later, we rolled into the town that no one can drive to. A sign said, "Welcome to Whittier." Disembarking was a piece of cake.

Whittier is mostly boats, lots of fishing boats. One store sells everything from fishing tackle to bread and rubber boots, and two condominiums made over from the barracks of World War II accommodate the few residents and transient fishermen. A ferry departs at three P.M. five times a week for the seven-hour trip to Valdez, an experience that almost rivals for sheer beauty the sight of Mount McKinley in full sun. We had little time to explore Whittier before boarding the *E. L. Bartlett* and setting out across Prince William Sound in an afternoon of sparkling sunshine. The snow-covered Chaugach National Forest rose on the left. Judy, the accompanying naturalist, pointed out in the course of the afternoon a rookery of Black-legged Kittiwakes beside a roaring waterfall, salmon leaping like popcorn completely out of the water, and at least three killer whales, one with a baby at her side. But Mack and I found the Northern Fulmer all by ourselves, life bird number 398.

No one needed to point out the Columbia Glacier as we approached it some six hours into the trip. The ice floes beside us grew larger and colder. Portage, Exit, and Holgate Glaciers had been only preludes to Columbia, which is bigger than the state of Rhode Island. It was nine o'clock. The fading light and the clanking of the ice against the hull created an eerie feeling. Passengers, who after six hours of surfeiting beauty had settled back to their books and conversations, came to life again. They scuttled along the decks, pulled coat collars up against the increasing cold, and strained to take in the enormity of it all.

The brochures are right: seals do float atop the little bergs. With my camera poised, I waited to get just a little closer only to have them slip one by one into the water again and again. We reached Valdez at ten P.M. and were allowed to park (no campsites were available) on the edge of Bear Paw Campground for two nights.

After Valdez was wiped out in the 1964 Good Friday earthquake, it was rebuilt four miles inland on property donated by a local resident. Ten years later builders of the Trans-Alaska Pipeline selected Valdez for the terminus because of its ice-free port, eight-hundred-foot-deep harbor, and proximity to the interior. It won out over Cordova, which sixty years earlier had won out over it as the railroad terminus for the copper mines of the Copper Valley.

We woke the next morning engulfed in fog. Valdez, almost completely surrounded by snowcapped mountains, is supposed to be the little Switzerland of Alaska. I knew the peaks were there. I had seen them the night before. But with its population almost doubled by those who had come to help clean up the Exxon oil spill, in the cold reality of morning fog, the crowded campground, the tents, the hastily erected shacks along the waterfront looked something less than a Swiss village. And yet, some beautiful log homes, an impressive hospital, well-designed schools, a museum, the visitors center, and numerous gift shops suggested money as well as oil flowed from the pipeline that ends across the bay.

Touring the town in Dick's van didn't take long, and checking out the gift shops not much longer. The real business as always was birding. We drove along the Richardson Highway leading out of town. An eagle's nest captured our attention. Discovering an eaglet in it, we hung around, hoping some parents would show up, but they didn't. A little later Mack spotted a swan on Robe Lake. But was it a Trumpeter or a Tundra swan?

"More likely a Trumpeter," Dick observed. "It's locally fairly common, according to the field guide."

" 'in its few remaining areas,' " I said, reading on in the guide. We checked black facial skin, forehead, bill, and whether the neck "kinked back at the base" or was "held straight up from the breast." Was the head rounded or flat? It gave neither a noisy, high-pitched whoop nor a single, sonorous honk, either of which would have settled the question. Finally we agreed the head was slightly rounded and the bill imperceptibly concave.

"It's a Tundra," Mack declared.

"Our 399th lifer," I added, checking the score sheet. Speculating on what the 400th would be, we drove around looking for an answer. But we didn't find one, and the next morning we left Valdez.

The first car in Alaska was delivered to Valdez in 1905. The original so-called road followed the old trail over the Valdez Glacier. Today's modern road, however, ascends more gradually from Keystone Canyon, one more example of Alaska's limitless variety of magnificence. Leaving Valdez, we climbed past Bridal Veil and Horseshoe and other thundering waterfalls. The spray spotted our windshields. Far, far below, between us and the falls, the water churned up in great white clouds. As the road climbed, the air cooled from chilly to chillier. Eight-foot stakes, painted black at the top to guide snowplows, were all that separated us from the rocks and streams below. We emerged from banks of fog into a world of sunshine and rode along beside the mountaintops, some still embraced by clouds. Colossal dimples of snow filled crevices along the road, snow that never entirely melts, miniature glaciers in themselves.

The road rippled with frost heaves before we reached Glenellen. I thought to myself, *perhaps this is what the woman back in Tok meant when she said the road from Valdez is dreadful.* Then we turned onto the Tok Cut-Off and found out what she really meant. The unpaved road was under construction. Delays were welcome respites from the bumping and the jostling. After one stop of twenty minutes for one-way traffic, our turn came to wind our way through swirling dust, bulldozers, dump trucks, and jackhammers. The speed limit was twenty miles an hour. A sign warned, "Loose stones. Drive slow." Moments later an impatient Alaska cowboy in a light pickup truck zoomed past, zinging a stone at our left front window with the accuracy of David slaying Goliath. The window shattered on contact with an explosion matched only by

96

the outburst of expletives from the driver. I CBed to Dick up ahead, who pulled off, and like the good scout he had been over and over, he found a piece of cardboard and constructed a temporary window that kept the airflow tolerable for the rest of the run into Tok.

In fairness to the Tok Cut-Off, it was more than a window-breaking, body-shaking, dust-choking experience. The aspens on the hillsides had turned to gold seemingly overnight and the fireweed that lines the road had dropped its blossoms, leaving soft, pink pods as pretty as the flowers themselves. Furthermore, we followed the Wrangall National Park for miles with one snowcapped mountain after another—Mount Drum (12,000 feet), Mount Wrangall (14,000 feet), and Mount Sanford (16,000 feet). In retrospect it was another day of extraordinary adventure in Alaska.

Valley of the Eagles

Avoid the reeking herd
   Shun the polluted flock
Live like the stoic bird,
   The eagle of the rock.

—Elinor Hoyt Wylie

Fast-flying fog—scudding clouds really—engulfed the motor home as we climbed up Chilkat Pass. We floated in a spectral world, crisscrossing mountain streams, winding through boggy tundra. The motor groaned and strained but never faltered. A blue glacier hung on the right. Mountain peaks came and went through clouds to the left. At the crest the road started its downward plunge. Emerging finally from the clouds, we followed the Chilkat River eighteen downhill miles through the valley of the Eagles into Haines. Occasional eagles fished along the stream but not the thousands that come in winter to feed on the salmon drawn by the warmer waters.

Main Street, Haines, stretches a half mile from the intersection with Haines Highway where we camped to Portage Cove where the cruise ships dock. The north side is lined with stores, gift shops, and several bars. Across the street against a backdrop of snowcapped mountains stand the primary and upper schools. Both sides of the street were generously garnished with masses of brilliant flowers.

Fort William H. Seward overlooks the cove just to the south of Main Street, an historic district that includes Totem Village with replicas of Indian tribal houses. We wandered among the totem poles, inspected a trapper's cabin with its food caches, and returned in the evening for a salmon bake on the Parade Grounds.

The annual Southeast Alaska State Fair was in town only a few blocks from the campground. From our RV we could hear the emcee announcing awards, upcoming events, lost dogs, and found children. After a fruitless early morning search for grouse, Mack and I wandered over to the fair. Folks said we could *do it* in a half hour, but we took two. The pig race alone consumed thirty minutes. Though small it had all the trappings of a state fair and was wonderfully Alaskan. Even the pigs in the pig race were advertised "All Alaskan pigs, born and raised in North Pole, Alaska."

Items in the Farmers' Market ranged from prize-winning vegetables to braided rugs ($135–$145) and a 1975 Alaskan license plate ($5). A miniature carousel with lively calliope music and a bouncy "moon landing" thrill added the carnival features. Log rolling and most of the horse shows had taken place the day before. Nine-year-old Hillary, proprietor at times in our campground, entered her seven-year-old cockapoo in the 4-H dog obedience class. She could have taken the blue ribbon for diligence and faith, but in the end only illustrated it is hard to teach an old dog new tricks.

I checked out sweaters from Nepal, T-shirts galore, ice cream in purple cones, halibut and chips "$4.75 per five-inch plate," and Belgium waffles with strawberries but eschewed instant portraits, a ten-dollar haircut, painted face or an attempt to win a large stuffed moose in a challenge called BREAK THE BEER BOTTLE. It was all there—the popcorn and cotton candy, the sounds and smells, the sights and fun.

But birding was our business, and we were up the next morning at 5:45 determined to find some grouse—Spruce, Blue, or both. Dick drove us out Mud Bay Road toward Chilkat State Park and the Old Cannery. Spotting a fisherman beside a stream, Dick slowed and called out, "D'ya ever see grouse around here?"

"All the time," he said. "Lookin' fer some?"

"Tryin'."

"Park at th'end o' the road and walk out the loggin' trail. You'll find grouse."

And we did. At the second bend in the path sat a Spruce Grouse, eyeing us as though we had been expected. A lifer at last! Then for good measure, Mack found a Townsend's Warbler, the fifty-seventh life bird since joining the caravan in Edmonton and the seventy-sixth since leaving home. We walked on, but found no Blue Grouse that morning.

Back in town the State Fair Parade was forming. We joined the throngs at the corner of Third and Main. Notably absent were marching bands, but not music. A young woman played Scottish bagpipes for a folk dancing group. Some red-shirted youngsters performed their rope-jumping stunts to the accompaniment of a chorus. Children on fire engines threw candy to children on the ground.

The floats were distinctly Alaskan. One youngster rode in a Conestoga wagon (a little red go-cart) hand-lettered "Alaska or Bust." A crowd of river-rafting youth nestled high atop a pile of eight rafts stacked on the back of a truck. The Exxon spill float, a "boat" propelled by numerous feet, tipped and tilted. Lettered on the side was

Exxon-Valdez
rhymes with disease.

Behind it trailed long black streamers.

We spent the afternoon birding, first on the Chilkat Eagle Preserve, where a few eagles fished on the river. Then still looking for Blue Grouse, we drove to the Chilkat Peninsula. The scenery was beautiful. We talked with a woman who told us exactly where to find Blue Grouse. We would have to walk after parking the car. "The trail is rough and a little hilly," she explained as I carefully noted her directions of where to turn off the main trail. Then she said, "On second thought perhaps you should forget all I've said. I just remembered Joe saw a bear out there a couple of days ago. They're after the berries, you know."

Semi-confident we wouldn't let ourselves startle a bear, we were up again at 5:30 the next morning headed for Blue Grouse, the possibility of meeting a bear ever present in our minds as we frequently rustled branches and repeatedly called, "Here, Bear. It's only me, Bear." Actually we were retracing yesterday's route but going quite a bit farther along the logging road. It was a beautiful morning—no fog on the mountains, the snowcaps sparkling, the woodsy smells refreshing. Blueberries hanging lushly from the trailside bushes did make me a little nervous. We did find two lifers, a Hammond's Flycatcher and a Gray-cheeked Thrush, but no Blue Grouse. "Let's try again around dusk," Dick suggested.

Back in camp by midmorning, I was beginning to feel like a cuppa'. So Mack and I walked two blocks along Main Street and turned left onto Fifth Avenue, a short two-block dirt road, to the Chilkat Bakery. It was so busy that the maitre d' was taking reservations, but we found a table in a window nook and ordered Old Dutch apple cinnamon rolls at $1.25 per (10 percent off for senior citizens) and oh, my! They were worth every penny and more.

After lunch we drove out to Chilkoot Lake in the opposite direction from the logging road. No one said the words Blue Grouse, and no one expected to see Blue Grouse in the middle of the afternoon, but we knew what each other was thinking. The weather was still beautiful, and the day had grown warm. A camper at the state park reported having seen a bear fishing near the parking lot that morning. We strolled along some trails in the nearby woods. Conclusion: good fishing, luckless birding.

On the way back to town, Dick slowed for us to watch the lumbering operations in the harbor. An eagle lit in a tree overhead, distracting us for a moment. Dick picked up speed as we approached town as though to say, *Well, so much for this afternoon,* when Liz cried, "Stop, Dick! Grouse!" Two pairs of grouse were pecking around like dooryard chickens in a driveway right off the busy street. Dick slammed the brakes. We stared in disbelief, hardly daring to say, "What kind of grouse?"

Camera in hand I crept stealthily toward them. I started snapping. Walked a few steps and shot. Walked again. Shot some more. They went right on pecking. We came so close no one could doubt even without binoculars that we had found our Blue Grouse at last. A car stopped at the edge of the driveway. A woman called out, "What's the problem?"

"Blue Grouse," Liz cried excitedly.

"Is that all?" she grumped and drove on. One birder's gold is another woman's dross.

The Chilkat Dancers were performing that evening in the Tribal Village. They are, according to the program, "authentic performers of the unsurpassed art and dance of the Northwest Coast Indians." The Chilkat and the Chilkoot were the war leaders of the Tlingit (pronounced CLINK-it) Indians who gathered many songs and dances from various tribes on their trading expeditions from Seattle to the Yukon. Some thirty years ago, their descendants, feeling their culture was declining, formed the Chilkat Dancers to perpetuate the songs and dances they now perform around the world.

We were privileged to experience an evening of these dances recreating various Indian myths and traditions, how an old woman held back the tide so that the Raven clan, which was starving, could eat clams, how a Ptarmigan wins his mate, how the Cannibal Giant was caught and destroyed. The original totem pole of the Cannibal Giant stands today at Klukwan, the home of the Chilkats at the head of Bald Eagle Preserve on the outskirts of Haines.

The Chilkat Blanket Dance pits the Eagle and the Raven clans against each other in a tempestuous dance in which a chosen representative of each clan wears an authentic Chilkat blanket, each one a work of art itself. I could only guess at the weight, decorated as they are with dangling strings of shells, shards, tusks, and bones. I saw one in a museum insured for over twenty thousand dollars. Many of the dances were performed with masks, some with movable parts. And interestingly, children as young as three and four danced along with their elders, learning "the unsurpassed art and dance" on the stage first hand.

We were reluctant to say good-bye the next morning to our favorite Alaskan city. After breakfast Mack and I walked to town once more. We wanted to say good-bye again to Helen in the gift shop where we had found several Alaskan treasures. Haines Hitch-up, I thought as we left for the State Ferry Terminal, was one of the loveliest campgrounds we'd been in—all grassed with immaculate facilities, spacious sites, and gracious hosts. Clouds obscured the snowcapped mountains as the ferry set out for Skagway.

Forty-five minutes later, we drifted into the narrow harbor and docked beside a luxury cruise ship from the Princess line. A sheer wall of rock rose two hundred feet on our right. All of Skagway lay in a little cluster of streets before us. This was the end of the waterway for those headed for the Yukon in the mad days of the Gold Rush. From here they had a choice of heading up White Pass Trail (later known as Dead Horse Gulch) to the right or clambering over the glacier on the left. Both were treacherous routes, fraught with murder, suicides, disease, malnutrition, and death from hypothermia. The twenty to thirty thousand goldseekers, outfitting themselves for the arduous journey, created the tent and shack towns that became Skagway and Dyea.

Three blocks up Broadway and two blocks left on Fourth Avenue, we found Hoover's Chevron Campground, the only campground in Skagway. What a contrast to the grassy sites that we had left three hours earlier. How Mack laughed when she and Liz shook hands without either leaving her rig.

"Where is the shower?" Mack asked the garage man who parked us.

"In the garage," he said. "My wife will show you when you pay. Give her ten dollars when you go that way." But we chalked up a first in that bumpy, lumpy, right-off-the-sidewalk garage parking lot campground. For the first time ever, we leveled the camper in two strokes of the button to a perfect balance. Furthermore, this tiny little town of quaint shops and restored buildings lay right at our feet. Two blocks east and two blocks north was the post office on the outskirts of town. Two blocks south and two blocks west, Dee served savory baked salmon. The Visitors Center in the restored railway station near the dock shows a documentary video that vividly recreates the aspirations and the anguish of the Gold Rush days.

"May we stay another night?" Dick asked the garage man the next afternoon.

"Why not? Give the wife another tenner when you see'er."

Early the next morning, we set out on a wild ptarmigan chase to Summit Lake (3,292 feet), which we reached from sea level in a little more than eleven miles. Despite thick fog Dick pursued the chase as far as Log Cabin, a town marked only by a railroad crossing five miles beyond Canadian Customs. No ptarmigan—Willow, Rock, or anything else. Rock was high on my wish list.

Jefferson Randolph "Soapy" Smith's name figured prominently in the tales about Skagway. Back in the 1890s, he would meet the steamers and bilk the newcomers in devious ways. He could both ingratiate and intimidate. But when after the avalanche of April 1898 he appointed himself coroner and with his gang dug up victims from their snowy graves and robbed them, Frank Reid, city engineer, said enough was enough. Reid and Soapy exchanged shots. Soapy died from a shot to the heart. Reid lingered two weeks. Both are buried in Skagway's Gold Rush Cemetery, a forest of wooden markers identifying many who died in the Gold Rush of 1897–98.

We drove also the nine unpaved miles out to the Slide Cemetery in Dyea at the start of the old Chilkoot Trail. Most of those buried there were victims of the avalanche that ultimately and indirectly caused Soapy's demise, too. A raptor (potentially lifer 407) crossed our path and disappeared in the woods before anyone could attempt an identification. But returning from Dyea, we came upon it again, this time in a more cooperative mood. It flew but never very far from the car. I took several pictures from fairly close range, two of them in flight. The vote favored its being a Goshhawk, the only lifer of the day. We saw eagles, too, along the Taiya River.

Strange, how Skagway in less than forty-eight hours captured my affection. Departing at 7:30 the last morning, I noted the beautiful mountain ash on the hillside. Autumn tints were taking over, mostly the yellow of the aspen and the pink-and-white of the fireweed gone to seed. It was too early for the ponies with their poopy bags to be clip-clopping along, pulling the tourist buggies. I thought once more of the Bank of Alaska midway down Broadway with its half-dozen oak rockers in a semicircle around a pot-bellied stove in the lobby.

Twenty miles up Klondike 2, we left Alaska via Carcross and the Tagissh cutoff back to Jack's Corner on the Alaska Highway. The cutoff was newly completed and saves many miles for those going south. Not far along the Tagissh, an eagle swooped down in front of Dick, made a turn, and dived for something right in front of Mack and me. From there it flew to a tree just ahead of us and perched not forty feet from the ground. I CBed Dick that we were pulling off for a photo opportunity, not to wait. That bird sat there for the best eagle pictures that I'd taken on the whole trip. And stoic bird that he is, his embarrassment at having tried to pick up a stick that he must have mistaken for something juicier did not show in any of my photos.

The next morning the sky was unclouded as the sun rose over the spruces lining the Alaska Highway. The temperature was thirty-eight degrees Fahrenheit at 6:00 A.M. It would rise to sixty-four before we reached our campground in Fort Nelson. We had come this route in reverse in July, but as Hyakawa points out, "You can't step in the same river twice." Just so, this was not the same road it was in July. For one thing the potholes were gone and it was much (not all—no, no) improved. Frost heaves still prevailed.

Dick called, "Birds on the left. Didn't see 'em in time to identify." With that warning we slowed, watching on the left, and then ground to a halt. A family of Ruffed Grouse were deliberately crossing the road. Grouse, I have concluded, have an unshaken faith that they have the right of way whenever crossing the road.

We saw sheep near Stone Mountain, darker now than they were six weeks ago. Erosion in the stone of the mountain has created pillars that bear an eerie resemblance to human figures. Moose grazed within sight of the highway. We loitered over lunch on the banks of Muncho Lake.

After our first impulse to stay a second day in Fort Nelson to rest, Mack and I both revived and were ready to set out with Dick and Liz at 7:00 A.M. the next morning. Actually we were a wee reluctant to bring this show to a close after 4,056 miles of companionable traveling. That was the score on our rig, not counting the unrecorded miles that Dick had put on his van, birding on location. So we traveled tandem one more day.

The next morning we parted ways. Liz and Dick headed back to Edmonton; Mack and I chose the Hart Highway to Prince George and from there southeast through the Columbia Mountains to Jasper. We would not return home for another six weeks, but the Alaska adventure ended in Dawson Creek.

In Search of a Ross's Gull

All day thy wings have fanned,
At that far height, the cold, thin atmosphere,
Yet stoop not, weary, to the welcome land,
　　Though the dark night is near.

And soon that toil shall end,
Soon shalt thou find a summer home, and rest,
And scream among thy fellows; reeds shall bend,
　　Soon, o'er thy sheltered nest.

　　　　　　　　　　　　—William Cullen Bryant

"How are we going to top Alaska?" Mack asked once the dust had settled from four months on the road last summer, once the slides had been sorted, and the Alaska story told and retold.

"How about Churchill?"

"Where's that?"

"I'm not sure, but James Lane has a whole book, *A Birder's Guide to Churchill*. So it must be a birding hot spot."

"What's there?"

"Thayer's and Iceland gulls, Baird's Sandpiper, King Eider, Red-throated Loon, Snowy Owl . . ."

"Snowy Owl! Let's go."

"But the rarest is Ross's Gull."

Churchill, Manitoba, on Hudson Bay is the most likely place short of Siberia to find a Ross's Gull. Mack and I, in our seventies, traveling alone in a motor home, had never seriously considered Siberia. Churchill, however, was a temptation we couldn't resist.

It wouldn't be exactly an everyday outing either. The AAA Trip-tik ended in Winnepeg with the notation "See local maps." The road itself ends in Thompson, 443 miles north of Winnepeg and still 300 miles south of Churchill. From there we had a choice of plane or train.

We chose the thirteen-hour train trip, confining our luggage to bare essentials—insect repellent, binoculars, spotting scope, cameras, tripod, fruit juice, granola bars, heavy sweatshirts, warm jackets (for the winds can be vigorous even in June on the banks of Hudson Bay) and toothbrushes. What knapsacks and camera bags could not hold we wore. Thus on a dry, warm summer evening, we arrived at the railroad station in Thompson in winter jackets and rubber boots, ready to head out for our Churchill adventure.

About an hour north of Thompson, the train stopped at the Indian village of Pikwitonei. Three-wheeled ATVs and many dogs of ambiguous ancestry stirred up clouds of dust as they varoomed in to meet villagers returning from a day in Thompson. After that brief furor, we seemed to leave civilization behind. Except for the three-legged, perma-frost-proof telephone poles stringing their sagging lines beside us, all we could see was endless taiga with its scrub spruce, stunted tamarack, and soggy muskeg. By ten-thirty the sun was putting the finishing touches on another spectacular sunset. Glad that we had reserved a sleeping section, we retired to the click, click, click of the wheels carrying us to Churchill and, we hoped, a Snowy Owl and a Ross's Gull.

I woke the next morning to what seemed a barren vastness. But that barren vastness produces over three hundred varieties of plant life and nurtures over thirty species of mammals from the boreal chorus frog, hares, beavers, foxes, and wolves to bears, moose, and caribou. And birds! Even though

109

this was the end of June and migration was over, the bird book promised more than fifty species that would be really hard to miss and forty more that we should not have to work hard to find. The latter included the Ross's Gull, an Arctic species that first showed up in Churchill little more than a decade ago. The first nests, built on hummocks in a shallow pond, were ravaged by predators. Now, however, the population is slowly growing.

The heart of Churchill is one block deep and eight blocks long with peripheral, unpaved streets wandering around the edges. It is bounded by Churchill River, Hudson Bay, great, gray boulders, and the tundra. The population varies from six to twelve hundred, depending upon the season. It peaks in October when tourists come to see the polar bears. But this was June, and we were looking not for polar bears but for a little eleven-inch, rosy-breasted gull, which flies like a pigeon and comes rarely and briefly during the second week of June to breed on the edge of Hudson Bay. By mid-July it moves from the "not hard to find" to the "you might see" category. You have to be lucky to find one in August. Then it is gone, migrated to Point Barrow or Siberia.

The train arrived late morning. We paused at our motel, one block from the railroad station, only long enough to pick up a rental car. Our first goal was Akudlik Marsh four miles out of town, where we should find Ross's Gulls feeding on the ponds or even nesting along the highway. But such is the nature of birding that the hours often go by faster than the miles. Our roadside birding started immediately. Smith's Longspurs scratched in the grass beside the road. Oldsquaws with their knitting-needle tails swam in the tundra lakes. White-rumped Sandpipers fed in the weeds. I photographed Horned Larks, Hudsonian Godwits, and Lesser Golden Plovers from the car window. We did not even get to Akudlik Marsh the first day, but we did clinch six lifers.

The next morning we started near the mouth of the Churchill River just above where it flows into the bay. Our gull had been seen flying there with other both common and uncommon gulls, but if it was there that morning, it was too fast for *my* eyes. We did identify one Common Eider, some Harlequin Ducks, and a Sabine's Gull. Later, following the Coast Road, which eventually would take us around to Akudlik Marsh, we were sidetracked by specks far below us in the surf of the bay. Abandoning the car, we clambered, scope and camera in hand, over the tundra, which rose and dropped like sand dunes. Still the water remained far below, but the scope finally revealed not White-winged Scoters, as we had first guessed, but a rarer find, Black Guillemots. Back on the road, we had not gone far before we found a Thayer's Gull nesting on a hummock in one of the many ponds that lined our route. The thought *with a lifer an hour, who needs a Ross's Gull* evaporated before I could say it. We did want a Ross's Gull.

After lunch Mack suggested we walk to the Granary Ponds before starting our afternoon search. This cluster of shallow, muddy-bordered, boulder-strewn ponds was only a three-minute walk from the motel. They swirl with Greater Scaup, Oldsquaws, Northern Pintails, American Wigeon, and more. Red-necked Phalaropes putt-putt around like bathtub toys. Arctic Terns swoop and bank amid a flurry of Bonaparte's Gulls. Eventually we worked our way to a group of birders on a far bank who, we noticed, had been watching one spot intently for some time. As we approached, one woman, squatting on the edge of the water, raised a finger of caution and mouthed "R o s s ' s   G u l l." There it sat, sharing a splinter of rock with two Arctic Terns and a Bonaparte's Gull, only fifteen or twenty feet from the shore.

I am not an overconfident birder. I would not trust myself to distinguish between a Herring and a Thayer's gull unassisted in a habitat common to both. But bless that little Ross's

Gull. I knew it when I saw it. That does not really call for any new medals on my birding hat, though, because not only is it the only gull with a wedged tail, it is positively identifiable in breeding plumage by its unique black necklace. We silently joined the other admirers, watching while it preened, as oblivious of us as the terns and other gulls sharing the little piece of the pond. A half hour later, it tucked its head into its shoulder as much as to say, "The show's over." The next afternoon we again found it in the same place, this time with its mate by its side.

Finding the Ross's Gull almost in the backyard of our motel epitomizes birding in Churchill. Of course we had to search, but on the whole, the birds were cooperative. They were dependable. They were approachable. Well-camouflaged Canada Geese and their young, sometimes two or three families and sometimes dozens of families, commonly fed among the tundra flowers. We could go back to the banks of the Churchill River near the pump station at the end of Goose Creek Road and find Buffleheads and Tundra Swans right where they had been the day before. A Long-tailed Jaeger, as if to say, "Look me over," flew low over our heads as we poked along the edge of the bay. A Willow Ptarmigan in full breeding plumage took my breath away as it posed nonchalantly for a picture before crossing the road to join his mate and chicks in the grasses. I would have missed them without his help.

Alone and unguided except for the field guide to Churchill, we found over fifty species of birds in four days. But that doesn't call for any medal for my birding hat either. We missed many, too many, including the Snowy Owl.

"Next time," Mack said as the train pulled out of the station, "next time the Snowy Owl."

The Dry Tortugas

There is a singer everyone has heard,
Loud, a mid-summer and a mid-wood bird,
Who makes the solid tree trunks sound again.

—Robert Frost

Mack and I were among the last of the twenty-some passengers to arrive at the *Yankee Freedom,* rocking gently at its moorings in Key West that April evening. Bruce, one of our birding guides, greeted us cordially. "I see you took me at my word. You're traveling light," he said, noting I was burdened only with a small knapsack and one camera bag. "You'll be glad."

The cabin was a buzz of voices. Crew and passengers mingled around the few tables, chattering and sipping sodas. Anticipation was palpable. "Follow me," Bruce said, pushing through the throng. "I'll show you where you'll sleep. Watch your step on the stairs. They're narrow, steep, and winding." At the bottom several little recesses of bunks opened in a circle around us. "That's yours," he indicated, pointing to one of them. "There'll be six of you—all women. Dump your gear and come topside for greetings and prelims."

After remarks and instructions from the first mate, the chef, and our guides, the captain concluded the remarks with "We'll be sitting a few miles off Green Key at sunrise. 'Twill be a pretty sight for anyone who wants to get up early." Then after a pause, he added, "That's probably all of you."

I had not slept at sea since I crossed the Atlantic on the *Queen Mary* thirty-five years before. Any similarities between

113

the two vessels escaped me that first evening except that we were afloat on the briny.

"What're you going to do with your sleeping bag?" I asked the young woman standing at the bunk across from me.

"Oh, I'm sleeping on the upper deck tonight. I'll be out of your way in a sec. And tomorrow night I'll sleep on the island."

"Do you have a tent?" I wondered out loud.

"No, don't need one."

"What about mosquitoes?" I asked naively.

"Mosquitoes? There're no mosquitoes on the Tortugas. The *Dry* Tortugas? There's no water. And so no insects."

"Super," I exclaimed. Not admitting how much insect repellent I was toting.

"Yeah, it's great for sleeping under the stars but tough on the birds making first landing here, exhausted and hungry."

Double bunks lined the three walled sides of our *stateroom*, leaving a three-by-six space in the center (three square feet per person, I figured) in which to disrobe and en-cot. *Hammock* would be a better word for the interwoven leather straps hung from metal frames.

I soon realized why the birder we met last evening looking for a White-crowned Pigeon on Islamarado Key said that though he has made this trip many times he has never slept below deck. It's not for the tall or the bulky. If I'm five feet eight, the cot, I judge, is about five feet seven. Our pigeon-searching companion was at least six two or three. Shortly after midnight the engines, which had been throbbing, revved up and we were on our way to the Dry Tortugas, a small group of islands sixty-eight miles west of Key West. The magic of the sea was working its spell.

Most of us were on deck the next morning to supervise the rising of the sun, my camera poised to catch the first slice of red to inch above the horizon. We were rock-a-byeing in a gentle sea. Fort Jefferson, a silhouette two or three miles to the right, bathed in the blush of the dawn's early light. Like the Ancient Mariner, we sat "idle as a painted ship upon a painted ocean." Gulls cried; waves slapped the hull. While the ship waited permission to proceed to the limited mooring, I contemplated Fort Jefferson and its checkered history.

Ponce de Leon discovered the islands in 1513 and named them the Tortugas for the great number of huge sea turtles that he found there. Later visitors added *Dry* because the islands have no natural water supply. Engineers in the mid-1800s envisioned a fortress, which could effectively defend the entire Gulf of Mexico against any intruder, an American Gibraltar, and set out to build it. It was to be, and still is, a huge six-sided, three-tiered structure encircling the entire ten acres of Green Key.

But from the first, Fort Jefferson was ill conceived. The development of a sophisticated cannon made the towering, eight-foot-thick walls obsolete before they were finished. Furthermore, the fort was half constructed before the engineers discovered they were building not on a coral island but a mound of sand and shells piled up by ocean currents. Millions of tons of bricks, stones, mortar, and steel were squeezing the sand and shells out like the filling of a jelly sandwich. The island, which had been barely three feet above sea level at the beginning, was now sinking and the walls were crumbling. Instead of abandoning their noble vision, the engineers built a moat to keep the waves and tide from further undermining the foundations and continued building.

Through the years Fort Jefferson has been a way station for galleons of treasure en route to Spain from Mexico, a naval base, a prison, a quarantine station for smallpox victims, an army base, a coaling station, and in the 1920s a stopover for rum runners. In 1935 after much abuse and neglect, Fort Jefferson and the Dry Tortugas were made a national monu-

115

ment. Today the rookeries and migrating birds are protected by law.

By midmorning we had reached the fort. Even before disembarking I had claimed two lifers. Sooty Terns and Brown Noddies nest on Bush Key not more than a football field's length from the fort. The sooties, like other terns, nest on or near the ground. The noddies in low-growing bushes. To hear the racket and see the air constantly filled with banking wings, I wondered who was left to tend a nest. Both birds surface fish in flight and flight was perpetual. The clamor of the terns' piercing, nasal *wide-a-wake, wide-a-wake* and the noddies' lower-pitched *k-a-a-a* didn't cease from the time we arrived until we left three days later.

Because a slip was still not available, we were sent ashore in a skiff, seven or eight at a time. Numerous small crafts bobbed at anchor just off the shore. Several seaplanes parked on the narrow airstrip, reminding me that we were only minutes from Key West by air. To those in our group who come out here every spring or even several times during the brief migration season, this landing was as routine as birding in the city park. But in my mind's eye, the Dry Tortugas were a miniature Galápagos, and I went ashore with the same eagerness I hope someday to approach the giant sea turtles on those islands. Boobies and noddies and Magnificent Frigatebirds were waiting. And if I were really lucky, a White-tailed Tropicbird would show up. So with the excitement of a child turned loose in Santa's toy shop, I hurried across the moat to collect my treasures.

To read about Fort Jefferson is one thing. To stand within its enclosure is quite another. I recalled Mr. Pickwick's reaction to Rochester Castle: "glorious pile—frowning walls—tottering arches—dark nooks and crumbling staircases." I would climb those crumbling staircases faithfully each morning at ten, for if the White-tailed Tropicbird were coming, it was wont to show at that hour. I stood upon the parapets with the believers and scanned the skies for the bird that didn't come.

The Magnificent Frigatebirds were reliable, though. Every morning before the sun warmed the air, a dozen or more glided overhead on the thermal waves. They floated, soared, hovered, lazed immediately above the frowning walls, so close their inflated red pouches were clearly visible.

As I have already noted, the Tortugas have no natural source of drinking water. The Coast Guard brings in water once a week for the few people who live in the barracks and maintain the park. And for the birds, someone has humanely constructed a tiny fountain, an oasis after a long flight from Mexico or South America. Some of the saddest stories are acted out close to that trickle of water, for these birds arrive hungry and weak. Some of the songbirds are so feeble that they are unable to ward off the attacks of starving Cattle Egrets. Nor are the egrets immune to death from starvation. Only the strongest survive to make the next leg of the journey to the mainland. With no insects and only one small, dripping fountain, the island is not a friendly depot for birds. Still, the majority do survive, do rest, recuperate, and fly on. Because they are weak, they are more approachable than they would be under normal circumstances.

Also because this is a way station for so many migrants, more species are found here together than would ever be true once they've dispersed to their natural habitats. Within the space of an hour and three or four acres, I saw Hooded and Chestnut warblers, Orchard and Northern orioles, Yellow-billed Sapsuckers, Summer and Scarlet tanagers, an Indigo Bunting, and Shiny Cowbird and the Ovenbird.

The Ovenbird had been on our wish list until three days ago. Although it breeds all over the eastern United States and winters near my home, it had eluded both Mack and me until we stopped at Costello Hammock near Homestead on our way to Key West. "It's very secretive," the naturalist warned. "But if you wait quietly, it will in time come to the edge of the woods." Our patience had been rewarded, but we could have saved our time.

"Come here," Mack called to me from where she was exploring the towering walls. "What's this bird?" knowing very well what it was.

"An Ovenbird," I exclaimed. We sat on some fallen boulders and watched it. There not ten feet from us, in the shelter of one of the arches, this little bird was hopping about in search of a seed or any edible morsel, regardless of the numerous passersby.

"So much for secretiveness when you're hungry," Mack commented.

In contrast to the universality of the Ovenbird, the Shiny Cowbird cannot under normal conditions be found anywhere in the country except in the Dry Tortugas. It was a must before we left there. The suspense was short-lived. Before lunch one of our leaders had found one in the grasses among the several trees that grow within the fort.

"Are we birding or are we birding!" Mack exclaimed. "Five lifers before lunch. Can you believe it?"

"The Galápagos can wait," I commented.

But lunch wouldn't. We had been urged to be prompt. I had crossed the moat and was about to board the ship, which was now in dock, when Mack called. Her attention had been drawn to a crowd by the pilings on the left. "It's time for lunch," the Capricorn in me reminded her.

"Lunch kerplunch," she said. "I'm going to see what's going on even if I have to walk the plank."

What was going on was that Bruce had found a Black Noddy perched on one of the pilings at the abandoned coal station. Now a Black Noddy is not to be confused with the thousands of Brown Noddies swirling and squawking over-

118

head. That is, it is not to be confused if you have a good leader who is able first to find it and then distinguish it for you from the hundreds of Brown Noddies also perched on the pilings. The Black is two or three inches smaller than the Brown, is black, as its name suggests, has a slender bill (Bruce said), and is very exciting to find because it cannot be found anywhere else in the United States. And it is not easy to come by on the Tortugas.

On our way to lunch, we were detained again. This time by a flock of Ruddy Turnstones feeding in the seaweed along the beach. They were literally turning stones, rooting in a frenzy through the beach debris.

Our group went to Loggerhead Key one afternoon, another island in this cluster of eight. It is larger than Green, more thickly wooded, with no man-made structures, except for a solitary lighthouse. We broke into two small groups, each with a leader, and birded opposite ends of the island. An hour later we traded territories. In that short time, we saw eighteen species of warblers, three of them lifers for Mack and me. Flashes of color darted through the branches—an American Redstart, a Yellow-billed Cuckoo, Rose-breasted Grosbeak, Painted Bunting. With a Black-whiskered Vireo here and a Northern Waterthrush there, here a thrush, there a thrush—Gray-cheeked, Swainson's, and Wood—Mack and I saw ninety-six species, including twenty lifers, before we returned to Key West.

One evening about dusk, traveling by skiff, seven or eight at a time, everyone who chose had a close encounter with thousands of Magnificent Frigatebirds in their rookery on still another nearby key. Because the birds are protected by law, no one is allowed to disembark. And so the skiff stopped short of spooking the birds, who themselves were in such a state of squawk and flux that I don't know how we would know if we were disturbing them. We were close enough anyway to see those old fellows in the trees seeming to contend with each other as they inflated their huge red pouches. If their object was to attract females, the ladies had a wide selection from which to choose. On our way back to the *Yankee Freedom,* we swung by Bush Key for a closer look at the rookeries of the Sooty Terns and Brown Noddies, our constant midair companions around the ship.

On a second trip to Loggerhead Key, we had several options—swim, bird, fish, snorkel, read on the sunny deck, loll in the cool cabin. Mack went with the birders. I wandered the beach with my camera. When Mack returned late afternoon, she said, "Come with me. I've two lifers for you."

"What? Where?" I asked in some confusion because the last of the birders were returning, and we were about to raise anchor.

"Not five minutes from here. Hurry!"

"How do ya know they'll be there?" I was reluctant to dash off on a futile chase.

"They'll be there. I promise. Come on!"

Not more than a hundred feet into the woods, Mack paused. "It's right around here," she said. "It's too tired to have gone far."

"What are we looking for?"

"A Worm-eating Warbler. It's fairly near the ground. I don't think it has the strength to fly very high."

A motion on a bush not a foot off the ground caught my eye. "That's it," Mack cried. "See that heavily streaked head? And plain breast? That's a Worm-eating Warbler."

"It looks like a sparrow to me."

"Believe me. It's a Worm-eating Warbler. It's supposed to look like a sparrow. Check the book."

"Gee, I don't even need my binoculars. Where's the other one?"

"Just a little farther. This will be easy. It's a Kentucky

Warbler. It has *bright* yellow underparts, a dominant yellow eye-ring, and a black mustache. It'll be near the ground also. Look for yellow." We walked along.

A leaf moved. A tiny fleck of yellow gold hopped and rested. Not fifteen feet from where I stood.

"This is the way to hunt warblers," I said as we made our way back to the ship. A dominant characteristic of warblers is their fidgetiness, never sitting still among the leaves for more than a second or two. Under normal conditions, these two would never have waited five or ten minutes for me to find them. "Two lifers in five minutes," I said. "Thanks for fetching me."

The skipper finally got all snorkelers, birders, fishermen, photographers, and stragglers on board and set his sights on Fort Jefferson where the kitchen staff was preparing a barbecue on the greensward between the moat and the fort.

No account of our excursion to the Dry Tortugas would be complete without kudos for the chefs. They not only prepared bountiful and tasty meals, they actually caught the fish, sometimes far out in the ocean. And having caught it, they knew what to do with it—grilled, in salads, hors d'oeuvres, chowders. Johnny had a recipe that some would have walked the plank for. In addition to three hearty meals a day, they offered a midmorning cheese board and an afternoon buffet for anyone who happened to be around. We were rarely out of touch with food if we so chose. It was almost gourmet around the clock.

Although pig and poi were missing, the feast at the island's edge that evening had all the festivity of a luau. If someone had strummed a guitar, I could have believed I was in Hawaii as the sun set beyond the palms to the west.

Our birding, however, did not conclude with the luau. The journey home the next day extended into the Gulf Stream in search of pelagic birds. En route to the deeper waters, we came upon three Brown Boobies perched on a channel marker. They looked us over thoroughly and voted to let us pass. Not far beyond twelve Masked Boobies rested between flights on a small key. It is a beautiful bird in flight. All the flight feathers and face are black, contrasting dramatically with the white shoulders and body. It is a relative of the Northern Gannet, but smaller with more black on the wings. Once out in the deeper water, we did see a Northern Gannet for comparison, the third lifer for Mack and me that morning. With how many to go? Three actually, both Bridled and Roseate Terns and an Audubon's Shearwater. So often at sea, the birds fly by too fast for me to appreciate, but not so the Roseate Terns that day. They flew close and low. And as if to say, "Would you like another view?" they swooped around us once more.

Though I can't count them on my life list of birds, one of the most surprising sights was the flying fish, which I had never seen before. Once they caught my attention, I was fascinated by the dozens that burst from the water and flew beside the ship fifty, a hundred, or more, feet, just skimming the surface before dropping back into the water again.

Late afternoon found us back at the dock in Key West, well tanned, well fed, and well rewarded.

Up and Down the Rio Grande

One of the ones that Midas touched,
who failed to touch us all,
Was the confiding prodigal
the blissful oriole.

—Emily Dickinson

The birding spot that Mack and I have returned to more frequently than any other is the lower Rio Grande. Campers go to Bentsen–Rio Grande State Park for various reasons, but they are all spelled B-I-R-D-S. We went there first to expand our life list, to satisfy our curiosity, and, if we were really lucky, to feed popcorn to a pair of Clay-colored Robins. A birding newsletter had alerted us to the robins' partiality for popcorn.

Arriving late at the campground, we found a sign in the window: Copeland, take Site 6. In the fading light, we set up camp, took a stroll through the park, and went to bed early. About daybreak I slowly became conscious of muffled sounds outside. Raising the shades slightly, I saw fifteen or twenty birders homing their scopes in on the woods beside us. I woke Mack, who hurriedly pulled on her jeans and quietly stepped outside.

"What's up?" she asked the first scope she met.

"Clay-colored Robins," it whispered back.

"Where?" she asked incredulously.

"The Rare Bird Hotline is reporting: 'Go to campsite 6, Bentsen State Park, Mission, Texas, for a pair of Clay-colored Robins.' "

She opened the door and called softly to me, "Start popping corn."

In the days that followed, Chachalacas and woodpeckers gobbled up most of our freshly popped corn before the shy robins dared emerge from the protective undergrowth. But they did ultimately succumb to the temptation—tentatively and unpredictably—coming for stray kernels after the big birds left. Chachalacas must have looked like King Kong to a pair of skittish robins scratching in the leaves. Still, one of the robins did fly bravely to the tabletop, which was always strewn with bird seeds, popcorn, and oranges. We grew accustomed to the robin seekers, who came from sunrise to sunset. Whenever they found one of us home, they would ask in awed whispers, "Have you seen *them* today?" We developed a rather proprietary feeling for *our robins.*

In contrast to the muted steps and voices of the first day, a racket, the likes of which I had never heard, jolted me out of bed the next morning. Believe me, to wake to the clamorous chorus of Chachalacas is literally a rousing experience. Their performance is precisely orchestrated. It bears no resemblance to the desultory caws of early morning crows. With no preliminary chucks, no clearing of throats, Chachalacas burst ensemble from utter silence to full voice. No crescendos here; no diminuendos. The females by nature (not conductor's direction) sing one note higher than the males, a subtlety I should have missed had I not read it somewhere. The chorus stops as suddenly as it starts. No inattentive countertenor spoils the performance with a straggly note. But don't applaud yet. This is only the pause between movements. At the flick of a baton, they are again in full voice. Chachaláca! Chachaláca! Stress the third note. To hear them once is to remember them always.

Of an afternoon some members of the chorus saunter into our campsite in small, sedate groups of four or five, walking with the aplomb of guests at a garden party. They come about teatime when the little birds take their siestas. Their iridescent tails catch the sunlight as they haughtily peck from popcorn to sunflower seeds. Those who pause to drink from the Tufted Titmouse's bath imbibe with dignity, raising their long necks to swallow, modestly revealing the little pink patch on each side of their throats. They scarcely lose their composure in the flurry of flying to the tabletop to check the fruit counter. But they rarely tarry there. One murmurs, "Table hopping does not become us." Soon another reminds the rest in a throaty alto voice suggestive of Bea Arthur, "Time for choir rehearsal, girls." Off they quietly fly. Before long from another corner of the campground comes the startling cry: Chachaláca! Chachaláca! Chachaláca!

We would have been well entertained had we never left our campsite. Great-tailed Grackles rattled in the trees overhead. Great Kiskadees called from the woods. A Brown Thrasher with an amazing repertoire sang in a nearby tree. The little birds came to our milk-jug feeders—chickadees, cardinals, Black-crested Tufted Titmice. Flocks of goldfinches scavenged on the ground. But my favorites, flashing their vivid colors as they cruised throughout the campground in search of oranges, were the Golden-fronted Woodpecker, the Green Jay, and the Altamira Oriole. By keeping our orange depots well supplied, we assured the visits of these three throughout the day.

Oranges are a staple. At our site alone, the birds consumed half a bushel in a week. Chachalacas like theirs on the ground or table. The others prefer their halves impaled on a spike or twig on a reclining tree trunk or horizontal limb. The Golden-fronted Woodpecker is the most demanding. He'd scream, "Where's my orange? The oranges are empty!" And empty they were every morning. Most shells end up completely excavated even without the help of squirrels. But squirrels take their share.

One afternoon I placed half an orange in the crotch of a small tree near our rig. Then I set up my camera, focused on the orange, attached flash and cable release, stepped back, and waited. An Orange-crowned Warbler was my first customer. It lit on the edge of the orange and drank comfortably, but that stance did not work for the big nine-to-ten-inch fellows who had to stand back from the orange. The Green Jay gave up after a few abortive attempts to find a footing. With a little hint of sour grapes, the Golden-fronted Woodpecker decided he wanted a more isolated location. Then the Altamira Oriole lit with one foot on each limb of the Y, several inches above the orange. After studying the situation, without moving his feet so much as a comma, he dropped his head and stretched for the prize. Undaunted by my flashing camera, he kept stretching until he made contact. With one more thrust, he plunged his beak deep into the nectar and drank. When at last he righted himself, still straddled between the two limbs and perhaps a little dizzy, he looked me straight in the eye and asked, "What do I do now?"

Despite the entertainment in our own backyard, the park had much more to offer. At site 42, a Great Horned Owl kept vigil high in a tree all day, stoically ignoring periodic attacks by a mockingbird, which seemed to bear him a grudge. Near another site, if we were lucky, we could binocular a Blue Bunting, which had taken a fancy to the particular ambrosia featured there. And if we were very lucky, as we were one morning, we saw the male, female, and juvenile feeding together. This was the *Blue* Bunting, not to be confused with the Indigo, which commonly breeds from Texas to New England. The Blue Bunting is a Mexican bird. And a Screech Owl was a permanent resident at site 105 in the primitive campground. He was often visible during the day and could always be counted on to depart for his nightly hunt promptly at seven o'clock.

After our initial visit, every February found us back at Bentsen State Park. The visits extended from a few days to a week to two weeks. Time flew as we enjoyed the birds, pursued the trails, and enjoyed the friends who met us there. Marjory and Eleanor came twice from Connecticut, Jean from Dallas, Becky from Austin, Jenny Kate and Wally from Boulder, Jean and Fred from Longmont, Colorado.

Others who like us returned year after year became friends. Louise and Red Gambill spend their winters in Mission and come regularly to the park early every morning. We first met them the year the Rose-breasted Becard was the rare bird in the park. Louise and Red knew its pattern, for it didn't conveniently settle down and wait to be discovered. We soon learned they were as dedicated and helpful as any birders we could ever hope to meet. Morning after morning they would be in the park ready to help another group of birders find the Rose-breasted Becard.

Bentsen regularly had a different rare bird or two each February. One year it was the Hook-billed Kite on the River Trail. He gave himself away by the piles of snail shells under the trees. Another year a Tropical Parula showed up, "resident but rare in the Rio Grande Valley of Texas," my field guide said. So rare the National Geographic Society's *Birds of North America* has no map for it. But rarer still another year was the Masked Tityra, which turned up in a tree in the primitive campground one afternoon. It was so rare that it didn't appear in the bird guides of North America and for a while the American Birding Association wasn't sure whether it was countable for life lists this side of the border. But lists or no lists, that stray, pale gray (so pale it looked white to me) bird with black wings created an exciting moment for forty or fifty birders who suddenly materialized from all over the park (and miles beyond) once Louise and Red put out the word.

Bentsen State Park is conveniently located between several other good birding spots up and down the lower Rio Grande. The year the Crane Hawk, another Mexican stray, was discovered at Santa Ana National Wildlife Refuge, I got up in the dark to be at Santa Ana by sunrise. The Crane Hawk had established a hunting routine, generally being sighted from just before sunrise through the next hour or hour and a half in the vicinity of the woods south of the levee. On this particular morning, the early birders broke into two groups, each hoping to psyche the wanderer out.

I went with those who took to the woods after crawling over or under a fence and breaking a trail through the underbrush. We scanned the skies, moved on a little farther, and scanned some more. We scoped the trees. We talked quietly among ourselves. We theorized. We rehashed tales of earlier sightings over the past week. After a couple of hours, I decided the hawk had probably outwitted us all. Mack and Heidi were waiting back in camp. We were departing later this morning. I headed back toward the levee and the car. Three men on the levee were at their scopes. As I drew nearer, one motioned for me to hurry.

"We've got it!" They urged me on. I reached the scope in time to see a black dot fade into oblivion.

"Well," Mack said back in camp when I related my tale, "you can't win them all."

On other occasions Santa Ana treated us much better. We found our first Least Grebe and our first Great Kiskadee there, and our first Buff-bellied Hummingbirds. They were darting back and forth in a huge patch of shrimp plants. I associate Santa Ana with White-faced Ibis, Black-necked Stilts, and kingfishers. The Ringed Kingfisher, a little larger than our Belted and with more rust than the female Belted, usually shows up somewhere in the refuge. He's a rather commanding figure. In contrast the little Green Kingfisher is half the size of the Ringed but with a proportionately longer but indisputable kingfisher beak. It amuses me. It looks like a little kid trying to do a grown-up's job.

On our most recent visit to Santa Ana, we were specifically looking for a Northern Jacana, another of those Mexican wanderers found only accidentally in the ponds and marshes on the southern tip of Texas. One had been sighted at Santa Ana.

"Look by the sluice at the end of Pintail Lake," we'd been told. We looked at the sluice and up and down and around Pintail Lake. Finally someone spotted it across the lake from the sluice. As the small group of birders talked among themselves, the Jacana flew.

"Where'd it go?"

"To the right. See it on that island of weeds?"

"That's a little closer."

Over the next hour, it gradually worked its way toward us. Patience. By noon it had come to the weeds and underbrush not thirty feet from the sluice. Its extremely long toes (feet, I suppose) allow it to walk on floating weeds and plants, giving the effect of its walking on water. It's only two-thirds the size of a Common Moorhen but with feet that look twice as large. If we hadn't found it at Santa Ana, we would have had a second chance at Falcon Dam, where three immatures had been reported.

Falcon Dam, upstream from Bentsen, has one advantage over Santa Ana. It has a campground. Mack and I found our first Verdin there, a sprightly little bird not much bigger than a hummingbird. One windy day Mack and I started to walk across the dam. We could have driven but didn't want to cross into Mexico. Nor did we want to get into an awkward situation turning the motor home around this side of customs. I was trying to take a picture of the Rio Grande, an impossible task in the fierce wind that was slapping us around. Mack was trying to persuade me to give up the project when suddenly a great, hawklike bird appeared, circling overhead. It seemed to enjoy being buffeted by the gale. Actually it was standing up against it better than we were. But what was it? Nothing that resembled anything in our North American guides. But back in the shelter of the rocking motor home, we found it in the Mexican bird book. It was a Gray-headed Kite.

"Shall we count it?" I asked Mack.

"Sure. Why not?"

"Was it on our side of the border?"

"Who cares? We earned it."

Driving from Bentsen State Park to Falcon Dam, one passes Santa Margarita Ranch. Here and there on a few thousand acres, a few hundred heads of cattle munch among the cacti, rocks, and stubble. For a dollar given to whoever comes to the door of the main house, birders are allowed to park and walk through the trees to the river. Mack paid our dollar, and we set off in search of a Brown Jay. It was a beautiful spring day. The huisachi trees were in full bloom. A pair of Harris Hawks lit briefly in a burst of yellow blossoms. But the Brown Jays must have gone shopping that afternoon. We sat on the riverbank, contemplating the beauty around us before deciding upon our next move. As we sat, a border patrolman drove up in his truck. We exchanged a few pleasantries before Mack asked, "Where can we find a Brown Jay?"

"Should find 'em right here."

"But we haven't."

"I haf'ta walk downstream aways. If ya wanna come along, we should see jays."

He led the way, ducking under low-slung branches and detouring around inlets. The river was low, the water being controlled by the dam farther upstream. Some Mexicans on the south bank were hoeing corn in a dry, stony plot of land.

"Do you have many illegal crossings here?" Mack asked. "It looks as though they could walk across."

"Walk er swim," our companion said, "but I'm not patrolling for them. I'm looking fer cows."

"Cows?" Mack and I both exclaimed in surprise.

"Yep. Cows swim across here 'n' bring their diseases with 'em. The Mexicans don't inoculate the way we haf'ta. Illegal cows keep us on our toes."

Surprised that we were not seeing any Brown Jays, he finally said, "I'll tell you where to find your jays. Go to the little village of Salenino." He gave us directions to turn left just before the Falcon Dam road and go down the road a couple of miles and through the village square until we could see the river.

"You'll see a campground on the left with three or four camps. They feed birds. You'll find your jay there or they will tell you why." That's how we came to meet Pat and Gale DeWind.

I would be hard pressed to name a more hospitable couple than Pat and Gale. Although Gale claims he's not a birder, don't be put off by his nonchalance. Theirs is the first camp in this tiny community of birders. The gate says, "Cars, no; Birders, yes." The sprawling, large-limbed trees beside their trailer hang with feeders to satisfy every taste, style, and size of bird. Peanut butter and grain mixes fill a variety of holes and crevices. A row of miscellaneous chairs set back thirty feet from the main stage provides an opportunity to watch the nonstop flutter and parade of birds at leisure, to rest one's feet, and to chat with other birders. We have never stopped that Pat, and usually Gale, were not in the yard to welcome and inform their guests, patiently distinguishing between Audubon and Altamira orioles, between Olive and Lincoln sparrows for novice birders, and asking them to sign the guest book. During a recent winter, they had had over two thousand visitors by the end of February. "The birders are beginning to drift off," Pat told us, "but the birders keep coming."

On our first visit to Salenino, we did, as the border guard promised us, find a Brown Jay, the biggest and probably the shiest of all jays. After that a stop at Pat and Gale's was a must on our every visit to Bentsen. If the Brown Jay was not in residence at the moment, Pat knew when it was last there and how soon its feeding schedule would bring it back. Usually within ten or fifteen minutes. I found my first Cassin's, Olive, and Lincoln sparrows at the DeWind's trailer site. And my first Lazuli Bunting. What a magnificent work of nature that is! Pat and Gale also know what is going on in the birding world all around them.

"Have you heard the White-collared Seedeater has moved down to Zapata?" Gale asked.

"Somebody said they heard it had. Is it true?"

"Would Louise and Red kid you?"

"They've seen it?"

"Within the week."

"Where is it?"

"Behind the library."

"Let's go," Mack said. And we did.

The White-collared Seedeater from Mexico is a rare winter visitor to the Lower Rio Grande. One has spent the past two or three winters in or around San Ygnacio farther up the river, but Mack and I had not seen it. If it were willing to meet us halfway, we should do our part. After all, it was a life bird. And so we went to Zapata, thirty miles farther upstream at the head of the International Falcon Reservoir, which the Falcon Dam creates.

The seedeater in question is a tiny finch, smaller than a Blue-throated Hummingbird. True to its name, it eats seeds

132

A Greater Roadrunner Streaked across the Road

Home on the Road, Daingerfield State Park, Texas

"Woof! I think it's an
ACORN Woodpecker."

Waiting for a Clay-colored Robin to Appear

Harris Hawk Atop a Saguaro

White-winged Dove: "All those babies to feed!"

Northern Pintail, Connie Hagar Preserve, Rockport

Marjory and Eleanor at Big Tree, Goose Island, Rockport

Like Kids with New Toys We Set Up Our Scopes

Mack Spotted a Loon; Dick Set Up the Scope

Black-legged Kittiwake over Prince William Sound

George Grilled His Fresh Salmon for the Whole Gang

Happy Hour in Fairbanks after a Long Day of Birding

A Bald Eagle Swooped Down between Dick's Rig and Ours

Author on Exit Glacier

Willow Ptarmigan, Churchill

I Recognized Ross's Gull at Once by His Black Necklace

Greater Yellowlegs

Razor-billed Auks, Machias Island, Maine

We Scaled the Slippery Rocks to the Atlantic Puffins

"Kids! They never get filled up."

Becky Befriends a Lost Blue-footed Booby in Texas

Snowy Egret with a Coiffure Problem

Limpkin on Wakulla River, Florida

**Iceland Gull to Great Black-backed Gull:
"When I do the kicking, I'll do the eating,
thank you."**

Iceland Gull, Saint John's, Newfoundland

Gambel's Quail, Green Valley Campground

Montezuma Quail, Fort Davis State Park, Texas

Sharp-tailed Grouse: "Don't you scare my babies."

At Last, a Snowy Owl!

Mack and Jean on Polar Bear (and Snowy Owl) Expedition

in weedy, grassy areas. I've never looked for a needle in a haystack, but I wondered whether a four-and-a-half-inch bird in a marsh behind a library would be less difficult.

Feeding on seeds that have dropped to the ground, a seedeater spends much of its day out of human sight and not much interested in showing its face to accommodate birders. After a half hour of aimless wandering along the grasses behind the library, Mack said, "Ah'm hungry. Let's eat."

While we lunched a carload of birders drove up and parked beside our rig. "They have a tape," Mack noted. "Maybe we're in luck."

Birders are usually willing to share, and they said we were welcome to tag along. A bird, hearing a recording of its voice, will often come out of hiding from sheer curiosity—or to protect its territory. On about the third try, we heard a high, distant *wink*. "It's here," one of the fellows whispered. Then, "There it is!" And there it was, bobbing on a stalk of grass that bent under its weight.

Was it annoyed with us? Or was that expression the result of its thick, short bill, turning up like a miniature grosbeak bill? It looked so stern on that tiny head. We stared at each other maybe five seconds before it said, "I'm hungry" and sank into the grasses.

That conquest was easy compared to finding the Ferruginous Pygmy Owl. For that expedition Wally and Jenny Kate, whom we had met on the Alaska trip, Jean, Muriel, and Melba—all from Dallas, Mack and I congregated at Bentsen. Wally knew a woman who would find a Ferruginous Pygmy Owl if we'd meet her at the foot of Falcon Dam the next morning. Because some of us don't do mornings as well as others, we all moved in our various rigs to Falcon Dam Campground the night before.

The next morning Wally piled all seven of us into his motor home, and off we bounced to the base of the dam.

Linda said as we started down the trail, "This shouldn't take long, but look sharply. Remember this owl is small, no bigger than an Eastern Bluebird—or any bluebird for that matter."

Two hours later we were still looking. We'd been up and down the path a mile or more. We'd split into separate groups. We'd left the trail and birded to the river's edge. Other birders joined the search. At 9:30 Linda had to leave.

"I know it's here," she said apologetically, "unless a hawk ate it last night."

"No problem," Wally assured her. "It's the challenge of birding. Makes the finding that much sweeter."

"Well, I wish you luck," Linda said as she reluctantly departed.

For another hour a dozen of us spread out, trying to cover every tree and bush over a half-mile stretch. Then came the word, mysteriously wafted through the leaves, that a Worthen's Sparrow had been seen behind the post office in Falcon Heights. It was a first-time sighting in this area.

Revived by the new challenge, Wally's harem hied itself back to the motor home and we jostled a couple of miles to the post office. Pouring out of the rig, we joined the others who were already scouring the field. I was getting a feeling of *déjà vu* when one of the fellows we'd left behind at the river came rolling in with the news that the owl had been found.

Back into the motor home we crammed and back to the river Wally rattled. Now I have never denied some birders are more dedicated than I. I'd been at this game five hours and was getting weary. I chose to stay behind this time and play with my notepad and pencil.

Fifteen minutes later Wally came huffing up the path, saying, "We've got it! You have to come. We have it in the scope."

His enthusiasm was not instantly contagious. "How far?" I asked, but Wally was already assembling his bicycle.

"The path's too rough for a bicycle," I started to protest.

"Come on," he commanded. "It's only a short way. You'll see a pile of stones in the middle of the track and a stick pointing to the right. Get off there and go into the woods. You'll see the others. They're waiting for you."

Wally tossed the bike over the gate, and I mounted the steed.

"Watch the stones," he warned as I went bouncing down the trail.

I soon came to the little cairn and the stick pointing to the right . . . and the owl. In about fifty feet, I came to the others and the young man waiting for me to see the Ferruginous Pygmy Owl in his scope. It was well camouflaged in a bush about ten feet tall.

"That small!" I exclaimed. "And its eyes are open!"

"Those aren't its eyes," the scope man said. "They're false eyes, black nape spots on the back of his head. You are looking at his back." As if to prove the point, the owl turned his head 180 degrees and blinked two big yellow eyes at me.

"Who *ever* found him?" I asked. Excitement was running too high for any very lucid answers at that moment, but I pieced together that Kim, the state-of-the-art bird guide from Minnesota, had found the bird and put the marker in the path. But by the time our little group arrived, the owl had flown to a nearby tree. It was our Jean who had found it there for us.

As for the Worthen's Sparrow, we did see birds in the field behind the post office. One of them was doubtlessly a sparrow. But was it a Worthen's?

"Ah'm hungry," Mack announced. "What time is it?"

"One-thirty."

"Ah'm STARVED!"

I am often asked, "What is your favorite bird?" That's impossible for me to say. But ask me what my favorite camp-

151

ground is, and I will tell you Bentsen State Park, not only because it has never failed to produce one or two rare birds and not only because of its proximity to several birding hot spots up and down the lower Rio Grande but also because I can recline in a chaise lounge at the campsite and be surrounded by large, colorful, active birds. I can feast my ears and eyes all day on the fiery flame of the orioles, the raspy *cheh-cheh-cheh* of the Green Jay, the haunting cry of the elusive Great Kiskadee, the self-possessiveness of the Golden-fronted Woodpecker. And when night falls, the little Elfin Owl at the campground edge flies bravely into the night and the Pauraques with their miners' lantern eyes when caught in the headlight call *pur-wheeer, pur-wheeer.*

Churchill Calling
Part I

At once a voice burst forth among
 The bleak twigs overhead
In a full-hearted evensong
 Of joy illimited;
An aged thrush, frail, gaunt, and small,
 In blast beruffled plume
Had chosen thus to fling his soul
 Upon the growing gloom.

       —Thomas Hardy

"Next time the Snowy Owl," Mack said when the train pulled out of Churchill last July. Bonnie Chartier, the local bird guide, had said we should see it in May, might see it in June, but how lucky could we be in July? Not lucky at all, although one had been seen recently with a flock of Canada Geese. Now Mack and I were off again to Churchill, traveling in our new twenty-seven-foot Catalina in search of a Snowy Owl.

The old RV had served us well—two trips across the United States, one to Alaska and another to Churchill last summer. Why press our luck? Besides, the price of gas was going up. 'Twas time to downsize. We sold it and bought a conversion van. It had everything the thirty-six-footer had had—dining nook, fridge, furnace, shower, closets (albeit small), sofa, bed, and bath. Everything except space. After two short trips, we knew it didn't have *any* space. Accustomed to starting a trip with enough homemade dinners in the freezer

153

for at least three weeks, I said to Mack as we started to think about Churchill, "Let's face it. This freezer will hold either two packages of your homemade spaghetti sauce or a six-pack of Dove ice cream bars. Which do you want to take?"

"Well, let's face it, indeed," Mack agreed. "Where are we going to put winter jackets for Churchill? Or enough yarn for my needlepointing?"

"What about books? Just bird books even if we don't take the crossword puzzle reference library?"

So we tooled down to our local RV dealer and did some fast haggling. Two days later we picked up the Catalina. Five days later we left for Churchill.

The trip list of birds began with the usual crows, robin, jays, mockingbird. In Tennessee we added Bob Whites, a Western Meadowlark, and in the campground a Summer Tanager that chirped nonstop variations of *See, here, hear me. Hear me? TV! Right here! Right here! TV! See me?* No lifers crossed our path. In Indiana a Red-eyed Vireo, resident soloist in the campground, made the list. We spent the weekend with Essie Crocker in Kalamazoo. She had goldfinches vying for thistle seeds at her feeders. An Indigo Bunting fluttered his colors, and a robin spun herself dizzy shaping a nest until it was perfectly round and every grass and twig lay smooth.

We didn't do any active birding until we reached Michigan's Upper Peninsula. At Blaney Park we turned north on Route 77, which traverses the Seney National Wildlife Refuge, reaching eventually the headquarters in Seney. The town's population of three hundred was nearly matched by the Canada Geese at the visitors center. In all stages of ages, they waddled, unk-unking, around the parking lot, swam aimlessly in the pond, or slept under the ornamental shrubs. The man at the counter in the visitors center recommended the seven-mile motor loop, which winds through pines and around numerous small ponds. It seemed a pleasant way to spend an afternoon.

A small bird flew in front of us and disappeared in the cat o' nine tails. "Challenge number one," I said, pulling off the road. It turned out to be a big tease, popping up briefly to bounce on a blade of grass before dropping again among the reeds, only to reemerge in a completely different spot just long enough to say peek-a-boo.

"We can play that game, too," Mack told it. "We're in no hurry." Working between bird and bird book, Mack finally convinced me it was a Marsh Wren, not a lifer but fun to spend a half hour with on a warm spring day. At the edge of another pond, a Swamp Sparrow was gathering nesting material from the fuzz of the cat o'nine tails. Numerous other familiar birds added to our trip list, but we found nothing new.

Back at the visitors' center, Mack asked, "What are our chances of finding an American Woodcock around here?"

"I'd say your chances are pretty good," the naturalist replied.

"That bird has so frustrated our efforts in Florida," Mack explained, "that I would gladly spend the night in Seney if we could find one."

"Ya need t' drive outta town west on the main drag 'bout eight miles t' Driggs River Road, just before the bridge. It's a dirt road on yer left. It'll take ya back into the refuge. Go, oh, mebbe a mile or so. Go 'bout dusk . . . nine er nine-thirty. Ya should get yerselves a woodcock. 'N' mebbe some snipes, too. Don't let 'em skeer ya when they explode with those whistling wings."

"Is the refuge road wide enough for a motor home?" I asked.

"Oh, sure. Ya won't meet enybuddy." We talked a little longer about the birding prospects in the area. He added a few more details to the directions. We thanked him for his help.

As we started for the door, he added, "Oh, ya'll probably hear a Whip-poor-will."

"How're we going to kill nearly three hours 'til dusk?" Mack asked.

"Let's explore the town."

That took about twenty minutes. Then we tanked up at the only gas pump in town two minutes before it closed for the night.

"It won't hurt to get out to the refuge early," Mack commented. We were both excited at the prospect of at last finding an American Woodcock. Of the ten patrons at the only restaurant in town, we were obviously the only two *from away*.

'Twas hardly dusk when we turned off the highway to Driggs River Road. It wasn't labeled, but the fellow had said, "If ya cross the bridge, ya've gone too far." The bridge was just ahead.

"How far do we go on this?" Mack asked.

"He said a mile or so."

Branches brushed the sides of the RV, but the track was hard and dry beneath the wheels. We searched the sides for a break in the brush, a path, an opening, remembering the spot at Saint Marks Wildlife Refuge in Florida where, we've been told, in the spring woodcocks fly straight into the air and then explode, spiraling down, the wind whistling through their wings.

"We've been a mile," Mack reported. "Shall I go on?"

"A little way, I think," I said tentatively.

We came to a fork in the track. "Ah, yes, he said we wouldn't have to go beyond this split. This should be a good spot."

It was full-fledged dusk by now. "What do you say I turn around while there is still some light?" Mack asked.

"Capital idea!" After a few backwards and forwards, we were in position for watching and eventually retreating. Water splashed quietly in the stream to our left. Driggs River, I suppose. The ground between us and the river seemed moist, maybe swampy. 'Twas hard to tell. The bushes on the right formed more of a thicket. Such a habitat should make any woodcock if not sing for joy at least whirr and chirrr. Our eyes adjusted as dusk turned darker. A Great Horned Owl hooted from deep in the refuge behind us. Closer by a Whip-poor-will began to sing. An hour passed. We still waited. At 10:15 we agreed we couldn't see a woodcock if it did show, or a snipe either.

"Shall we call it a day?" Mack asked.

"Might as well," I said. "Foiled again."

Mack started the motor. But when she turned on the lights, we had no headlights. She tried again: on/off, on/off. No headlights.

"Let there be light," I commanded.

"Very funny. Who do you think you are? Now what do we do?"

Why is the dark so much more eerie when you can't turn on a light? We sat there and contemplated our options. The owl hooted.

"We can stay right here till daylight," I suggested. "We are self-sufficient . . . beds and breakfast."

"But we don't have electricity, and it's supposed to get cold. The furnace won't ignite without electricity."

"How cold?"

"Maybe in the forties."

"Oh," was all I could think to say.

The outline lights around the edge of the rig were on. They shed enough light to keep us between the thickets as Mack cautiously made our way back to the highway.

"Doesn't it seem odd that some of the lights go on but

not the headlights?" I asked more to make conversation than get information.

"Different fuses probably," was all Mack replied.

With the highway came the real challenge. We had planned to camp in Munising, thirty-five miles west of Seney. Of course that was now out of the question. Somehow we would have to creep eight long miles back to town. And then what? They had rolled up the sidewalks two hours ago. But as Mack pointed out, we didn't need sidewalks.

Fortunately traffic was light. The road was faintly visible, and thanks to our trim lights, oncoming cars could see us. Each one flashed lights and shouted "Lights!" as we met. It was now eleven o'clock.

The motel was still open. Maybe we could at least tell our troubles to someone. We knew Seney didn't have a campground. Was there a . . . no, no garage would be open at this hour. *Was* there a garage?

The woman at the motel listened sympathetically, made some phone calls, and finally thought of Elijah, who owns and operates Fox River Automotive. He might have a suggestion. Elijah had retired for the night, but he would meet us at the motel in twenty minutes. We could park at his shop. Guided by his taillights, we followed him down Fox River Road out of town to his shop, where he found an extension cord and plugged us into electricity.

"You'll be safe here," he assured us. "I'll be back at eight to check your problem."

The rest of the night as uneventful. The furnace did kick on. Someone said the temperature that morning had been forty-two degrees Fahrenheit. We were so snug I couldn't vouch for that. At least the heat wave of the past few days had broken.

Elijah arrived early and set in immediately to solve the

problem of the lights. After some time he discovered the only thing wrong was they had never been properly connected.

"While you're at it," Mack said, "can you find out why our generator won't stay on?"

Before he solved that one, a woman with three children drove into the yard. They all piled out and gradually wandered over to where Elijah was working. "All mine," he said proudly, stroking his beard. Come, I suspect, primarily to see the strangers. If we had wondered before, we knew now by their dress they were Amish.

By ten o'clock Elijah pronounced us ready for the road again. "What do we owe you?" I asked.

"I'll write you a bill," he said. I waited while he figured at the counter. Finally he handed it to me. It read in its entirety: Light and generator $20.

"But what about rescuing us in the night? What about the electricity we used overnight? What about camping in your parking lot?"

Elijah smiled and said, "If you like, send me a postcard from Churchill." I gave him thirty dollars and assured him he would receive a card from the banks of Hudson Bay.

That was Tuesday morning. We were to meet Jean in Winnipeg on Saturday. We'd have a day to spend in Agassiz National Wildlife Refuge north of Thief River Falls, Minnesota, where we had birded two years before on our way to Alaska. At that time I was eager to find a moose. But despite three days in four refuges, I hadn't seen one. Since then I had met several moose, and they were far from my thoughts when we started out on the motor drive through Agassiz that morning. Our target bird for the day was a Least Flycatcher. It should be there, and it would be a lifer.

A Yellow Warbler crossed the road and perched briefly on a limb to the right. As we watched it, a tiny bird flew into the same tree. A Least Flycatcher perhaps? It flew into the air and back to the tree. "Acts like a flycatcher," I mumbled.

Our attention was riveted on the little twit, flitting behind some leaves, when a motion in the road caught my eye. There in broad daylight in the middle of the road a moose was ambling directly toward our rig.

"Excuse me," I said, "am I in your way?" At such moments my impulse always is to take a picture. And as always at the sight of my camera (and me, I suppose), the moose turned slowly and dissolved into the woods. During the distraction the Least Flycatcher, if that is what it was, escaped, and three more hours in the park did not produce another. However, we saw two more moose. Or did we see one moose two more times? Anyway, the time had come to move on. Churchill was calling.

This year instead of driving to Thompson and taking the train to Churchill, we left the RV at the airport in Winnipeg, safely plugged into one of those umbilical cords that Canadians use in winter to keep their cars from freezing. Jean, bewitched by tales we told of last year's adventure, joined us there, and the three of us flew on to Churchill.

What a contrast our arrival was to last year's. A sharp northeast wind blowing across the frozen bay whipped snowflakes into dizzying swirls. Freezing rain cut my face like flying icicles. I pulled the cord tight around my hood and braced against the gale as we pushed toward the shelter of the shed. Five naked telephones hung on the wall, each with the name of a Churchill hotel. But we didn't have to phone. Louise from the Polar was waiting. The reunion was joyous.

"I have a surprise for you," she said giggling as soon as the preliminary greetings were over.

"What's that?"

"I brought my baby with me."

"You have a *baby*?"

160

"Yes, come see him while we wait for your bags."

We pushed through the crowd in the tiny terminal and stepped out into the parking lot. "Be careful not to slip on the ice," she warned. She opened the front door of her van, revealing a basket on the seat. From a bundle of blankets stuck one wee nose and two blue orbs.

"Louise!" Mack exclaimed, "you didn't bring that baby out in this weather!"

"What weather?" she asked in surprise. "This is one of our first good spring days." Jean looked at me with a raised eyebrow.

"How old is he?"

"Four months."

We fetched our bags and camera gear, climbed into the van, and started for the town five miles away. Once on the road, we could look down on the tumble of great gray boulders, boulders worn smooth by centuries of ice, wind, and water, boulders that dwarf the occasional polar bear that clambers around among them. Through the mist and the rain and the snow, Hudson Bay was barely discernible a mile to our right except to see it appeared to be solid with huge chunks of ice.

"I warned you it might be rugged," Mack said to Jean.

"I LOVE it," Jean's muffled reply came through the scarf she held to her face.

A mile from the airport, the road bears right past Akudlik Marsh and the ponds where we would go in coming days to look for the Ross's Gull, the bird that brings more birders to Churchill than any other bird. In four more miles, we reached the Polar Hotel. Louise's brother Dan came out for the luggage—shy, curly-headed, big-brown-eyed Dan. There was another happy reunion, for he had stolen our hearts the summer before. He with Louise and her husband own and run the eleven-room hotel.

161

Our room would be comfortable, with two double beds, telephone, TV and refrigerator. But no sooner had we dropped our bags than we went next door to rent a car for the week. Time should not be wasted with so much good birding to do. We stopped only long enough to say hello to Rémee who, now free from his cocoon, gave us an endearing smile.

"There is one blessing that comes with the wind and the cold," I said as we stepped outside.

"What's that?" Jean asked.

"No mosquitoes or black flies."

Churchill Calling
Part II

A bird sings the self same song
With never a fault in its flow
That we listened to here those long
    Long years ago.

                  —Thomas Hardy

"Our top priorities," Mack reminded us as we climbed into the car, "are a Ross's Gull for Jean and a Snowy Owl for Ev and me."

"Then let's start at the Granary Ponds where we found the gull last year," I suggested.

Jean immediately spotted an Oldsquaw on the first pond without raising her binoculars, a lifer for her. "Oh, I love birding in Churchill," she hurrahed. We ticked off Arctic Terns, Northern Pintails, Gadwalls, Northern Shovelers, and American Wigeon faster than a bear licks honey. But not a Ross's Gull. Before the afternoon was over, though, we found a Pacific Loon in Churchill River behind the grain elevators. That was a new bird for all of us.

The next morning the wind had shifted, the rain had stopped, and the temperature risen to fifty degrees, only four below the average summer temperature. Jean and I, the photographers, wanted to get down to the bay for pictures of the jam-packed icebergs. Then we could follow the Coast Road to Akudlik Marsh for the gull. But to our amazement, when we reached the water at Eider Cove, only two or three random bergs floated in the bright blue waters of Hudson Bay.

"What's going on?" I asked, completely baffled. "Was yesterday a figment of my imagination? Wasn't the bay solid white with ice when we arrived?"

When I questioned Dan that evening, he explained simply, "The wind shifted."

"It must be some wind to blow all that away."

"That it is," he agreed.

"Is it gone now for the summer?" I asked naively.

"Oh, no. The winds keep shifting. The ice comes and goes until it melts."

True enough, it did come back, and Jean and I got our wintery pictures, including a stretch of the Coast Road hard packed with snow.

The next day the great chunks were gone again except for the few stranded on the beach, taller than we, looking like giant ice carvings of birds and bears.

We visited Cape Merry, the rocky promontory where the wind never stops raging. Far below, the waters of the river meet the tides of the bay in a turbulence that attracts ducks, loons, seals, and whales. Overhead jaegers, terns, and gulls wheel and scream. Maybe a rare Sabine flies among the Herring, Bonaparte's, Glaucous, and the Thayer's gulls. Maybe even a Ross's? But the action over Cape Merry is too frantic for any of us to isolate a lone gull. Back up the river a couple of miles, behind the grain elevators, they come to rest on the sandbars at low tide. Jean was confident she would find her Ross's there one day.

Churchill has fifteen miles of paved roads and forty-eight of graded. The rest are *unmaintained.* It is a small area to bird, but the diversity of habitat makes it one of the prime birding spots of North America. It has both tundra and boreal forest, brushy taiga, willow thickets, streams, ponds, marshes, Chur-

164

chill River, and Hudson Bay. Goose Creek Road, stretching ten miles from the Highway, as the main thoroughfare is called, to the Pump Station at the river's edge, has within those ten miles all the habitats except the bay.

Birding Goose Creek Road, we came first to a forest of stunted black spruce, which over a period of a week yielded an American Robin, Gray Jays, a Gray-cheeked Thrush, Common Flicker, Boreal Chickadee, and a Blackpoll Warbler with its lisping Johnny-One-Note *zi-zi-zi-zi*. The most amusing bird in the forest was Lesser Yellowlegs. I wonder whether any Texas or Florida Yellowlegs has ever contemplated sitting in a treetop. They are shorebirds, marsh sandpipers, cousins of curlews and godwits. But a Lesser Yellowlegs in Churchill favors treetops for perching.

After two miles the spruces give way to wet tundra. Water in the roadside ditches is deep enough for Mallards, Green-winged Teal, Pintails and Greater Scaup. What spills over runs into shallow puddles beloved of Black-bellied Plovers and White-Rumped Sandpipers. We saw also Spotted, Solitary, and Stilt sandpipers.

Common Redpolls, Yellow and Wilson's warblers, and a flurry of sparrows—Savannah, Song, and Tree inhabit the Willow thickets along the tributary before it joins Goose Creek. From there to the river spreads a wide expanse of marsh. We often saw Northern Harriers skimming the bogs, probably in search of dinner. It was a likely habitat for Snowy Owls, but we couldn't find one.

The river is wide, maybe a mile across. Buffleheaded and Black ducks swam near the shore, and through her scope, Jean found three Tundra Swans midstream farther up the river.

We set out another evening for this same spot on the river to watch the sun set. Before we reached the river, I stopped to photograph Stilt Sandpipers still feeding in the puddles at ten o'clock. Clouds were gathering. A storm was approaching. By the time we reached the river, clouds obscured the sun. Forget the sunset. While we waited a pelting storm, so characteristic of summer, exploded. The winds didn't know which way to blow. I stepped from the car and could hardly stand against the onslaught of rain and wind. Quickly retreating, I rejoined Mack and Jean, who were scanning the river for Tundra Swans. The storm passed almost as fast as it came. Buffleheads bounced on the waves like yo-yos.

"There's something out there besides Buffleheads," Jean said, straining at her binoculars. "Maybe it's only flotsam and jetsam, but it looks like a cluster of birds all stuck together."

"Where?" I asked.

"About twenty feet to the right of the Buffleheads and a little farther from shore."

"I see 'em," Mack said. "I'm getting out." The rain had eased to a drizzle. Rays of the sinking sun broke through the clouds, turning the mound of stones beside the Pump Station into a pile of rusty gold. Color began to fill the sky over the river.

"Look behind you, you photographers," Mack cried. The brightest rainbow I had ever seen arched between us and the horizon, planting one pot of gold back by the Stilt Sandpipers and the other pot of gold in the marsh to my right. Low on the horizon, tiny points of stunted spruce looked as though someone had trimmed the fading blue sky with pinking shears. Over the river the clouds were aflame.

"The poetry of earth is never dead," I murmured to myself.

"Who said that?"

"John Keats."

The flotsam and jetsam would have to wait. They were too dark for identification tonight. We sat, awed by the tapestry of Nature. Finally someone asked quietly, "Shall we go?"

The sandpipers were still foraging. It was eleven o'clock.

But what about the Snowy Owl? Two miles out of town, RX Road turns left off the Highway and climbs quickly to a ridge of boulder-strewn tundra spotted with little ponds. Bonnie Chartier's guide to birding in Churchill says Snowy Owls frequent the area in winter and "once in a blue moon will linger into summer." Well, it was only spring, late spring. We checked faithfully and optimistically as we came and went on the Highway. What we did find one day was a pair of Lesser Golden Plovers. And, a bird we did not readily recognize. It was trying to balance on a utility line, not an easy trick on a blustery day. "It's not a Lesser Yellowlegs. That's for sure," Jean said. "It's almost twice as large and the bill's too long."

I headed across the bogs and hummocks to take a picture. It was not disturbed by my approach. It was more concerned with stabilizing its teetering position on the line. When I came almost under it, I could see its white panties and recognized it was a Hudsonian Godwit, a cousin of Lesser Yellowlegs.

Another adventure took us to the town dump, renowned for the polar bears that once scavenged there, though they are rarely seen today. Nor did we find any birds on our first visit. But we went again under different circumstances. We had started the evening with a boat ride. The two-hour excursion offered by Sea North Tours promised to carry us out among some of the bigger icebergs and let us hear through special magnification the Beluga whales talking. But high winds churned the already turbulent bay to the danger point. After a rough half hour, the captain aborted the trip. In the meantime, however, Mack had talked with a woman who said we'd have a good chance of finding a Red-throated Loon near the dump.

Safely back on terra firma, thankful for less terra and more firma, we headed for the dump. "Keep to the right of the general garbage," the woman had said. "Then turn left past the pile of discarded refrigerators and follow the road as far as you can drive." *As far as you can drive* meant as far as we trusted the car in the wet ruts and slime. From there we were to scale the embankment and scan the pond straight ahead of us.

At the dump the winds had subsided, the sun was setting, and the mosquitoes were ravenous. I opted to stay and protect the car.

"From what?" they wanted to know.

"Against the unforseen," I quipped.

Mack and Jean climbed onto the levee and disappeared from sight. I scarcely gave polar bears a second thought. "They are still out on the icebergs," I told myself. When the explorers returned twenty minutes later, groping through the gloaming and slapping mosquitoes to the tune of "Old Susanna," something in their step told me their mission had succeeded.

"We'll get you one tomorrow," they promised. And they did . . . at another pond.

A mile beyond the dump, the road climbs the rocky ridge and winds through a jumble of huge boulders. Polar Bear Alley (unmaintained) bears (pun intended) to the left. Bears have been known to summer there. Bonnie's guide says

> Before starting up the faint road among the rocks, be sure that you have purchased numerous copies of this bird-finding guide and mailed them to your friends. It would be nice for them to have something to remember you by.

We eschewed Polar Bear Alley.

Instead we moved farther down the Highway to a large rocky area where Willow Ptarmigan, Water Pipits, and Horned Larks nest. "Occasionally," the guide says, "a Snowy Owl will linger here into early June," and continues, "and you may stumble on a bear."

"Not in June," I humphed.

168

We searched the area as extensively as we could—and still stay within running distance of the car. Horned Larks? Yes. Snowy Owl? No.

The next road to the right was more productive. Jean had just turned off the Highway when a Canada Gander, waddling in the middle of the road, showed no inclination to give ground. Rolling like a sailor just off his ship, he made his deliberate, wobbly way for some distance before taking to the bushes. We were still pondering his odd behavior when Jean spotted a male Willow Ptarmigan on the left partially camouflaged in a pile of rocks near a thicket. With a mixture of wariness and curiosity—or was it a confrontational challenge?—he met Jean part way as she approached with her camera. "He was just being hospitable," she said when she returned to the car.

We were primarily looking for Hoary Redpolls on this particular side road—never forgetting, of course, the Snowy Owl. The road, once past the Ptarmigan thicket, came to some stunted spruce and then rose to Spruce Ridge. Beyond the Ridge at road's end stretches open tundra. Luck went with us. Short of the tundra in a patch of willows, a flock of Redpolls was feeding. But were they *Hoary* Redpolls? The Hoaries flock with the Common, look like the Common, and sound like the Common. They both have red caps and black chins, deeply notched tails, and two white wing bars. So what is so great about finding Redpolls? Like mountain climbers who climb the mountain because it is there, birders seek a Hoary Redpoll because it is there . . . somewhere. It *is* different in two respects. The short, curved mandible is too fine a distinction for me, but one bird did finally sit long enough to reveal its paler back and the light, almost white, unstreaked rump. Light enough to call it *hoary.*

Returning to the Highway, we looked for but didn't see either the ptarmigan or the gander. But without the latter to

169

distract us, Mack spotted on the bank scarcely ten feet from the car Mrs. Goose lying flat and motionless. Only the down sticking out on all sides gave a clue she was on a nest. Did I feel the hairs at the nape of my neck prickle? Jean inched the car quietly away.

"Where next?" she asked.

"Let's go back to Goose Creek Road and look for what we couldn't identify the other night," Mack suggested.

"You mean the flotsam and the jetsam?"

"That's it."

Back at the river, the cluster was still bobbing.

Whatever it was was animate, ducks of some kind or some close relation.

"A huddle of puddle ducks," I decided.

"They are divers," Mack observed.

"Some have orange beaks" was Jean's contribution, studying them in her binoculars. They bobbed in the water, not seeming to be headed anywhere.

"I think they have—or some of them have—a white wing patch that shows only when they rise on a wave," Mack said.

"Do the ones with the orange beaks have a black lump on the beak?" I asked, thumbing through the bird books.

"Yes, yes they do," Jean said.

"Well, I think they are White-winged Scoters." The others agreed after checking the field guides. A first for all of us.

Bonnie Chartier not only has written the birding guide for Churchill, but she also owns and operates the Wilderness Encounter Tours. Outside her office across from Akudlik Marsh, she maintains a large bulletin board where birders record the dates and sites of outstanding finds. On our way back to town, we stopped to see whether the scoters had been noted. Talking with a couple of other birders who were also checking the board, I asked, "What are our chances of finding a Snowy Owl around here?"

"Awfully slim" was the candid reply.

"What about a Boreal Owl?" Jean asked.

"Remotely possible," he said. "They are a permanent resident and so they are here, but they are rarely seen. Your best chance would be to pull off the road in the open area across from the airport. Go at dusk and watch the spruces at the edge of the tundra."

We positioned ourselves, the car facing the trees, the sinking sun at our backs. Jean's camera was loaded and ready. "Just in case it flies by the window," she said, laughing.

I suggested we concentrate. "Never underestimate the power of believing."

"Shhh." This from Jean. "Look on the ground at the edge of the trees," she whispered. A fox, poised and alert, sniffed the air. Jean moved her camera to the window's edge. We hardly dared exhale. The fox took a few cautious steps into the open. He froze again. Sniffed. An ear twitched, a nostril quivered. Sensing no harm, he trotted toward us and right past the car, completely ignoring Jean's clicking camera. His coat was a mixture of brown and white.

We waited 'til dark for the Boreal Owl, but willingly settled for the fox.

"Probably an Arctic fox," Dan said back at the hotel, "just changing into its summer coat."

We did find an owl, a Short-eared Owl, one evening. Driving down Goose Creek Road once more to see what the fading light might produce, Mack stopped for us to watch a bird chasing what turned out to be an owl. When the chase ended, the owl lit in a tree some distance from us. With our binoculars homed in on it, it took off and flew directly toward the car. From the back seat, I shouted, "Put up your window!" Mack, keeping her binocs on it, was so mesmerized all she could do was watch. Within what seemed ten feet of the car, it turned sharply skyward and disappeared. When Mack regained her voice, she said, "I could see its tonsils." Whether it had caught the glint of someone's binoculars or what its intention had been, we couldn't fathom.

Bonnie's guide says the road to Bird Cove, "although rutted and bumpy, is usually passable most of the way" to the abandoned ship that lies stranded in the cove. The *Ithaca*, like the wrecked Lambair plane lying on its belly a half mile short of the airport, is a bleak reminder that Churchill played its part in World War II.

We took the "rutted and bumpy" road through tundra carpeted with netted willow, Lapland rose-bay, and reindeer moss to the point where the tides had washed it out. Leaving the car, we walked toward the rocky beach. As I watched, the whole desolate expanse of tundra between us and the horizon came alive with hundreds of Canada Geese. Roused from their slumbers, or feeding, or whatever, they made a coordinated, slow, deliberate waddle farther into the bogginess. But the Snowy Owl was not among them.

The week was going all too fast. It was Friday evening and we had found neither target bird. "I'm beginning to think this Ross's Gull is a hoax," Jean said. "And I'm going to forget all about it and take a buggy ride this afternoon."

For an exploration of the tundra, she had two choices: Len Smith's monstrous vehicle with tires six feet in diameter and two feet wide with six-inch tread or Bonnie Chartier's van. Mack and I had gone in the tundra buggy the year before. "This is going to be a rough ride," the young driver explained when we set out. "Fight it and you will have sore muscles tomorrow. Let yourself bounce and roll with the buggy."

Off we had gone over no road, for the tundra is fragile and must be treated tenderly. Tenderly? With an army truck? Limp as bean bags, we were tossed forward and backward, up and down. I stiffened briefly when we plunged dead ahead into a pond. Mack stiffened even more when the driver scared a Herring Gull from her nest on a rock in the middle of the pond. Though the gull squawked, "Help! Help!" and stuck to her grasses until we were within a few feet of her, she did finally fly, leaving two downy, helpless chicks in the grassy nest. Mack lectured the young man severely for endangering the lives of the babies to say nothing of the trauma suffered by the mother.

Dan recommended Jean go with Bonnie, since she is a naturalist. She would be more likely to spot birds. I joined Jean, partly to compare the two means of getting across the tundra. *She will probably skirt the ponds,* I thought. She didn't. Hung up on a rock in the middle of one pond, she rocked the van back and forth.

"We are in no danger," she reassured the half dozen passengers. "I just don't want to wreck the transmission." Then she added with a twinkle in her eye, "You can see it isn't deep. We could walk."

She stopped for a botany lesson: White Mountain Avens, Snow Cinquefoil, Bog Rosemary, and the azalialike Lapland Rose-bay. We stepped on Caribou Moss as soft and deep as sponges. A caribou to our left paused in his grazing to watch us pass. Bonnie knew of a fox den. She hoped the kits would be playing outside, but before we reached them, a handsome male Willow Ptarmigan intercepted our path. Bonnie opened the sunroof for Jean and me to take pictures. She explained, "This is the way professional photographers take the polar bears."

"You come out and mingle with the bears in this van?" Jean asked incredulously.

"Sure, every October."

"Are we likely to see a bear today?" someone asked.

"Not likely, but I never say no when it comes to bears."

The Willow Ptarmigan approached the van. "May we get out?" Jean asked.

"Sure. He may come right up to you." His winter white

was splotched with summer brown. He may have been distracting us from a nest, but he seemed a friendly fellow. The reddish brown feathers from the breast up had a sheen punctuated by a black beak, white lores, and a prominent red eyebrow. He let us come as close as we wanted for full-frame photos. I offered him a tip, but he said he didn't accept gifts from women.

The tundra is sparsely dotted with spruce, one tiny spruce at a time. I photographed one not more than six feet tall. Its few branches all grew to the south. Despite its puniness Bonnie said it could be eighty to a hundred years old. Small shallow ponds like the occasional trees were scattered everywhere, too, all the way to the horizon.

Our destination was the bay, where we scanned the beach, gravels pits, and tundra as far as binoculars would reach for polar bears. Not finding any, we were forced to turn our attention to the Arctic Terns, which were turning their attention to us. We were invading their nesting grounds. Since they lay their eggs on the tundra with very little in the way of a nest, it behooved us to step cautiously. The reward for negligence was a severe peck on the pate.

"Oh, that's why Bonnie said, 'wear your hats' when we left the van," Jean said, taking a direct hit as she said it.

"Hey, that would've been a great picture. Let him do it again."

"No, thanks," Jean said, rubbing her head.

Back in town, Jean made her routine check of the Granary Ponds before dinner. A small crowd was gathered on the banks of the third pool. Jean hurried ahead.

"Anything good?" she asked the first person she met.

"There's a Ross's Gull with those other gulls across the pond."

At the same moment, the cry went up, "There it goes." Heads moved like robots on a signal control, following the flight until it disappeared around the grain elevators. As one, the crowd hustled across the railroad tracks, around the elevators, to the river's edge. The tide was low. Hundreds, probably thousands, of gulls were sunning along the banks and on the sandbars. Had the Ross's settled in among them?

Time passed. Small flocks would suddenly rise, fly over the river, bank, and redistribute themselves on the sandbars. "'Twould help if they'd stay put," a birder near me commented. We were not alone in the search.

"I think I have it," someone said. He tried to tell others where that single gull with a black necklace was huddled down among the others. That was all the help Jean needed.

"I *have* it," she said with a touch of awe in her voice, hardly above a whisper. Seconds later it took off in a cloud of gulls, not the ideal sighting that Mack and I had the summer before, but a lifer nevertheless.

Our last full day in Churchill was spent at Twin Lakes, the outermost area one can drive to in Churchill. Lapland Rose-Bay carpeted great stretches in pink. We walked in the woods, strolled along snowy paths, even found a Northern Shrike, which had eluded us all week. We spotted a flock of beautiful Pine Siskins, White-winged Scoters, Common Goldeneyes . . . but no Snowy Owl.

When we wearily trudged into the restaurant of birders' choice that evening, the seven or eight tables were already crowded. Before we could find a seat, someone asked, "Did you see the bears?"

"What bears?"

"A mother bear and cub were wandering along the RX Road this afternoon."

"Are you kidding?"

"Boy Scout's oath," he said.

"Did you see 'em?"

"No, the bear patrol whisked 'em outta town before I even heard about 'em."

"How far out of town?"

"Don't know."

Jean, Mack, and I looked at each other: three minds with a single thought. Our weariness vanished instantly. We gobbled our dinner and drove to the RX Road. "If not a bear, maybe a Snowy Owl," Mack said. "It's almost our last chance."

Of course the bears were long gone, but we drove along the Coast Road, scanning the bay and hoping for a glimpse of two bears swimming into the midnight blue of Hudson Bay.

"Something's in the water," Mack said as we came to Eider Cove.

"A bear?" I asked hopefully.

"No, ducks of some kind."

"I've got 'em," I said. "Surf Scoters?"

"Let's scope them," Jean suggested. Out came the scope. The heads were all black. That eliminated Surf Scoter. Jean thought they were too small for any scoter.

"Let me look again," Mack said, coming back to the scope. After more deliberation she gave her verdict, Black Guillemots.

I was busy checking the guide. "According to Bonnie," I reported, "Black Guillemots don't come until mid-June and then 'how lucky can you be' to find them."

"This lucky," Jean thought. "And it *is* June 16."

"What's that behind the guillemots?" asked Mack, who was still working the scope. "Hey, you guys, have a look! It's a . . . it's a *King* Eider."

"Gorgeous!"

"But no bear."

The next day we had to say good-bye to Louise and little Rémee. Dan drove us to the airport. As we parted, I said, "Next time the Snowy Owl *and* a polar bear."

"Next time," said Dan, smiling, "try October or November. And book early."

The Land of Canyons

I caught this morning's minion king-
    dom of daylight's dauphin, dapple-down-drawn Falcon, in
      his riding
  Of the rolling level underneath him steady air, and striding
High there, how he rung upon the rein of a wimpling wing
In his ecstasy!
                    —Gerard Manley Hopkins

The July monsoon came early to southeastern Arizona this year. Hard showers had pounded the plains with increasing frequency in recent days. And this was only May. Dark clouds were already gathering over the distant mountains to the east this morning, but we were headed west. At Fort Huachuca, Mack showed our pass and drove on into Garden Canyon. The road wound a few miles through grasslands interspersed with shooting ranges and warnings not to leave the pavement. Low hills rose on either side. We drove slowly, searching for a Botteri's Sparrow, a secretive summer resident of these dry plains. It is almost impossible to find before it begins to sing in July, but . . . we might be lucky.

Our main objective was a Buff-breasted Flycatcher. This smallest of flycatchers is only five inches from its feathery top knot to the tip of its forked tail. We'd have to climb to find it—up the canyon two or three miles to an elevation of five thousand feet at least, maybe seven thousand. Eventually the road began to rise gradually past a couple of picnic areas with sparrows, but no Botteri's. At the third picnic ground, the pavement ended.

The gravel road now rose sharply, twisting into curls of S-turns. A half mile into the canyon, a marker on the left was crudely lettered SCHEELITE. Somewhere behind those limestone cliffs, a path led into Sheelite Canyon and a pair of Spotted Owls. "We'll have to climb on foot for that one," I said to Mack as we drove by.

We continued jolting and crunching up the trail, scanning the trees on either side for Stellar's Jays, a Northern Pygmy Owl, Hepatic Tanager or, best and rarest, an Elegant Trogan. We were almost two miles into the canyon when the first raindrops hit the windshield.

"What's that?" Mack asked.

"Angels' tears."

"Crying because we're doomed?" We knew these showers did not come gently. Nor singly.

Mack had hardly, but skillfully, maneuvered a turnaround before someone unzipped the heavens. Hail ricocheted around us. Lightning flashed. Thunder reverberated through the canyon. In a flash—flash of flood—we were a piece of flotsam in a rushing mountain stream. Through a foggy window, I glimpsed an empty car near the entrance to Sheelite Canyon.

"I wonder where those folks are," I said more to myself than to Mack.

But she responded, "In a limestone cave, I hope."

Early the next morning, we were back on the trail. At the upper picnic area, we struck up a conversation with a couple from California. They were also looking for the Buff-breasted Flycatcher. We continued in tandem up the rocky course until a washout called a halt. It was only a short walk from there to the deserted cabin, James Lane's landmark in his guide to birding southeast Arizona. The land opens into a flat, grassy area with a scattering of conifers and oaks. Here, Lane says, in Sawmill Canyon six to eight pairs of Buff-breasted Flycatchers make their summer home.

"All I need is one," Mack said as we spread out to start the search.

"We should get a Greater Pewee up here, too," one of the Californians reminded us.

The sun was shining. The air was clear and cool. Four little human beings wandered around in a world silent except for a few bird *chips* and the rustle of oak leaves. How privileged I was to be one of them. A half hour went by. I was heading up the canyon, trying to keep my mind on the search. Something flitted among the conifers. Was it a butterfly? Maybe a bee? Maybe a twig? I raised my binoculars. Nothing. No, there it was again. I signaled the others. "I think I have it. Maybe." I did.

What a little gem you are, I thought. *Well worth two arduous trips up this mountain.* We stood, admiring its cinnamon buff breast as it darted for an insect and then returned to its perch in the pine. We stood chatting, Mack and I congratulating ourselves on life bird number 547. Suddenly Mack held up a finger and said, "Listen! Who says Jose Maria?"

"The Greater Pewee."

"I just heard it. On the left. In the woods." Everyone listened. Shortly came a clear, whistled *ho-SAY ma-REE-ah.*

"That's it!" our companion said.

We waited. It came again . . . once, twice, *ho-SAY ma-REE-ah, ho-SAY ma-REE-ah.* Mack spished softly, *psh-sh, psh-sh, psh-sh,* drawing out the sibilant *shhh.* Out of the thicket flew a Greater Pewee to sit for several seconds on the branch of a nearby oak. Then, his curiosity satisfied, he flew away.

"Five. Four. EIGHT," Mack mouthed. After a moment of reverent silence, she added, "Keep 'em comin'. In fact, an Elegant Trogan about now would be very acceptable."

A trogan was possible but not likely in this open area. Nevertheless, we fetched our lunches, found some boulders to sit on, and put ourselves into a receptive mood, which didn't exclude conversation.

"Have you seen Fat Albert?" one of our companions asked.

"Who's Fat Albert?" I wanted to know.

"It's a dirigible, the government's fair-weather surveyor along the Mexican border."

"For drug trafficking?"

"Right."

"Yes, we saw it a couple of days ago," Mack said, "when we were coming down the Hamburg Trail over in Ramsey Canyon. But I didn't know its name."

"You went for the hummingbirds?"

"Yes."

"Did you see the White-eared?"

"Fleetingly, but long enough to count it for a lifer."

"It's been stirring up a lot of excitement even among the veteran, die-hard birders."

As we talked, a pair of Painted Redstarts, deciding we meant them no harm, continued with their nest building in the overhang of the bank across the gully from us. One at a time, they disappeared into the hole with a mouthful of weeds or grasses and then vanished into the woods for more. What a sight—bold white wing bars contrasting with the black of their bodies. And he with a vivid red breast. As they twitted and fussed, they fanned their tails, showing off the white outer feathers.

I hadn't paid much attention to the swallows flying around the clearing until a Violet-green lit atop a pole near the old cabin. Caught in a shaft of sunlight, it fairly shimmered. A memorable moment!

By midafternoon we gave up on the Elegant Trogan. The

California couple had already left. "No point in being greedy," I said philosophically.

"Or playing cutsey with these afternoon showers," Mack added.

Quarter of a mile down the mountain, Mack had just navigated a hairpin turn. A tributary of Garden Creek flowed in from the right and splashed along beside us. From somewhere upstream came a raucous cry. "What was that?" Mack asked, jamming the brakes and crunching to a stop.

"Sounded like jays."

"No, too hoarse for jays, too . . . too unsustained."

"Crows, maybe?"

"I doubt it."

So did I. "Then what do *you* think it was?"

"An Elegant Trogan. It was more of a croak. More of a squawk than jays make."

Walking at this point was out of the question—too many rocks, too much water. We sat in the car, binoculars searching the treetops. The habitat was ideal for trogans, streamside woodlands at an elevation of five thousand feet. But the cry did not come again. Nor did either of us see a flash of color in the trees.

"Shall we wait?" Mack finally asked, "or shall we try to beat that black cloud back to camp?"

"Driver's choice." We drove on.

The next day we left Sierra Vista without a Botteri's Sparrow or even looking for the Spotted Owl, but not without going down to the San Pedro River to look for an Abert's Towhee. Birds, however, cannot be ordered and delivered on demand. We didn't find the Towhee, but we were pleased with the Tropical Kingbird, lifer number five hundred and forty-nine.

On to Madera. If you have only time for one canyon, James Lane's guide says, make it Madera. We camped in Green

182

Valley, twenty-five miles south of Tucson and an easy run into the canyon. Before dinner the first night, we found two life birds in the campground, a Brown-crested Flycatcher and several pairs of Gambel's Quail. The latter, always in pairs, were constantly monitoring the grounds, pecking, grunting, crying a sad little *qua-el,* as though telling their name. They were shy, though. They scurried away, pretending the telephone was ringing, whenever we approached, he always a little in the lead.

Our trips into the canyon traversed first a giant cactus garden, seven miles of Prickly Pear, Staghorn, Teddy Bear and Buckhorn colla, and a variety of Barrel cacti, all in bloom. Some days Mack thought she would never get me and my camera past the cacti. Next came the Florida Wash, where birders seek Scaled Quail, Phainopepla, Brown Towhee, and more. The best bird there because it is the rarest is the Rufous-winged Sparrow. That's what we were walking up and down the wash looking for the morning a car paused at the bridge and a woman called out, "There's a pair of Elegant Trogans on the trail above Santa Rita Lodge this morning."

"How far up?"

"Not far. Length of a football field, maybe."

"Have you seen them?"

"'Bout a half hour ago."

"Thanks," I said. "Forget the Rufous-winged Sparrow." We were already scrambling up the bank to the car. I recalled how cavalierly we had dismissed this bird the first time we came to Madera five years ago. And we hadn't been lucky in Sawmill Canyon last week.

Jean, who had come from Dallas for the weekend, led the trek up the trail. We heard one before we saw it, a kind of parrotlike squawk. Then Jean spotted it, all twelve inches of iridescent bronze with a bright red breast and yellow bill. On the branch above, his spouse sported brown above and a pinky breast. They sat erect, high in a sycamore tree but not so high that we couldn't see the black bands at the tip of their long, square-cut copper tails.

The word had spread fast. The crowd was gathering. The trogans took all the hullabaloo in their stride. They must have had a nest nearby, for ordinarily they are shy and stay much farther up the trail. This pair stood its ground, uttering only an occasional *co-ah*. Staring at them, I felt they were the ones that should have had binoculars, studying the hype in all the gawking creatures down below. Jean had soon shot a roll of film.

"I'm going back to the car," she said, "for my tripod and another lens. Can I bring you anything?"

"I'll go with you and get the lunch," Mack volunteered. "We've waited long enough for this pair. We might as well stay and enjoy them."

If we hadn't settled in there between the mountain stream and the trogans, we probably never would have found the Northern Beardless-Tyrannulet. What a preposterous name for a tiny four-and-a-half-inch bird, which raises its crown slightly in a bushy crest that gives it a quizzical look. It is so shy it is more often heard than seen, and that's not often. For such a little bird, it has a loud, clear, whistled *pee-yerp*, which could be heard over the splashing water. It shares the trogans' fondness for sycamores beside a mountain stream.

In the days that followed, we found other lifers in Madera Canyon. At the hummingbird feeders outside Santa Rita Lodge, where Mack once provided TLC for newly banded hummers, a Scott's Oriole sipped nectar, and some friendly Yellow-eyed Juncos instantly became Mack's favorite bird. A mile and a half further down the stream, a Lucy's Warbler played hide and seek, and a Gray Vireo flicked its tail as it foraged restlessly through the chaparral and mesquite undergrowth.

One evening we drove to Bog Springs Campground high in the canyon to hear a Whiskered Screech Owl's Morse code call before it took off for a night of hunting. That turned out to be a *threefer* with a Western and an Elf owl completing the trio. Another day at Bog Springs, I lured Gray-breasted Jays to my camera with popcorn and caught flashes of Painted Redstarts and Bullock's Orioles streaking through the pine-oaks. Five years ago we were the only RV in this park. This week we couldn't have found a site if we'd wanted one.

One piece of unfinished business remained before leaving Madera Canyon, the Rufous-winged Sparrow, which the trogans had upstaged. Back at the Florida Wash, the weather was ideal; the birds scarce. Had we dawdled too long over breakfast?

"It's here or nowhere," Mack said. "Its range is as limited as the trogans' if not more so. Just a wee corner of the United States."

"At least it's the right habitat, rocks and tall grasses."

Other birders were scouring the wash, too, looking for various birds. We searched together up and down the—for the most part—dry riverbed. At one moment I thought I had found the long-sought Abert's Towhee, but it was a Brown Towhee, very similar but no cigar. The Rufous-winged Sparrow fleetingly passed before our eyes and disappeared in the grass. Or was it? The call was right, a trill of *chips*. Another birder assured us we had found it. Iffy, but we had other things to do than play games with Rufous-winged Sparrows.

Throughout birddom mention of certain landmarks establishes instant rapport between birders: "the dump" in Churchill, "the fountain" on Green Key in the Dry Tortugas, "the cabin" in Sawmill Canyon. The roadside rest area on Route 92 in Arizona is such a landmark. Every birder worth her birding cap knows the modest pulloff on the right, driving east from Nogales. Several first sightings of birds in the United

States have occurred nearby. It also alerts anyone looking for one of the most productive birding areas in Arizona to take the next left, ford the Sonoita Creek (if the water's not too high), and proceed a short way to the Patagonia–Sonoita Creek Sanctuary. Thanks to The Nature Conservancy, this narrow strip for a mile and a half along Sonoita Creek has mesquite thickets, fields, and stands of willow and cottonwood instead of golf courses and high-risers. We had scarcely crossed the creek than we came upon some birders rejoicing in their discovery of a Thick-billed Kingbird, a lucky find north of the Mexican Border. They found it for us, first lifer of the day. Way to go!

For the next few hours, we wandered through birdsong, following the trails across the fields, through the cottonwoods, and along the stream. I collected yellows: Yellow-shafted Flicker, Yellow-breasted Chat, Lesser Goldfinches, Yellow Warbler, kingbirds, and flycatchers. The Dusky-capped Flycatcher was a life bird. A Black Phoebe and a saucy Bridled Titmouse amused us. The Gray Hawk (a rare find) did not amuse us when it snatched a baby something—maybe a Mississippi Kite—from its nest. How the mama beat her wings and screamed. A Vermilion Flycatcher and a Summer Tanager, studies in red, lit briefly in a mesquite bush within four feet of each other. Now that was a sight to remember. But it is the Gray Hawk that I can't forget. Northern Harriers and Kestrels were hunting, a Gila Woodpecker, pecking, Bronzed Cowbird, Brown Towhee, Bewick's Wren . . . it *was* a day!

Along the riverbank, we met a young woman in a wheelchair. My compliments to The Conservancy that its two or three miles of trails are navigable by wheelchair, though they might not have been for someone with less grit than Terry had.

"Have you seen the hummingbird nest?" Terry asked. We hadn't.

"What kind of hummingbird?"

"Black-chinned."

"Where is it?" I asked.

"Bear left at the main entry and follow the trail up the bank. Turn left again and go along toward the old dam. It's on the left just before the dam."

After a little more conversation, we made our way to the hummingbird nest. We found the place. We found the tree, thanks to a naturalist who was standing nearby. Mack even found the branch, but the bird flew in and out so fast that she couldn't pinpoint the nest. Eventually we all found it under a sprig of leaves—all two inches of it. Just enough for mama to sit on, not in, covering her two wee ones, the size of peas.

Leaving the sanctuary, we stopped at the Paton feeders just beyond the border of the sanctuary. A sign on the gate says, "Birders Welcome." The Patons even provide chairs in the shade at a discreet distance from the comings and goings at their dozen hummingbird feeders.

Birding hot lines in recent weeks had reported a rare hummer among the regulars at the Patons', and we hadn't sat long before the lone Violet-crowned Hummingbird showed up to put the icing on a very productive day.

During the weekend Jean spent with us at Madera Canyon, we took a day to climb (by car) Mount Lemmon in the Santa Catalina Mountains northeast of Tucson. For sheer beauty, spectacle, and variety, this trip would be hard to beat. The diversity of animal and plant life from the base to the top is, to quote James Lane again, like traveling from Mexico to Canada in forty-two miles. For the first ten miles, saguaros and palo verde of the Sonoran desert dominate the landscape. Then they give way to evergreen oaks, pinyon pine, juniper, and prickly pear. Agave stalks grew fifteen to twenty feet tall, what Mack called Arizona asparagus.

At Bear River Canyon, we walked along the stream under

Arizona Cypress and the first Ponderosa Pines. Bird calls were numerous and varied, and the Hepatic Tanager was a life bird. The Hepatic is to the mountain forests what the Western Summer Tanager is to the valleys. Is there any redder red than tanager red?

Round and round, zig and zag, the road climbed from one breathtaking view to another. "I'm glad I'm here to do the driving for you guys," Jean said. But she wasn't there to do the driving the next two times we came up. We just couldn't get enough of Mount Lemmon. At Windy Point the panoramic view looks back at the valley four thousand feet below. The road below ribbons up through dry hillsides splashed with blooming yucca, agave, and sotol, around forests and along mountain streams. Free-standing boulders at Windy Point look ready to tumble to the valley below. As we roamed about, looking for the best camera shots, a group of young climbers with ropes, spikes, and all the rest of their mountain-climbing gear rapelled themselves up the perpendicular wall of a hundred-foot boulder at the edge of the parking lot.

Two miles farther along at seven thousand feet, our birding began in earnest. Leaving the main road, we drove into Rose Canyon, hoping to find a Red-faced Warbler, rarely seen below six thousand feet. The search was short. Though tiny, it is so distinctive that I recognized it instantly. In fact, recognizing it was easier than believing it. It has an ordinary enough gray back, gray wings and tail, and very white underparts. So far so good. Nothing unusual. But add to that a pair of black over-the-head earmuffs, a white skullcap slipped down on the back of its head, and wrap the rest—forehead, face, and throat halfway down the breast—in a bright red muffler out of which sticks a sharp little black beak. I couldn't tell whether it was terribly embarrassed or was bundled up against the cold.

It was a modest, but friendly enough little fellow—or gal.

Both male and female look alike. It popped up several times foraging among the pine cones and grasses, jerking its tail sideways, as we picnicked in the Ponderosa grove. Unlike other warblers it nests on the ground, but we didn't seem to be disturbing a nest. Such an independent little mite. Another for my memorable list.

The squirrels in Rose Canyon were memorable, too. I'd never seen a tassel-eared squirrel before. Mack couldn't believe her eyes. "What *is* it?" she cried, running after it. "I want to take one home." Personally I would have settled for a pair of Red-faced Warblers. We found a Grace's Warbler also before we left Rose Canyon, a beautiful little gray and yellow bird . . . but a bit anticlimactic after the Red-faced.

At eight thousand feet, Douglas Fir and White and Yellow pine began to show up among the Ponderosa. "Yellow Pines," Jean exclaimed. "This should be Pygmy Nuthatch country." She'd hardly turned into Spencer Canyon before Mack spotted one upside down pecking at a pine cone. "And there is another."

"And another," I added, wanting to be part of that exultant moment. "The book says they roam in loose flocks. I think we've come upon a loose flock."

As we reveled in the pygmies, a streak of blue crossed the road, a Western Bluebird. Several others came and went in the field across the road. The competition for our attention was getting crucial.

The Irondoor Inn stands across the street from the ski lift at eighty-five hundred feet. Outside Broad-tailed Hummingbirds darted from feeder to feeder, the wingbeats of the males making a loud trilling whistle. Inside, having our snack on the screened porch, Mack was thrilled to find her Yellow-eyed Junco friends from Santa Rita Lodge hopping around the floor between tables, cleaning up dropped crumbs.

"Wonder how much they pay 'em," I pondered.

"And who says birds don't have personalities," Mack said defensively.

By now the change in temperature from the high nineties of the desert floor was noticeable, especially to Jean and Mack in shorts. Five hundred feet higher in white fir and quaking aspens, we rounded a bend to face snowbanks. At the top elevation (9,185 feet), the whole world spread out before us. An afternoon storm was approaching across the desert. I photographed the rain coming straight at us. Then it hit—lightning, thunder, hail, and snow. Jean started the motor and turned on the heater. Gale winds rocked the car like a boat. Between chattering teeth Mack managed to say, "Who'd a thought it?"

The storm passed. We wandered around looking for anything the mountain had to offer, maybe a Red-breasted Nuthatch, an Evening Grosbeak, or Warbling Vireo? What we found was a lone Broad-billed Hummingbird hunkered down on a snow-covered sprig of Engelmann Spruce. He echoed Mack's "Who'd a thought it?"

A Western Tanager in breeding plumage—red head, yellow breast, black tail, black back, and yellow wing bars—flew across our path as we started our descent to the desert and warmer temperatures.

Jean had to return home the next day. Mack and I broke camp and headed for Cave Creek Canyon in the Chiricahua Mountains.

Portal at the entrance to Cave Creek Canyon has a post office (open five days a week from 10:30 A.M. to 12:30 P.M.), a library, a combined store and lodge, and seventy residents.

"What do you suggest we do first?" Mack asked.

"Let's find a campsite. We have three campgrounds to choose from—all primitive, no hookups."

The first was full, and we chose not to ford the brook to

get into the second one. A fifty-foot stream, coursing over a river of rocks, separated us from our third option, Sunny Flat.

"Well?" Mack asked.

"I vote for this one. It's more open than the others." She drove cautiously down the bank, entered the stream, and splashed our way into the campground. We circled the area once and selected a flat, shady spot to be our home for a few days. I walked back and put our three dollars for the first night into the box on the post.

"We're going to be at some disadvantage, trying to bird this narrow, steep-walled canyon in a thirty-six-foot motor home," Mack remarked.

"We'll have to walk—as good birders should," I said.

"But how are we going to get out of the campground?"

"A very practical question," I admitted, eyeing the two- and three-hundred-foot cliffs on three sides of us and remembering the stones in the fast-moving stream. We had tried unsuccessfully to rent a car in Douglas. "But first things first. Let's settle camp."

"What's there to settle?" Mack wanted to know. "We have no hookups."

"We can put up a couple of hummingbird feeders and pop some corn for the other birds."

"How are you going to pop corn?"

"Touché. Make it bread crumbs."

After settling into our little Eden, we drove back to Portal and phoned Dave Jasper, a local birder whom friends had recommended. Could he help us find some target birds?

"How about day after tomorrow?" he asked.

"Excellent."

"In the meantime be sure to visit the Spoffords' feeders here in town. They have a Berylline Hummingbird coming fairly regularly. And bird locally around South Fork Road.

You'll find a lot on South Fork where you can park your rig. It's not far from the trail."

"I've read bears roam that trail," I said.

"Farther up than you'll go. But should you meet one, be sure *not* to turn your back. Bears get really excited when you run away screaming 'Bear.'"

Cave Creek is more isolated than the other canyons we'd been birding. With the exception of the Mexican Chickadee, which is found nowhere else in the United States except here, all the birds in this canyon can be found in more accesible areas. Because of its remoteness and lack of creature comforts, Cave Creek attracts only committed birders who cherish its remoteness . . . and its beauty. It is an Elegant Trogan's heaven, a steep-walled canyon with perpetual water. It is named for the many holes in the soft canyon walls, the homes once of cliff-dwelling Indians.

In addition to the remoteness and beauty, the Spoffords draw birders to Cave Creek Canyon. The Spoffords, like the Patons at Sonoita only more so and forever, have hung or mounted twenty-five to thirty feeders of every sort throughout their yard. They offer something to please any bird with the slightest inclination to accept a human handout. We went there, as Dave suggested, to find the Berylline Hummingbird. A half-dozen others were strolling around the garden or just sitting and watching the feeders when we arrived. I sat down on one of the benches the Spoffords hospitably provide.

"Have you come for the Berylline?" the young man beside me asked.

"Yes, that and everything else. I've never been here before."

"The Berylline was here about ten minutes ago. It favors that feeder on the right," he said, indicating a string of three hanging from a Honey Mesquite.

"When will it be back?"

"It's been coming about every forty minutes today."

I moved on to a bench nearer the feeder that he had indicated, checked my camera settings, and waited. Other hummingbirds—Broad-billed, Broad-tailed, Magnificent, and Blue-throated—darted constantly between the feeders, but I was looking for one that would be green above and below with a chestnut rump, wings, and tail. Would I be able to isolate it from all the others?

Twenty minutes passed. A man with a camera appeared.

"You waiting for the Berylline?" I asked. He nodded. I sensed he was not going to waste any time talking. More cameras arrived, no-nonsense cameras with long telescopic barrels. If I were going to see this Berylline, I'd have to leave my seat and find a place among the silent cameras.

"It's been thirty-eight minutes," one camera whispered to another.

I seriously doubted any tiny rare bird was going to come feed within five feet of what had become a small mob of jostling photographers jockeying for position.

"That's it!" somebody murmured under his breath. And I suppose it was.

The excitement over and the photographers gone, folks again strolled quietly among the birds. Acorn Woodpeckers competed at one of the platform feeders. Titmice, House Finches, a Hooded Oriole, and some Black-headed Grosbeaks ate at various feeders around the garden. White-winged Doves and Gray-breasted Jays fed on the ground. A Solitary Vireo called from the trees. A Black Phoebe appeared briefly at the edge of the brush. A Yellow-eyed Junco pecked aimlessly about, as though tidying up after the others.

We didn't see the Spoffords to speak to. They were too busy replenishing nectar, seeds, cracked corn, and peanut butter. And they call this retirement? Whatever they call it, they have provided pleasure for thousands of visitors for years.

Back in camp an Acorn Woodpecker, a clown of a bird, was going through contortions trying to sip from a hummingbird feeder. Gray Jays gorged themselves on our bread crumbs. The soft light of dusk highlighted the green lichen that covers the rose-colored cliffs towering hundreds of feet above the Arizona Sycamores, Black Walnut, Apache Pine, and Mountain Mahogany. I was sorry I had used up so many superlatives on earlier canyons. *Awesome* did come to mind. We scanned the cliffs for a Prairie Falcon until the light faded.

Dave picked us up at 6:30 Saturday morning and within an hour had found both a Bendire's and a Crissal thrasher for us in the grasslands to the east of Portal. We came back then to Portal and climbed the old mining road to Paradise, a town of thirty the last time the census was taken. We splashed through so many washes that I began to wonder *who needs bridges?* as we made our way up the canyon. Way up there somewhere beyond Paradise, a position I had never found myself in before, a Plain Titmouse was whistling its spring *weety-weety-weety* song among the juniper and pinyons. In its gray-brown somberness, it would never be confused with its cousins, the Tufted or the Bridled titmice. But since it was the third lifer of the morning, I found it a very satisfactory little fellow.

Two more were waiting for us there among the oaks and conifers, but they made us work for them. We abandoned the car and wandered around for an hour before we had a good sighting of a Blue-throated Gray Warbler. Likewise the Western (recently renamed Cordilleran) Flycatcher. The latter, my field guide says, "seeks an inconspicuous perch." I can vouch for that. Without Dave, Mack and I would have found neither. Superb guide that he is, though, he stayed with the search until we had good identifications. If I couldn't see what was so clear to him, he was patient until I did see it. Or if the flycatcher flew prematurely, Dave would search until he found it again . . . or another one.

Toward the end of this productive morning, we were in the South Fork picnic area when some bird overhead let out a sharp *arrk*.

"Do you know what that is?" Dave asked.

"An Elegant Trogan?" Mack ventured.

"Right." And so we had our second sighting of a female.

The weather had been deteriorating. We were back in monsoon country with showers coming a little earlier each day. Our six good hours with Dave came to a sudden halt when thunder, lightening, and hail drove us undercover. Cognizant of those warnings at every wash: do not enter during flash floods, I was glad we were back in the campground.

I asked Dave, "Do these streams we've been fording ever become impassable for long at a time?"

"Some do. Some more than others. A friend of mine claims she drank coffee for two days at the lodge in Portal waiting for friends marooned in their campground across the creek."

We agreed the afternoon was probably a lost cause. "Keep an eye out," Dave said in parting, "for the Virginia Warbler and the Prairie Falcon. They are both possible right here in the campground, though the falcon will be high in the cliffs." He whistled once more the Virginia Warbler's song. "Listen for it," he said as he left.

We hadn't scratched the surface of Cave Creek Canyon. The trails go on and on up to heights of nearly ten thousand feet, canyon beyond canyon deep into the Chiricahua Mountains. Next time we will explore farther, but now the Texas canyons were calling, Hueco Tanks and Guadalupe, and we hoped a pair of Montezuma Quail were waiting for us in the Davis Mountains.

North Florida

I heard a bird at break of day
　　Sing from the autumn trees
A song so mystical and calm
　　So full of certainties.

　　　　　　　　　　　　　　—W. A. Percy

Some birders, probably fewer than one percent, rail against keeping lists. Another one or two percent may be indifferent to them, but the majority of birders keep some kind of list. Life, State, Year, Backyard are common. The kind, though, is restricted only by the whim of the lister: Birds with Red (or Blue or Black or Yellow), Birds that Nest on the Ground (or in Trees or Cavities), Birds with Green Legs (or Pink or Yellow or Black).

　　Charles Kennedy was leading a field trip in Mobile, Alabama, for an American Birding Association conference when we came upon a Bay-breasted Warbler sitting on a utility line. It was a lifer for me, but I was surprised when Charles said, "That's one for *my* list." Surely a birder as experienced as he must have a life list well into the seven hundreds, with probably every warbler in the book.

　　"What kind of list?" I asked.

　　"Bird on a Line," he replied.

　　The Life List Mack and I keep grew from a Backyard List. When the opportunities for finding lifers grew increasingly infrequent, we started an Annual List. That is not to say we abandoned the Life List. Oh, no, not with numero six hundred taunting us on the horizon. But while we awaited the next new bird, the possibility that around the next corner, in the next tree, on the next pond, under the next brush pile a bird could put us over last *year's* total added zest to the most familiar, around-the-neighborhood walk.

Marjory and Eleanor, annual visitors from Connecticut, have developed a game more challenging than scrabble, better exercise than hopscotch, and more fun than poohsticks. It began casually enough with their Trip List of our dooryard and lakeside birds, plus two local specialties, a Bachman Sparrow and a Red-cockaded Woodpecker, both inhabitants of Osceola National Forest on the east side of town. Then on a day's outing to Wakulla Springs near Tallahassee, they found their first Limpkin. A recluse, the Limpkin lives in wooded swamps here and there throughout Florida and southern Georgia, but we've never failed to find two or three along the Wakulla River.

You may never have seen a Limpkin, so named for its peculiar walk, but you may have unwittingly heard its penetrating *krr-oww*. When Hollywood came to Wakulla Springs to film the first *Tarzan* movie, it became so enamored of the Limpkin's cry that it ironically dubbed the haunting wail into a number of jungle films despite the fact the bird has never been closer to Africa than the Florida Everglades. Its fondness for apple snails keeps it from wandering.

Not far from Wakulla Springs, Saint Marks National Wildlife Refuge is a birders' paradise. The refuge harbors up to twenty-five thousand waterfowl in winter—wigeons, pintails, gadwalls, shovelers, teals, goldeneyes . . . ibses, egrets, and herons abound. A resident pair of American Bald Eagles has a nest within easy binocular reach. One of the pair keeps vigil in a bald tree overlooking several ponds not far from the road. Dozens of Osprey nest in old snags. Clapper, Virginia, and King rails are all possibilities in the marshes on the edge of the Gulf of Mexico. Brown Pelicans, grebes, and loons stay year round. Belted Kingfishers are as dependable as grandma's ginger cookies.

Eleanor and Marjory's first Florida list was made with no more concern than as a trip record, an extension of other diary items. The count when they left Florida was a modest sixty-four.

"I bet we could beat that if we tried," Marjory said as they were leaving.

The next November (for the Thanksgiving visit had become a tradition), Marjory announced as we waited by the baggage carousel in the Jacksonville airport, "We have to beat last year's sixty-four."

"Sixty-four what?" I asked innocently.

"I saw a crow near the runway as we were taxiing in," Eleanor said.

"Okay. That's number one."

A Mockingbird was caroling in the parking lot. A Cattle Egret fed on the roadside along Route I-10. No bird went uncounted. To everyone's surprise, a flock of Snow Geese was hunkered down beside a pond a few miles short of Lake City. And Ollie, our resident Barred Owl, came to Mack's call soon after we drove into the driveway.

During dinner Marjory asked casually, "What's on beyond Saint Marks Refuge if we keep going farther west?"

"Houston, Texas, and El Paso if you go far enough," I volunteered.

"You know what I mean," Marge said. "Birds. Maybe we could go out and stay overnight somewhere and explore?"

"We don't have to have a traditional Thanksgiving dinner on a traditional date," Eleanor reminded us, and we all agreed. We'd fit the turkey in wherever it least disturbed the other birds.

So we set out for the Florida Panhandle and a goal of at least sixty-five birds.

"*Seventy*-five," Marjory decreed.

The first stop was Saint Marks again. The regal eagle was perched aloft his personal tree. Most of the ducks from the year before were there, including both Greater and Lesser Scaup and a Common Goldeneye. One of the ponds was solid with coots. In another a Sora Rail was minding her private business. A flock of White Pelicans rode in the water so far away that we could not have positively identified them without a spotting scope. Almost at our knees, an American Bittern stood so placid in the reeds that we almost missed it. Sedge and Marsh wrens scuttled in the grasses along the beach where we walked patiently back and forth until we had identified them both. On the pilings extending into the gulf posed Brown Pelicans, Double-crested Cormorants, and a lone Reddish Egret. Terns wheeled in the air. Gulls mused on the sandbars rising from the receding tide.

On this second visit to Wakulla, we chartered our own boat, the better to leisurely scan the short mile allowed us for exploration. An occasional Limpkin probed the watery edges with its long bill in search of frogs and insects. Apple snails were out of season. The Limpkins, long accustomed to the jungle boats, allowed us to admire them. What appears at first glance to be a speckled bird with long legs is really beautifully designed. It is basically chocolate brown all over, but every brown feather has a white crescent tip. The result is a masterful camouflage. With a trip list in hand, however, no bird on the river was overlooked: Anhinga, White Ibises, American Coots, American Wigeon, Moorhens, Turkey Vultures, and Double-crested Cormorants.

"What's it doing?" Eleanor asked our pilot after a cormorant twice had flown over our heads and lit in the water right in front of the boat.

"It's fishing," he explained. "The boat stirs up fish, so the bird gets his pick of the best. While he feeds we get ahead of him. Then he flies up front again and starts all over."

"Smart bird," Eleanor commented.

During the next two days, we birded the southeastern corner of Apalachicola National Forest (good for the Red-cockaded Woodpeckers), Saint George's Island, and other barrier reefs to the end of Saint Joseph's Spit in Saint Joseph's Bay past Apalachicola almost to Panama City. But of all the beaches we walked, all the trails we pursued, all the birds we counted, Alligator Point on the coast a few miles west of the Ocholockonee River took the prize. It won hands down, partly for the Roseate Tern, a lifer for Marjory and Eleanor, but mostly for the sighting of a Swallow-tailed Kite.

We were exploring an abandoned road running along the east end of the point. Suddenly this most graceful of all North American hawks was hovering over our heads. Its striking black-and-white pattern and long swallow tail left no doubt as to what it was. I looked right into its beady eyes. We stood speechless as it drifted not more than twenty or thirty feet above us. Its great black-and-white wings spread a full four feet or more, scarcely quivering. Then with a little tip of one wing, it caught the sea breeze and floated away. We weren't what it was looking for.

"What are you planning for an encore?" Eleanor asked, the first to regain her voice.

"I wish it would come back," Marjory whispered almost in a trance. But it didn't. It was number seventy-nine on a list that reached eighty-four by the end of the visit.

"We didn't quite make eighty-five," said Marjory, sighing as we approached the airport.

"Seven dozen is an easy number to remember," I tried to console her.

They arrived at the airport the third year, Trip List in

hand. "We have to beat eighty-four," Marjory said before we had hardly finished our greetings.

"What's this year's goal?" I asked.

"Ninety," Eleanor said.

"For a starter," Marjory added.

"Well, since we're in Jacksonville, shall we bird the coast before we go home?" Mack suggested. "All those in favor say *bird*." The vote was unanimous.

Two or three miles beyond the Mayport Navy Yard, Fort George on the left and Ward's Island to the right offer some of the best shore birding in Florida. Mack and I have birded both with Steve and Diana, birding friends who used to live in Jacksonville. In Steve's Isuzu Trooper, we have charged sand dunes and challenged incoming tides with good results—both in driving and in birding. Even with two-wheel drive and two good feet apiece, we chalked up a list of thirty-four before moving on to Fort Clinch at Fernadina Beach. We'd counted Osprey, Royal and Forster's terns, Greater and Lesser Black-backed gulls, Short and Long-billed dowitchers, Semi-palmated Plover, Horned Grebe, Killdeer, and American Oystercatchers. The latter vied for "most exciting bird" with a Long-billed Curlew being driven off a sandbar by the incoming tide.

At Fort Clinch two rarities topped off the list, a flock of Purple Sandpipers and a Glaucose Gull. Both birds, though possible, are unusual in Florida. The Glaucous was a lifer for Marjory and Eleanor.

On another day Thanksgiving turkey took a back seat to the flock of wild turkeys that Marjory spotted near the Visitors Center at the southern end of Paynes Prairie, an hour's drive from home. The best of Paynes Prairie, which eighteenth-century naturalist William Bartram called *the Great Allatchua Savanah*, however, for my money is the north end off SE Fifteenth Street, Gainesville, for those willing to walk a mile and a half to the observation tower. The call of the Sandhill Cranes can be heard a mile away. And the stroll to them has many rewards of its own, especially for someone trying to break last year's Trip List.

From the parking lot, we followed the La Chua Trail down a steep slope, past the Alachua sinkhole and into the prairie basin. This large area and marsh was once a lake, traversed by steamboats in the nineteenth century. Today we travel on shank's mare. Alligators don't count on a bird list, but clusters of eight-, ten-, twelve-foot gators lazed on the opposite bank of the canal.

"Why are they all on *that* side?" Marjory asked.

"Maybe they're not," I commented, pointing out that the embankment on our side was so steep we really couldn't see what might be on it.

"Oh," Marge gulped.

Numerous sparrows—Savannah, Marsh, Vesper, and more—weren't hard to find. A Common Yellowthroat in the brush was a happy surprise. A Little Blue Heron hunted and a Pied-billed Grebe swam in the canal. Gradually the trail became wetter. A Greater Yellowlegs stood up to his knees in water in the cattail marsh, which gave way finally to a weedy slough as we approached the observation tower. White Ibises were easy to spot, but we probably missed some of the Black-crowned Night Herons huddled deep in the dark of overshadowing bushes. Our excitement grew as the call of the cranes intensified.

From the top of the observation tower, we looked out upon miles of prairie and an estimated three thousand cranes. Some fed at the foot of the tower, their reflections sharp in the shallow pools. As far as binoculars could reach, groups of Sandhills dominated the scene—sauntering, milling, feeding, calling. Their inimitable trumpeting, rattling *gar-oo-oo* never ceased.

A few coots and Purple Gallinules swam in the puddles. A Great Blue Heron, motionless as Michelangelo's *David*, waited for a minnow worth his effort. Great Egrets and some Snowies with the golden slippers snatched teatime tidbits. On the north side of the tower, a hundred or more Wood Storks congregated. I couldn't tell even with my binoculars whether they were chewing toothpicks, but surely they were discussing the woes of the world. I've never seen a jolly Wood Stork. With their long thick bills and naked black necks, they are no subject for a beauty contest either. But they never fail to excite me, especially a flock in flight. As many as ninety have paused at one time on Harris Lake near Astolat, and from time to time, a half dozen or more stop briefly on our own lake. But they never stay. Perhaps this gathering forty-five miles south of Astolat explains why. Storks of a feather and all that.

"How many birds on your list now?" I asked Eleanor that evening.

"Sixty-two, though we haven't double-checked yet."

"Where do you want to go next?"

"Could we go back to Saint Marks? We always have such a good time there."

"And maybe stay overnight in Panacea and go to Alligator Point?" Marjory suggested.

"She hopes to rendezvous with a Swallow-tailed Kite," Eleanor explained.

"So do I," Mack said.

After a day at home to enjoy Astolat and pay homage to the Pilgrims of Plymouth, we headed for Saint Marks and Alligator Point. The Bald Eagle was not in his tree, but down the road a piece, a pair perched together in another dead tree. They were doubtlessly discussing plans for the new brood early next year. 'Twas time to think about refurbishing the old nest.

In a brackish stream on our approach to the lighthouse, Mack's sharp eye caught a Virginia Rail darting from the mudflat into the protective grasses. This little bird, half the size of a Clapper Rail or about the size of a Hairy Woodpecker, is so elusive that we have doubtlessly driven by it many times unaware of its presence. This time, stopping at the spot, we lay in wait until it ventured forth again. That was a memorable moment, but still not as surprising as the Fulvous Whistling Ducks that we came upon a little later. Fulvous Whistling Ducks are fairly common in marshlands within their range along the Gulf Coast but not as far east as Saint Marks. They do occasionally show up during fall migration. Luckily this was one of those occasions and we were there.

The Fulvous Whistling Duck is an unduck-like duck. It flies like a heron, lands like a goose, and squeals instead of quacks. When frightened it stands totally still like a bittern. And everyone knows what a duck does when startled. Formerly called Tree Ducks, they rarely perch in a tree and never nest in one. But they do have webbed feet and duck bills, enough to qualify as ducks apparently.

Crouched with some ibises on the banks of a weedy pond at a turn in the road, they puzzled us for a long time until two of them stood, revealing their long legs, long necks, tawny underpants, white rumps, and dull blue legs and feet.

"That's our eighty-fourth bird. We've tied last year," Eleanor announced once the identification was agreed upon and the excitement subsided.

"So we don't need to go to Alligator Point," I teased. "You're bound to find another even if we go home now."

"But I was hoping for ninety . . . or maybe ninety-five," Marge said with a hint of disappointment in her voice.

"Okay," Mack chimed in. "Let's work our way toward Panacea where we'll bird Alligator Point tomorrow."

"And maybe see the Swallow-tailed Kite again?" Marjory said, suddenly cheered.

"We can hope."

November is a great month for birding in Florida. The summer heat is gone. The air is balmy and dry. November and April are Florida's driest months. The weather was ideal when we reached the beach the next morning. We checked first the spot where we had encountered the Swallow-tailed the year before, but no kite was in sight.

"We'll check again before we leave," Mack promised.

The road west makes its way between an inner waterway on the right and the Gulf to the left. Docks extending from private property into the waterway were lined with gulls, cormorants, and terns. Of all the gulls sunning there, the Ring-billed was the easiest to identify. Bonaparte's and Laughing gulls share more characteristics, but Bonaparte's are the smaller of the two and have red, not black, feet.

"That's three gulls without half trying," Eleanor had just said when Marjory asked,

"What's that *little* gull sunning with the Bonaparte's?"

"Maybe it's a tern," I proposed.

"The wings are too rounded," Eleanor said.

"Could it be a Little Gull?" Mack asked.

"Little Gulls can't be here," Marge countered. "My book says they're 'European stragglers and rare breeders' in North America."

"I'll get the scope," Mack offered.

The Bonaparte's took off in a raucous cloud of white, the smaller gull going and returning with them. Finally Mack had it in the scope.

"I still think it's a Little Gull. I think we have a rare bird here. Take a look, somebody." We each took a turn at the scope, checking out wing tips, underwings, wing linings, tail, legs. The black hoods of summer had mostly disappeared, eliminating that clue.

"Well, what do you think?" Mack asked when all observations seemed to have been made.

"I think it is a rare Little Gull," Marjory said.

"I don't see what else it can be, especially that size," Eleanor agreed.

"Because it's too small to be a Bonaparte's and because it has red legs, I'll vote for Little Gull, too," I said.

"So it's unanimous," Mack tallied. "It's a lifer for Ev and me."

"For us, too," Eleanor said.

"Not bad," Marjory conceded, "even if the Swallow-tailed doesn't show."

"But we haven't given up on that one," Mack assured her.

Some of the other good birds of the day were a Royal Tern, Solitary Sandpiper, Black-bellied Plover, American Oystercatchers, and American Avocets.

Returning along the beach, we stopped to study a flock of Greater Scaup, hoping to find some scoters among them. Brown Pelicans were diving for their supper. Then a Reddish Egret appeared just off shore. So unlike its patient egret cousins, the Reddish capers around in pursuit of its delicacies. It dashes, stops, starts, waving its wings to shadow the water, the better to spot its prey. It's one of my many favorite birds.

"What is your count now?" I asked Eleanor later as she and Marjory compared notes.

"Ninety-four."

"Only one more to go, Marge."

"Well," she said tentatively.

Leaving the Point, we looked once more for the Swallow-tailed Kite. It wasn't around. We reluctantly headed back for the main road. Before we reached it, Mack cried, "There's your ninety-fifth," pointing to a Northern Harrier flying over the marshes. "Now we can relax the rest of your visit."

"Well," Marge said again, "one hundred is a nice round figure."

"You're insatiable."

Back at Astolat we loafed for a day, frequently checking our own little bird sanctuary with its cardinals, chickadees, titmice, Carolina Wrens, and water birds. Marge had already counted them and the Pileated Woodpecker.

The next morning we drove to the west entrance of Okefenokee Swamp near Fargo, Georgia. The picnic lunch on the banks of Okefenokee and later a boat ride into the swamp, pleasant as they were, did not produce any new trip birds. In fact, the whole venture was remarkably lacking in birds except vultures in the skies and Eastern Bluebirds on the utility lines. But a black bear did lope across the road as we left the park.

"We should keep a mammal list," Eleanor suggested. "We have raccoons, possums, squirrels, gators, and now a bear."

"Don't forget the armadillos," Marjory reminded her.

At Occidental Petroleum's phosphate fields and ponds in White Springs, a Glossy Ibis was feeding with a flock of White Ibises. "Ninety-six," said Eleanor, the record keeper.

Farther down the road, Marjory called out, "Redshouldered Hawk on the utility line on the right."

"Ninety-seven and two more days to go," I calculated.

Back home Mack asked, "Do you have a Black Vulture on your list? They are so common that they sometimes get overlooked." Eleanor checked and found they did not.

"Two to go," Marge said.

Those two were found right at Astolat in the woods on morning walks: a Black-and-White Warbler and a Solitary Vireo. Then for good measure, a Song Sparrow joined the regular feeders as we ate breakfast the last day.

"One hundred and five next year," Marge called from the curb as Mack and I pulled away from the airport.

"I hope they get a hundred and ten," I said. "What a present that would be for Marge's eighty-eighth birthday."

The Coast and the Cascades

How do you know but every bird
   That cuts the airy way
Is an immense world of delight
   Closed to your senses five?

—William Blake

The map warned: *This road closed in Winter. Trailer travel not advised.* Well, this was mid-June, and Mack and I were traveling by car, having left the motor home in Florida this trip. The squiggly road snaked along mountain streams, rising ever higher toward McKenzie Pass in the Cascade Mountains of Oregon. Through occasional breaks in the forest, I caught glimpses of snow-covered Mount Jefferson miles to the north and of the Sisters—North, Middle, and South—sparkling white to the South. All four rose over ten thousand feet into the clear cerulean sky. The road climbed. The snow crept closer. As we approached the pass, snowbanks, sliced smooth as angel cake beside the road, rose higher than the car on the right and one or two feet on the left where they were melting into the boggy marsh.

"Imagine driving through snowdrifts this high in June," I commented. "Lucky the snowplow went through ahead of us."

"And not far ahead, judging from that meringue-white snow," Mack added. "Do you think we can find a Rosy Finch along here? How high are we?"

"Over five thousand feet. Five thousand, three hundred,

and twenty-four to be exact. If we were in New Hampshire, we'd be on top of Mount Washington."

Rosy Finches, fancying a certain delicious insect they pluck from snowbanks, spend their summers at high altitudes where the snow is deep. So at the peak of the pass, we went in search of Rosy Finches. We scaled the crude stone steps to the top of the observation tower from which we could see the shadowy outline of Mount Hood seventy-eight miles to the north but not a Rosy Finch within a hundred feet.

"The snow's too patchy," I decided.

A campground on the down side of the pass failed to produce a White-headed Woodpecker . . . or a walk along a waterfall trail, the Virginia Warbler we didn't get in Cave Creek Canyon last summer. Either one would have been a life bird.

This summer's birding excursion had a goal of twenty-seven lifers. Twenty-seven would take our life list to six hundred. We'd picked up a few along the way: a Yellow-green Vireo in Texas, Pinyon Jays in New Mexico, a Brewer's Sparrow in Canyon de Chelly on the Navajo reservation in Arizona, a Prairie Falcon in the Birds of Prey Refuge along the canyons of the Snake River in Idaho. That was the way it would be from now on. Here a lifer, there a lifer, plucking them one by one from the treetops, sky, beaches, and sea. Gone are the days of finding thirty new birds during a weekend in Rockport or three or four days in the Rio Grande Valley. Mack and I had never seriously birded the Northwest until now. Therefore, we had great hopes of flushing out our six-hundredth bird in Oregon or Washington.

I had written to Ben Fawver in Coos Bay back in April, asking what our chances were of finding Hermit Warblers and Wrentits in his area and whether he could spare a day, or part of a day to bird with us. He predicted a ninety percent chance of finding a Wrentit and maybe even better of seeing a Hermit

209

Warbler. Then he added, "If you are interested, I can show you nesting Tufted Puffins, a nesting colony of ten thousand Common Murres, and some nesting Pigeon Guillemots." What birder wouldn't be interested?

And so Mack and I didn't dawdle long on Mckenzie Pass, for we were assured of some exciting birding on the Oregon coast. Besides, we would return to the Cascades later.

I had on previous visits to Oregon been impressed by the extent to which the three-hundred-mile coast is protected against human encroachment and at the same time has been preserved for human enjoyment. Those three hundred coastal miles average a state park every eleven miles while approximately fourteen hundred islands, rocks, and reefs are part of the Oregon Islands National Wildlife Refuge to which no one is allowed entry. The result is that every spring a place like Three Arch Rocks Refuge, for instance, north of Coos Bay has about seventy-five thousand Common Murres nesting on almost every available ledge.

We had not met Ben except through correspondence and telephone conversations until the morning we set out to find a Hermit Warbler, but he had indicated in the published list of ABA (American Birding Association) members that he was willing to guide visiting birders. We've never been disappointed by an ABA volunteer. Nor were we this time. He was eager to show local specialties and took care to provide the best possible sightings.

At seven o'clock, we were walking among the Ponderosa Pines in a forest near Charleston. "We shouldn't have much trouble finding a Hermit Warbler," Ben said. "They nest in these tall conifers."

Before long he signaled he'd heard one. I strained to isolate its song from the trickle of the mountain stream and other bird calls and chips. "I'll play the tape," Ben said, "and try to draw it in." The tape worked. The song came closer: a distinct high *seezle, seezle, seezle, seezle* slurred up at the end with a quick *zeeteet*. We walked up and down through the trees and along the road, following the song. But search as we did, not one of us caught a glimpse of that little yellow head.

Finally Ben said, "We should probably look for the Wrentit and come back here later." Over the next few miles, the coastal road dropped in elevation until Ben pulled off where a tangle of paths webbed through the chaparral to a promontory overlooking the shore. "The Wrentit is a weak flier," Ben explained as we selected a path of sorts. "It prefers to scrounge near the ground among this brushy stuff. You may hear it before you see it."

Although genetically a member of the thrush family, the Wrentit has several characteristics of wrens, such as its song and its tail. "You'll know it when you see it," Ben said. "It has an extra long, wrenlike tail, but without the bars. And, unlike wrens, it has a pale yellow or creamy eye."

"What's the song like?" I asked.

"It's a loud, clear monotone of *pit-pit-pit*, running down into a trill if it's a male. The female doesn't add the trill."

Ben was leading the way. He stopped to pick some salmon berries and had just offered me a sample when Mack called, "I have it." Not more than twenty feet behind us, she'd found the saucy little Wrentit foraging in the chaparral about three feet off the ground. Our presence didn't disturb it in the least. It hopped from bush to bush as we watched.

"Only nineteen to go," Mack said, ticking off No. 581.

Ben introduced us to salad berries, bland tasting, similar to huckleberries. On the way back to the car, he picked a small bouquet of tiny seaside asters and seaside rocket, the latter with four wee petals and a yellow center.

"You're a botanist as well as an ornithologist," I said.

"I find one as fascinating as the other," he replied.

"Is it time for the nesting thousands?" I asked.

211

"At your service," Ben smiled.

Off we went down the coast, hugging the shore as closely as possible. Great rocks and boulders rise starkly out of the Pacific, often close to the shore. More than sixty of them host nesting seabirds. Ben stopped at one on our way to Bandon to see a colony of Pelagic Cormorants.

"This is going to require a short walk through the scrub," Ben said as we set out.

"No problem."

In a little we emerged from the trees and brush to the edge of a cliff almost eye level with a few thousand whirling, swirling Pelagic Cormorants about fifty yards off shore. I may have stood like stout Cortez (or Balboa) "silent upon a peak," but the cormorants were anything but silent. Like all seabirds, they do not sing, they squawk. Some soared high overhead. Others fished along the rocky edges or in the tidal rips and surf and carried their catch to babies in seaweed nests on the narrow cliff ledges.

"Have you noticed," Ben asked, "the cormorants propel themselves in the water with their feet unlike puffins and guillemots? The latter, using their wings, literally fly under water."

"I know puffins fly under water, but I'd never thought about the cormorants," I said.

"What color would you say these cormorants are?" Ben asked next.

"Black," Mack and I agreed.

"They certainly look black from here, but they are really an iridescent violet green."

From the Pelagic colony, Ben continued south to the Bandon Wildlife Refuge. Several young men in the parking lot that morning greeted Ben with considerable warmth and reverence.

"The puffins have left, Dr. Fawer," one young man said.

"I'm sorry to hear that because I have brought visitors from Florida to see them. I thought they'd still be here."

"I was hoping, too," the young man said, "but there are murres and gulls, guillemot and lots of other stuff."

Ben set up his scope, and we scanned the rock islands. He pointed out a colony of probably ten thousand nesting Common Murres. They nest in denser colonies than the Pelagic Cormorants. Perhaps they have to, for the Common are well named. They are abundant off the West Coast and common in the East off the coast of Canada. "We estimate their population along the Oregon coast to be two hundred and fifty thousand," Ben told us.

Out of the water, a Common Murre sits in an upright position. With its white front and dark brown head, back, and wings, it looks like a penguin, while in the water at a little distance, it looks like a loon. But their young know which is which. Both murre parents share the incubation of a single, large, pear-shaped egg, taking turns resting it on their webbed feet. They don't build a nest. Even though the pear shape keeps the egg from rolling off the ledge, I wondered why the wind didn't blow it off on a windy day like this, especially when parents were changing shifts. But apparently the system works. The population is not decreasing.

I was interested in the hierarchy (or higher-archy) of seabirds. Black Oystercatchers build in the rubble at the water's edge. Pigeon Guillemot stake their claim in crevices ten to forty feet above the water level where they incubate two eggs for a month and then share the feeding of the chicks in the nest for at least another month. Pelagic Cormorants choose higher cliffs, and above them the Common Murre and Brant's Cormorants nest on flat cliff ledges. Higher still, if the outcroppings are steep enough to suit them, Double-crested Cormorants build their nests of sticks, bones, and feathers. At the crown where some topsoil has accumulated, puffins, auklets, and storm-petrels lay their eggs at the end of burrows. At the very top, maybe a hundred or more feet above the Oyster-catchers, on flat, grassy ground, Western Gulls raise their families.

Tufted Puffins return to the Oregon coast in April in their colorful breeding plumage—a jet-black body with orange legs and feet and creamy-white facial feathers. Pale yellow ear puffs flow back from their eyes, and yellow bill plates sheath their orange bill. They incubate a single egg for six weeks and then carry fish and squid to the chick for another six to eight weeks.

"The puffins must have just left," Ben said. "I saw them here three days ago."

"It's a magnificent show even without puffins," I said.

"Anybody getting hungry?" he asked.

"Yes, I'm starved," Mack said. "I can't believe it's after one. How time flies when we're watching birds."

Ben put away his scope, which, because of the high winds on the coast, had been of dubious assistance. "Perhaps I can find a spot out of the wind," he said as we climbed back into the car. He drove to a little park well back from the beach in the protection of trees, but I wouldn't say it wasn't windy. After snacking we wandered among the trees, looking for birds without much success. They were either taking siestas or seeking shelter from the wind. Mack strolled across the street and down to the beach. She returned, saying she thought she had found a White-winged Scoter. It was too far away to be sure.

"Let's scope it," Ben suggested. The scope, though, was useless in the whipping wind. Checking with binoculars, Ben agreed it was probably a White-winged Scoter. Since it was not a new bird for us, we did not pursue it further.

Ben thought looking for the Hermit Warbler would be fruitless in this wind, and we agreed. He returned to Coos Bay along an inland road through the country.

214

"I'm sorry about the Hermit Warbler," he said in parting.

"Well, at least we know now what we're listening for," I said.

Mack told him, "You've given us a marvelous day with the Wrentit, the Pelagic colony, and those thousand murres and more. It's been wonderful."

"Where do you go from here?"

"North, to Hillsboro. A friend is going to take us birding in the Cascades."

"Oh, you'll be sure to find your warbler there."

The next day we drove along the beautiful coast as far as we could before turning inland for Hillsboro on the outskirts of Portland. Jeff, who four years before had delighted in finding lifers for Mack and me, could not help us this time. He was completing preparation week at a camp where he would be nature counselor this summer. Luckily for us, his mother was willing to spend a couple of days with us on the bird trails. She's no mean birder herself. "How do you think Jeff got so bird-wise so young?" she asked with a twinkle in her eye.

Within an hour of our arrival, we had stashed our gear in Mary Anne's van and were off to Camp Baldwin four or five thousand feet up the side of Mount Hood in the heart of the Cascade Mountains to have supper with Jeff and two hundred newly arrived Boy Scouts. They were gathering around the flag for first assembly as we drove into the parking lot. Mack spotted Jeff in the distance—tall, handsome, and freshly graduated from high school. He grabbed time to welcome us before leaping off to take care of some pressing responsibility.

We ate with the Scouts at tables under the trees, marveling at the amount of food some youngsters put away. I studied the faces and antics of the young lads, just arrived from home—the boisterous, the outgoing, and the few with just a hint of *what am I doing here?* in their eyes.

We had no doubt what we were doing there. Evening Grosbeaks had already greeted us. After supper we sauntered through the trees.

"Shhh!" Mack whispered. "Listen."

It was the slightly hoarse *seezle seezle seezle seezle zeet-zeet* of the Hermit Warbler. Here among the conifers at the base of Mount Hood, we found the little fellow with his yellow head, black bib, and gray back with white wing bars—all five and a half inches of not only one, but two.

"I'll have to drop Ben a note," I said.

Other birds—Mountain Chickadee, Pine Siskin, Pygmy Nuthatch, and a Hairy Woodpecker—teased us to stay. We loitered until the dark, and mosquitoes, reminded us that we did not know where we were going to spend the night.

"I think we can find something at Government Camp, but we should probably start looking," Mary Anne finally said, a little reluctant, I thought, to leave Jeff, although by now he was tied up again with his duties.

One little town after another—Government Camp, Rhododendron, Zigzag—either had no motel or no vacancy. A little past midnight, Mary Anne commented, "It wouldn't be the first time I've slept in the van." Before I could ask where she figured I might sleep, we came upon what looked like a motel of sorts. All lights were out, but someone did answer the bell and found a room of sorts to accommodate the three of us for a few hours.

I was dreaming that I was trying to lasso sandpipers from a dune buggy. Mary Anne was driving, splashing recklessly in and out of the incoming tide. I had just heaved to rope when Mary Anne said, "If you want to find seven lifers today, we have to get going."

"Going? Where? It's hardly light."

"The least likely of your target birds to find is the Rosy

Finch, and the best chance—the only chance—is to get up into the snow on Mount Hood."

"Whose idea was this?" Mack asked as we drove up the mountain to a ski area where cars and busses were already disgorging skiers.

"Must be races today. We'll have to get away from all this activity," Mary Anne said. "Let's walk a bit." The wind blew. The snow swirled. I plunged my mittenless hands deep into my inadequate jacket.

"Let's face it," Mary Anne said at last. "We aren't going to get far enough to find a Rosy Finch. Let's spend our time looking for those we have a real shot at."

For the next ten hours and two hundred plus miles, Mary Anne proved to be a birder par excellence. Up and down and through the Cascades, she took us. In a deserted campground near the quaint town of Sisters, we found a Red-breasted Sapsucker and missed by inches—or minutes or fate—a White-headed Woodpecker. As we roamed through the campgrounds, we met a man who had just seen a White-headed Woodpecker within the past twenty minutes. So sure was he that he could find it again, he offered to take us to it. We followed him into the forest, across a stream, and along a corduroy road to the spot. The woodpecker, however, had moved on.

Mack and I had looked unsuccessfully in every coniferous forest from New Mexico to Oregon for a Townsend's Solitaire, a large, eight-and-a-half-inch, slender, gray bird. Its white outer tail feathers are conspicuous in flight, and the field guide says it is fairly common on mountain slopes. Mary Anne agreed and took us to another deserted area, parked, and led us down a path under towering pines.

"Your Townsend's nests on the ground," she instructed us. "It also catches flies from a perch. So you'll need to keep your eyes on both the ground and high places." The silence of the forest was sprinkled with the cheeps of invisible birds, the subdued hum of insects. The pungent odor of forest dampness filled the air. The trees were growing more sparse. I could see the opening at the edge of the forest not far ahead. Mary Anne, who had been walking in front, slowed for us to overtake her. "There's your Townsend's Solitaire on the ground," she whispered.

Anyone not a birder probably cannot understand the excitement, the thrill, the satisfaction of finding a species for the first time. It's not the thrill of winning the lottery after buying lottery tickets for years. No reward accompanies the 585th bird other than the moment itself, and it's the bird, not the number, that provides the thrill. At least for me. It's like panning for gems. In the sifting sands, you have found tidbits of garnets, chunks of amethyst, zircon, quartz, topaz, but you've never found a ruby. Therein lies the challenge. The Townsend's was a ruby. Not a diamond, but surely no agate either.

By the time we reached Lost Pond, where all day Mary Anne had confidently promised she would find a Barrow's Goldeneye, the rain had started. The Barrow's is much rarer than the Common Goldeneye that we know in Florida. It had eluded us all over Alaska and everywhere else. "This won't take long," Mary Anne said. "I know right where it stays."

Lost Pond, tucked away in a quiet piece of forest, is not big. And fortunately, considering the rain, Mary Anne was able to drive halfway around the pond. With binoculars we could scan the whole surface in detail. Of course, no rule in a bird's world says it must stay where it always stays.

"I won't give up on this one," she said, "because I know it is here." Rejecting her offer of umbrellas, we stepped from the car and scouted the water's edge where grasses and bushes overhung the water—and possibly the Goldeneye. Then Mary Anne spotted it, not where *it* always stays, but near the entrance to the pond. Swimming toward the bank where we had come in was not one but a pair of Barrow's Goldeneyes *with a family.* Let the rain come down. Who cares? Not Mack, not me, and certainly not Mary Anne, who had just won her fourth gold star in the past twenty-four hours.

"Friends," she said after we had looked our fill and everyone had congratulated everyone, including the happy couple on the pond, "we are a long way from home, maybe two hours. What else do you have on your Must See List?"

"Put that way, do I dare say?" Mack asked. "But before you say no, how about a Red-naped Sapsucker and a Vaux Swift?"

"If we haven't seen a Red-naped by now, we aren't going to find one today. But with a little luck, I can find you a Vaux Swift back in Hillsboro. It's five o'clock. Let's head for home."

Back in Hillsboro she stopped at a park along the highway at the edge of town. In the fading light, swallows were darting and swooping over a small body of water, snatching insects from the air as though the supply would not last the night.

"Among those swallows," Mary Anne said, "are a few Vaux Swifts. Maybe. They are dark on the back like the swallows and a little smaller, but the difference in size is hardly discernible. Your binocs won't help. They dart too fast. Concentrate on the tails. The Swifts' tails are short and stubby, squared off."

This is hopeless, I thought to myself, but I kept checking tails as they swooped back and forth. Then I saw one. My eye followed it through one loop-the-loop and back. "I have one," I cried in disbelief. At almost the same moment, Mack and Mary Anne each isolated one.

"How many lifers does that make?" Mary Anne asked.

"Five, counting last night's Hermit Warbler," Mack said. "The Vaux Swift is number five hundred and eighty-six. Only fourteen to go. Let's find some dinner. AHMM hungry."

After dinner we retrieved our car at Mary Anne's. In

parting, she said, "I'm sorry about the White-headed Wood-pecker and Red-naped Sapsucker."

"Don't you be sorry one bit," I told her. "Five lifers in twenty-four hours? That's by far our best birding day all summer."

And Mack added, "Tell Jeff you matched his performance of four years ago." We said good-bye and drove to our motel.

My friend Virginia resides in the Dearborn Memorial (and I might add *Private)* Library in Seattle, the only library I know where I can book a room but not borrow a book. "Of course you cannot borrow a book," she told a friend as they sat sipping tea. "Would I ask to borrow one of your teacups?"

Virginia's not a birder, but as I have said on previous occasions, she's a rara avis, a wit who can turn a phrase faster than I can say Calliope Hummingbird. For two years she had been promising us a Calliope Hummingbird if only we would come to Washington. We'd booked our rooms ahead and there we were.

"I'm not going to let the Oregon coast upstage ours in Washington," Virginia said after listening to me extol the wonders of the ten thousand nesting murres we had seen with Ben. "We'll go tomorrow to Tokeland on Wallapa Bay where I have a little cottage. And," she paused dramatically, "you will find hummingbirds at the cottage."

"Calliopes?" Mack asked.

"Maybe," Ginny said, a bit mysteriously.

How the sun did shine when we set out. Mount Ranier, close enough to touch, sparkled. Glittering amethysts, emeralds, and diamonds danced on the snow. "I bet we could find Snowy Finches up there," Mack commented.

"But the coast first," Ginny decreed.

At the coast we explored Wallapa Bay, lunched at the Dunes, dined on fresh crab from Nelson's Fish Market, admired a glorious flock of Brown Pelicans at Westport—a busy whaling village—and ate a "whale of an ice cream cone." And she did in truth, no spoof, have hummingbirds in the fuschia at her dining-room windows.

"Are they Calliopes?" she asked hopefully.

"No," I said reluctantly.

"I didn't think so. No steam whistles. Right? What are they?"

"Rufous," Mack told her.

"But a great trip bird, the first we've seen all summer," I added.

"You have a Dark-eyed Junco feeding on the lawn," Mack said.

"Do I *really*? But no dark-eyed gentleman, I suppose."

On our way back to Seattle two days later, I asked, "Do you know where we can find a Water Ouzel?"

"Yes, I do. I really do. Or were you teasing because you think I wouldn't believe there's such a bird? Marian in North Bend has one that feeds in Christmas Creek behind her cabin."

"How far is North Bend?"

"About an hour's drive into the Cascades from Seattle."

"May we go someday?"

"Actually Marian is expecting us."

We met Marian in town for lunch and then drove out to Snoqualmie Falls. In the woods between the parking lot and falls, a bird (not a Water Ouzel) darted among the leaves. Despite binoculars we caught only streaks of brown, flashes of pale yellow, but never enough to put a whole bird together. I dismissed it as just another LBB (Little Brown Bird) and walked on to photograph the falls, which drop with a thunderous roar two hundred and seventy feet to the river below. Even though Mack and Marian lingered, neither came up with a definitive identification. When we returned home three weeks later, a card from Marian was waiting to tell us she'd been back to study the LBB and had determined it was a Cedar Waxwing. Such a woman bears watching. With a smidgen of encouragement, she might find herself traipsing all over the country looking for lifers.

The rustic route back to town passed behind Mount Si and Little Si, two of the rugged mountains that we had gazed upon during lunch. Then up we went five or six miles into more mountains, to Marian's cabin and the Water Ouzel.

"I must warn you," Marian said. "We've had so much rain lately the ouzel's rock is covered. I haven't seen her for several days, although I did hear her this morning."

Not thirty feet behind the cabin, Christmas Creek, perhaps I shouldn't say rushed but at least fell trippingly, musically, with a sense of destination, a Water Ouzel's delight. Though I scarcely took my eyes from the creek while enjoying my Ben and Jerry's on pound cake, I did not see or hear the ouzel. But in the presence of all the other natural splendor, 'twas greedy to pine for an ouzel too.

When the time came to leave Seattle, we drove north from the city and turned east toward the Cascades once more. The climb through Stevens Pass was steep enough for signs marking "Chain up Area," something one doesn't see in Florida. The weather was windy but far from snowy. At Coles Corner we left the main highway and headed north to Lake Wenatchee.

"What are our priorities?" Mack asked as we neared the state park.

"A Calliope Hummingbird, Red-naped and Williamson's sapsuckers—and, if we get up high enough a Virginia Warbler."

Neither the woodland paths of the state park nor the piney forests of Sno-Park cooperated. A woman at the ranger's station advised, "Try Fish Lake and go early in the day before the wind starts. It always blows here in the afternoon."

Back at Coles Corner, we registered for the night at the Squirrel Tree Chalet and Restaurant. Walking from the chalet to breakfast early the next morning, Mack stopped abruptly. "Ev, Ev," she whispered, "look at the blue flowers in the garden. There's a hummingbird." We raised our binoculars. "It is! It's a Calliope. I can see the streaks on its white throat."

"It's so tiny! Can you believe how small it is?"

The Calliope at three and a half inches is not only the smallest bird in the United States, it is the smallest bird in North America.

"You don't know, little bird, how long we've waited for this moment," Mack said. As though to say *and a moment is all you get,* the Calliope darted out of sight. We moved on to our waffles and coffee.

At Fish Lake an Osprey fished and some birds twittered along the woody paths, but all the human activity around this fishing camp prompted us to move on to White River Road, which follows the White River into the mountains. Along the way a coyote was keeping a watchful eye on her two pups playing in an open field. A little farther up the river, a Common Merganser basked on a log midstream while her babies struggled to join her. Mack turned onto an old logging road and climbed up the side of Dirtface Peak. Viewed from a promontory, White River nine hundred feet below was only a ribbon of milky glacial waters, weaving through meadows on its way to Lake Wenatchee. Spectacular as the view was, we were not high enough to find a Virginia Warbler.

"What does the book say about Red-naped Sapsuckers?" Mack asked.

"Common in deciduous forests."

"And the Williamson's Sapsucker?"

"Uh, da-da-de-da Williamson's? Here it is: 'Uncommon in pine forests at higher elevations in summer.'"

We were poking along the river road, checking both sides

when Mack slammed the brakes, sending maps, AAA guides, notebooks, glasses, and potato chips slithering to the floor.

"What's *that?*" she exclaimed.

"What's what? Where?"

"On the fence at the entrance of that driveway about thirty feet ahead on your right."

"A grouse of some kind."

"But what kind? Do you think you can get a picture if I back up and you get out?"

"Can try. Will probably spook her."

I took a picture at fifty feet. If she spooked, at least I would have a reminder for the diary. I inched closer. I took another. She didn't flick a feather. At twenty feet I saw her eyelids blink, and she raised her head ever so slightly, inquiringly. At fifteen feet she turned with slow, deliberate steps and faced the road. From there I took a full-frame slide. I had no need to go closer, though obviously she was not to be outstared.

Not until I was back in the car and we pulled up beside her did we see why she had stood her ground. How did Thorton Wilder put it? If you want to see a mother, look a tiger in the face? Something like that. Out of the leaves poked two baby grouse. They hopped onto the bottom rail of the fence where mama stood directly above them and posed for a family portrait.

"They're Sharp-tailed Grouse," Mack said. She'd had time to study the field guides.

"Is it on our wish list?" I asked. We hadn't been looking for one. It was. It was a lifer that just happened like a present under the Christmas tree.

A little farther down the road, a Blue Grouse with three young ones emerged from the grasses on the right. She stalled in the middle of the road until three more caught up with her. Shooing them on across the road, she still stood in the middle.

"What's her problem?" I wondered out loud. Then a seventh chick poked its head out of the shrubbery.

"Hurry up," she said, taking a few tentative steps herself. But Pokey dallied, pecking inquisitively at bits and specks of debris while his family waited.

"There's one in every group," Mack muttered before they were all swallowed up by the roadside ferns.

"What do you say to some lunch before we look further for sapsuckers?"

"I'm in favor," I said.

The deer feeding on the far side of the river scarcely raised their heads when Mack backed into a picnic, or maybe fisherman's, clearing between the road and river. Lunch was postponed briefly to identify a Fox Sparrow lunching in the dense undergrowth. A warm sun streaked through the canopy of oak leaves. Peanut butter sandwiches had never tasted better. In my mind's eye, I was composing a picture, starting with a fallen tree trunk, which lay decaying in the water beside us and reaching back across the slow-moving river sparkling in the sun to the deer in the background, now munching their way upstream.

"I saw a flash of red," Mack said, dropping her sandwich and picking up her binoculars. At the same moment, a bird with a red, black, and white head, a red chin and throat, and a yellow belly lit on the tree in the water. We had a full, uninterrupted view of a Red-naped Sapsucker not twenty-five feet away. He posed, caught an insect, and returned to the treetop from which he'd dropped. Then, as though to ask, "Do you doubt your eyes?" he returned to the tree trunk and posed again.

"Can you believe that?" Mack asked after he had returned to the treetops.

"And can you believe it is our third life bird today?" Such success tends to breed greed.

225

"Let's look now for a White-headed Woodpecker and a Williamson's Sapsucker," Mack said. We looked, but we must have met our quota for the day.

We left the Pacific Coast and the Cascades eleven short of our six-hundred goal. Montana's MacGillivary's Warbler and magpies were only trip birds. Wyoming's Common Snipes, Lark Buntings, and Horned Larks were all exciting but not life birds.

"Do you think Wally can rise to the challenge when we get to Boulder?" Mack asked me.

"Well, not eleven. White-headed Woodpeckers aren't in Colorado."

"Williamson's Sapsuckers are."

"We'll see."

Between the Rocky Mountain National Park the day after a freak summer blizzard and the Pawnee National Grasslands, Wally did find four lifers for us in two days: a Rosy (Brown-capped, Gray Phase) Finch, a White-tailed Ptarmigan, a Virginia Warbler, and a McGown's Longspur.

"We probably wouldn't have *three* hundred on our life list if it weren't for friends like you," I said, watching Jenny Kate pack a savory bag lunch for the road. "I'm going to start a new list, *Birders' Helpers.*"

"And nominate them all for Oscars," Mack added.

Newfoundland Diary

He sings to the wide world
    she to her nest.
In the nice ear of Nature
    which song is the best?

—James Russell Lowell

Saturday, June 18

We disembarked from the ferry last night in a murky fog. We groped our way five miles to Placentia through murky fog and dark of night. When I woke this morning to more fog, I thought, *the guide book warned you.* Visibility was less than two hundred feet when Mack and I set out for St. John's after breakfast.

"How do you like Newfoundland?" I asked her.

"You mean judging from what I don't see?"

But the fog gradually lifted. By the time we met Marjory and Eleanor at the Best Western on the TCH (Trans Canada Highway), the sun was shining, the sky sparkling blue.

Our friends flew in yesterday from Connecticut to join us in this expedition around the southeastern corner of Newfoundland. Though small in area, nearly half of Newfoundland's population live on the Avalon Peninsula, joined tenuously to the rest of the province by a thin strip of land. On the map it looks like a piece of jigsaw puzzle waiting to be placed in the larger picture. Anyway, here we are, assembled and ready to explore.

First of all I called Ken Knowles, another ABA member

willing to help visiting birders. I'd written earlier, asking whether he could make some suggestions. His prompt, cordial reply had further whetted our appetite for this adventure.

"Come for tea—or coffee, will you?" were almost his first words. "We can watch the feeders while we talk birds and go over the notes I've made for you."

"Sounds good," I said. "You know there are four of us?"

"The more to enjoy the birds."

It was arranged. We would arrive two-thirtyish.

Ken and Kathleen live in Middle Cove near Torbay, a few miles north of St. John's. Their home sits back from the road amid numerous bird feeders and backs up, after three or four hundred feet, to a quiet *pond*. "Newfoundland has no *lakes*," Ken explained.

A Fox Sparrow ate at a feeder near the deck. More scavenged on the ground. Dark-eyed Juncos—some juveniles—fed on the ground, too. A Boreal Chickadee flew in from the woods to peck at the suet melting in the heat of this warm, sunny day. More birds came and went at feeders across the drive. As we sat in the living room sipping wine, going over detailed notes Ken had made for us, and watching birds through the picture window, the bluest Blue Jays I have ever seen snitched the peanuts that Ken had put out for them on the woodpile outside the window. Later, walking through marshy grasses and woods to the pond, we heard a Northern Waterthrush call.

When at last we were leaving (with a jar of Kathleen's homemade jam for future breakfasts), Ken said he could bird with us around St. John's tomorrow morning. "But," he added, "should you wake to one of Newfoundland's rare, sunny mornings, I recommend you take the Bird Islands Charter trip instead. It's a must. But not in fog."

Sunday, June 19

"What fog?" I asked, blinded by sunshine when I squinted through the drapes this morning. "Let's *carpe diem.*" Marge and Eleanor agreed when we met for breakfast.

Twenty miles south of the city, we embarked from the village of Bay Bulls on a trip to the largest puffin colony in North America, Mr. O'Brien, who runs the charter, claims. For the first half hour, as the boat sailed away from the dramatic vistas of the coastline and into Witless Bay, the crew of two entertained us with Irish jigs and Newfoundland ballads, kind of hurdy-gurdy renditions more in a festival mood than "I must go down to the sea again" and seriously look for life birds. But as we approached the first bird island, the taped music gave way to the sounds of thousands of birds soaring, wheeling, diving around the boat.

"Puffins on the right," the skipper called. Suddenly the water was dotted with the splashings of fleeing birds—murres, cormorants, auks, an occasional guillemot. But mostly puffins caused the splashings. They flailed their stubby wings, trying to become airborne, while Mack cried, "Aren't they ahhh-DAWWW-rable! Those ahhh-DAWWW-rable babies!"

The Atlantic Puffin was a lifer for Eleanor and Marge. It was our second encounter—Mack's and mine. Three years ago we had gone from Jonesport, Maine, to Machais Island to see puffins. Fifteen passengers for an extra fee were privileged to go ashore in a skiff and risk their necks, legs, and ankles scrambling across wet rocks covered with slippery seaweed before walking a plank across churning waters fifty feet below to reach the path up the hill through an Arctic Tern rookery to the puffins. Swinging sticks, bats, and hats warded off most of the terns. They, of course, were defending their nests by dive-bombing our pates. Those who survived the slimy rocks, the plank, and the terns were further rewarded with permission to clamber over more rocks and huddle with other photo

229

fanatics in a blind, looking out at a few hundred nesting Atlantic Puffins and Razor-billed Auks.

From the blind I photographed birds not six feet from my camera. Some paused (or posed?) a few cautious moments, their mouths dripping with silver fish, before waddling across the rocks to underground burrows and their hungry chicks. Others lit on the roof, the patter of their feet sounding like the first pelting raindrops of a sudden shower. We didn't see the young ones. No one ever does. When they are ready to leave their underrock homes, they fly at night, far out to sea, not to return until they themselves are ready to breed.

It is easy in a blind to take pictures worthy of an Audubon calendar, but today we were in a boat in Witless Bay, buffeted by offshore waves. Binoculars were more useful than cameras.

"Aren't they ahhh-DAWWW-rable?" Mack kept asking, moving from port to starboard with never a faltered step as the boat rocked from side to side. Marjory and Eleanor stretched across the rail, straining for a closer look.

"I wish they'd hold still," Marge said.

"Wouldn't you love to hold one?" Mack speculated.

"Whale!" someone cried before we reached the second bird island, "I saw it spout!"

"If you missed that one, don't worry," the skipper called over the mike. "It's feeding. It'll return." Three or four minutes later, it surfaced again. "That'll be its pattern," the skipper explained. "It's a humpback, twenty-five to thirty tons probably."

By now clouds had obscured the sun. Drizzle came and went intermittently. So did the whales. We must have seen five or six, some at close range. And the finale was best of all. With the passengers' permission, we stayed out an extra fifteen minutes to track a mother and calf. They dived, spouted, arched, and breached in a performance that Sea World would have envied. The skipper had no sooner said, "Well, folks, we have to get back to land," than mother and calf breached not fifty feet off the starboard rail.

"Bye, bye," they waved. Wow!

We dined in Flake Restaurant tonight in the quaint village of Quidi Vidi . . . a little high class for the likes of us in our birding togs, but the maitre d' didn't sniff. Actually we went to Quidi Vidi to look for a rare Iceland Gull that Ken had seen recently at the east end of Quidi Vidi Lake near the restaurant. We searched before and after dinner, but didn't find it.

After a day that had moved from sunshine to overcast to rain to clearing, we drove home after dark in a fog as dense as Sherlock's gloomiest fens ever knew. We did get lost, but only within a few blocks of the hotel.

Monday, June 20

The fog was gone this morning.

"I'm not leaving St. John's without the Iceland Gull," Mack declared resolutely at breakfast. And there it was this morning, a lone juvenile, dabbling in a pond full of Herring and Great Black-backed gulls. A feisty little thing it was, too, staking its claim against all others. Bobbing in one spot, it churned the water as though its webbed feet were motorized. It was apparently stirring up goodies for breakfast because when one Great Black-backed twice its size (from its perspective) approached with wings spread, Little Feisty said with neck outstretched like an angry goose, "Look, I do the kicking, I'll do the eating. Thank you very much." The big bully backed off.

"First life bird of the day," I said unnecessarily, noting it on the trip list with an asterisk.

Later at Cape Spear, the easternmost point of land in North America, we stood at the tip end of the boardwalk, facing Ireland with the whole continent of North America at our backs. Mack and I climbed the million steps, more or less, to the lighthouse. A deep, dark blue sea rippled below us. I could almost see Ireland on the horizon. The day had turned sunny.

It didn't seem sunny, though, for the gray fox limping along the side of the road. He was not only injured, he was skinny and hungry. When I tossed out bread left from feeding the gulls, he gobbled two slices up hungrily. Then he gathered up the rest and held it in his mouth. Was he rationing it for later? Or, we speculated after hearing his mate had recently been killed, was he taking it to some hungry pups nearby?

Being hungry ourselves by then, we continued down the highway to Bidgood's, a supermarket renowned for its Newfoundland specialties. Mainlanders go there to stock up when they leave for home. Some sweet rolls, a loaf of bread hot from the bakery, a chunk of cheese, and a jug of wine made an excellent tailgate picnic a few miles down the road with a wind coming off the pond strong enough to carry us out to Bird Islands again if only we'd had a boat instead of a station wagon.

Thanks to Ken's notes, we didn't miss the Arctic and Common terns nesting on an island just off the highway at Renews. As we watched, something startled them, and a cloud of the three or four hundred rose from the grasses. They must have been wing to wing on their nests.

After Renews and Cappahayden, leaving the coastal villages behind, we drove nearly thirty miles through scrubby terrain. The road had a gentle roller coasterlike quality of ups, downs, and arounds. Never sure what the next vista would reveal, we wouldn't have been wrong to guess a few small, blue ponds would be in the picture. It reminded me of the tundra in Churchill. As we approached Trepassey, we looked for caribou. When Marjory made our reservations with Jerome yesterday, he said, "I see caribou on the road as I speak." He was surprised that we hadn't seen any.

Tuesday, June 21

This morning we went in search of caribou and shortly came upon a pair grazing beside the road. I suggested taking the St. Shotts road to the left. It shouldn't have much traffic. In fact it didn't have any. All ten miles to the sea, the barren plains were dotted with caribou in groups ranging from two or three to maybe a dozen. One lone critter walked straight down the yellow line in the middle of the road. We stopped and watched it come toward us, head down, paying us no heed. Until it heard the click of my camera.

The tiny community of St. Shotts stands on a promontory overlooking the Atlantic. White breakers crashed on the rocks below. A Horned Lark lit on a clod of grass near the car. A Savannah Sparrow flitted up and down in the grasses. Three white and one black sheep nibbled stubble as they ambled along the skyline. In a sheltered cove far below, two sunbathers took advantage of the sunny day. The Floridians zipped their winter jackets to the throat.

This evening before dinner, Mack and I walked up a trail that starts behind the motel. After winding through the school yard, it climbs to a 360-degree view of barreness to the north and east, forests to the west, and pastel homes on the water's edge to the south. During an hour's stroll, we found three warblers—a Black-and-White, a Yellow, and a Wilson's. Before we returned to the motel, I was in my shirt sleeves.

"Pray we have weather like this tomorrow for Cape St. Mary's," I said to Mack.

"We can hope, but remember it's full moon."

"And summer solstice," I added. "My grandpa used to talk about bad storms during summer solstice."

Last night the Trepassy Motel was a beehive of activity. Seven of the ten rooms were occupied. In addition, Mary, guidance counselor at the school, was treating a group of high schoolers to a barbeque. We were all arriving at once. The jubilant youngsters (last day of school) greeted us like visiting aunties, offering to carry our bags.

Tonight, in contrast, only one guest is here, plus the four of us. Jerome, who owns the motel and does all the work when traffic is light, prepared our dinner of pea soup, grilled cod, baked potato, and salad. And served it.

"I'm not a waiter," he warned, toting two dinners at a time on a wobbly tray. "But how am I as a cook?"

"Super!" we assured him in unison.

I was standing with Jerome on the patio later, talking and admiring the full moon. The first stars were beginning to twinkle in the darkening sky. Looking down at the lights in the homes along the shore, I commented, "It's a pretty village."

"Will you please tell that to everyone you meet?" he responded dolefully. He's depressed by the lack of business and the economic conditions in town. A recent government ban on cod fishing has already resulted in four hundred of the village's fifteen hundred population moving elsewhere.

Wednesday, June 22
Today we drove through the saintly towns—St. Stephens, St. Vincent's, St. Mary's, St. Joseph, St. Catherine's, St. Bride's, and our destination was Cape St. Mary's. Of all the towns, St. Vincent's was perhaps the most attractive, larger than most along the way. Its typical boxy, colorful homes were scattered casually up and down the hilly terrain. We had especially looked forward to St. Vincent's because the brochures described sandy beaches and showed pictures of whales cavorting just off the highway. "This is your best chance of seeing whales from your own vehicles," they said. However, the one gravely beach was not easily accessible, and no whales showed. I can't say the same for mosquitoes. And *they* were huge!

Anyway, we were eager to get to Cape St. Mary's where we

would stand on a craggy headland not forty feet from ten thousand nesting Northern Gannets and thousands more kittiwakes, murres, and razorbills. Below us the sea would churn in that forty feet separating us from the nests. The birds would swirl and soar and scream.

Rain had been spitting off and on ever since our picnic in Hollywood Provincial Park.

"Just quickie showers," I said optimistically. But we didn't loiter in the park to bird.

When we reached our B and B in the fishing village of Branch, I was still dismissing the rain as a drizzle. "And if it does get worse," I pointed out, "we can always go out to see the gannets tomorrow." What did *I* know?

Rosemary, our host, said a big storm was blowing in from Nova Scotia. If it reached us by tomorrow, we'd have no chance of seeing Bird Rock. She advised that we head for the birds at once. Well, *at once* after a spot of tea and some homemade bread.

Once at the sanctuary, we could hardly stand against the wind. I tried to slip into my raincoat as I stepped from the car but managed only to clutch it to keep it from whipping out of my hands. It flapped and cracked like a frantic sail. My hands were frozen when we reached the visitors center fifty feet away. Slowly—more slowly for me than the others—it became clear that none of us was up to the twenty-minute walk to the headland.

"How many people have gone out today?" Eleanor asked.

"Twenty, mostly this morning," Arlene said. She'd be the one to go with us if we chose to go. "We had a hundred yesterday. Can you believe I was in my shirt sleeves?"

"So were we in Trepassy," Marjory said.

While we warmed up, we watched a video of the walk we wouldn't take, the Bird Rock we wouldn't see, and the birds I wouldn't photograph. Ken Knowles had said, "I hope you won't meet up with a storm from the south." Well, we had.

Back to the car we struggled. By now the rain was pelting like BB shot. We sat in the parking lot a few minutes, each thinking her own thoughts. This was to have been the highlight of the trip. For me, at least. Rain gushed down the windshield. Vague gray birds in a vague gray world wheeled in perpetual motion. The car rocked in the wind. Five draggled sheep came jogging toward us from the path we wouldn't take.

"I wonder where *they'll* find shelter," Eleanor mused.

Back at Whalen's Hospitality House, Rosemary made us a delicious chicken dinner, with homemade raspberry cake for dessert. Nicole, fifteen, needlepointed each of us a souvenir bookmark that said BRANCH. Carol, younger, introduced her two-month-old rabbit that likes to kiss people.

"It tickles," she warned.

Thursday, June 23

The rain has mostly ended, leaving only wind and fog. The radio at breakfast called yesterday's storm *wicked,* reaching sixty-mile-an-hour winds. Leaving our hosts, we paused at the foot of the hill to watch the crashing surf. If it were beating up on this protected cove, which cradles the 380 residents of Branch, we didn't even want to think what it was doing at Bird Rock.

Instead we drove north fifty miles to Whitbourne on the TCH. The inland route took us along paved and unpaved roads and through what should have been good songbird country, but the only bird we heard was a Waterpipit along a rippling stream.

Our afternoon objective was Bellevue Beach. Eleanor had read that it has smooth, colored stones. She fancies one or two for her rock garden in Connecticut. Thinking Bellevue Beach would probably be in Bellevue, we took off from Whitbourne in a northeasterly direction. Once off the TCH, one wee village followed hard upon another through Chapel Arms, Norman Cove, Long Cove, Thornlea. We'd left the saints of yesterday behind.

Mack turned off the secondary road onto a tertiary straight into Bellevue, straight past the church and half dozen houses, and straight into Bellevue cemetery.

"Did anyone happen to see a beach?" Mack asked.

We were facing Trinity Bay, which stretches for fifty miles or more to Cape Bonavista.

"This *is* Bellevue," Marjory said, map in hand. She is chief navigator.

"And there *are* some rocks," Eleanor added, not giving up without a try.

One by one we disembarked and made our way to the rocky pile, on the way frightening a gull tugging at a piece of plastic cup buried in the sand. For twenty or thirty feet along the water's edge, stones, worn smooth by the rains and winds of centuries, ranged in size from caramel candies to Idaho potatoes and loaves of bread. Many were colorful in a subtle way. We spent considerable time—all of us—picking them over, selecting, discarding, and deciding which treasures to carry away.

Taking a different route back, we came to a provincial park, always a good place for birds. The gatekeeper said eagles and woodpeckers had been reported at some campsites. We checked but didn't find any. The day was waning, and we had an hour's drive back to the motel.

"I'm going to take a quick look in the 'Day's Use' area before we leave," Mack said. And *there* was Bellevue Beach spread out before us at least the length of a football field—wide, sandy, beautiful. A few day users lingered, but the beach was mostly ours. Neatly lettered signs between the parking lot and the water asked PLEASE DO NOT REMOVE ANYTHING FROM THE BEACH.

"Good thing we stopped in Bellevue," Eleanor commented.

Friday, June 24

"Where do you think all these crafts are I read about before we came?" Eleanor wondered this morning while we waited for the short, hard shower to let up after breakfast.

As if to answer her question, we had not gone far up the east coast of Trinity Bay before coming upon a small shop, opened only this past week. If charm and enthusiasm count, this genial young lady's project should fare well.

Farther along in Whiteway, the Women's Institute Center has a large shop and a great variety of native crafts. Knitted wools predominated, tables full of blankets and sweaters, hats, babies' bonnets, gloves, mittens. While Eleanor and Marge examined crafts and Mack looked for birds, I explored the church and graveyard next door.

We often come upon a church before the center of a village. That was true in Whiteway. The church and Women's Institute stand alone on a rise before the road dips to the houses beside the water. From this vantage the view across the bay stretches to the horizon. The bays here, the big ones like Trinity and Conception, are wider than the land they separate. An unusual rock formation called Shag Rock stands off shore a mile or two like a phantom ship. The story is that *probably* it was named for a gull-like seabird called a Shag. What better place for that noontime rite than a pulloff beside the road overlooking Shag Rock and Trinity Bay?

Refreshed, my friends found the strength to shop again, this time in Cavendish. And I found the opportunity to take pictures of several lines of colorful clothes billowing in the wind.

In Heart's Delight (Wouldn't you love that for an address?) we skipped the craft shops, driving down to the water's edge instead. We weren't looking for gulls dropping sea urchins from the sky to crack their shells on the pavement, but that is what we found. The narrow lane was lined with empty shells, and two Herring Gulls were extracting juicy morsels from those they'd just dropped, too absorbed to make way for traffic. Great Black-backed Gulls busied themselves around the beach and boats of the tiny marina.

By mutual consent we bypassed the craft shops in the next town, Heart's Desire. In the third Heart, Heart's Content (I'm not kidding), we took a right and crossed the narrow peninsula to Victoria and Carbonear on Conception Bay. We will continue our explorations in and out of here a couple of days.

Saturday, June 25

Northern Bay Sands with its promise of warm waters within the cove—warm enough for swimming, the brochures said—had persuaded Eleanor and me to bring along our bathing suits. It's a big beach, the biggest we've seen except for Bellevue, the real Bellevue Beach, I mean. We walked across the greensward past some picnic tables, looking for a way to get to the water below. The most likely approach (hardly a path) was steep and stony.

"What do you think?" I asked.

Marjory dismissed it with, "It doesn't look like sand to me."

Except for us and some barefooted teenagers in shorts and shirts playing frisbee at the far end of the beach, the gulls had the whole cove to themselves. Squeals from the youngsters whenever they had to step into the water did not suggest they planned to swim. Eleanor and I looked at each other and zipped our windbreakers a little higher. Meanwhile, Mack, who was looking for pebbles for her new project, "Rock

Group," spotted birds far out in the bay. Far enough for her to unpack her scope for a closer look. They must be, we concluded, White-winged Scoters.

Back in the car, we proceeded up the coast. Like yesterday the towns came rapidly one after the other, but today the road rose to greater heights before dipping to the villages. The views of bay, headlands, and distant mountains were more dramatic. At Lower Island Cove, we left the main road and followed Mount Road to the water and large flocks of gulls. We made it our noontime pause for lunch and pictures.

Two things have eluded us all week, moose and icebergs.

"Where are the moose?" we ask daily. A clerk at the Moorland Motel said we should be glad we hadn't seen any. They are a highway hazard, and the highway is where they roam . . . at dawn and dusk when the light is dim.

But this afternoon we did see an iceberg. It must have been a few miles away because we continued to see it even after rounding the tip of the peninsula at Old Perlican and heading south where we had an eastern view of it. Shortly the road dropped dramatically into Bay of Verde and stopped. We'd reached the end of the line. A steam-belching, crab-packaging plant dominated the village.

"Where do you get the crabs?" Mack asked the young man who came to the car as we slowed.

"Just up the stairs at the end of the building," he replied.

"I mean where do *you* get them to process? Where do they come from?"

"Oh, I'm not sure of that," he pondered. "Maybe around Labrador. Many of 'em—most of 'em—are frozen and shipped to Japan. Japan is a big market for our capelin, too. The Japanese believe the caviar promotes longevity and sexual desire."

Capelin have turned up frequently in conversations this week. It is a small fish, resembling smelt. "You won't see many

240

whales until the capelin come in," Ken told us. "The whales follow the capelin, and the sea birds follow the whales." Imagine a thirty-ton whale pursuing a six-to-ten-inch fish. In a good year, though, the capelin come in in such abundance that people scoop them up on the beach by the pailful. The whales must go slurrrp!

Normally, some fisherman have told us, the arrival of the capelin is preceded by a period of bad weather, called capelin weather. If that be true, we may miss them, although they are already overdue. Fortunately we have not had a spell of bad weather. Au contraire. Probably the tardiness of the capelin explains why we did not see whales at St. Vincent's.

From Bay de Verde, we retraced our route, stopping at Northern Bay Sands to check on the White-winged Scoters. They were still bobbing like corks, but no closer to our beach than they'd been earlier. This time Mack and I picked our way down to the sand, which turned out to be much finer than we thought. I found a beauty of a stone for Eleanor's rock garden. She's sure it's the one she admired this morning. It must weigh nearly twenty pounds.

"Will you take it home for me in the car?" she asked.

"Is your suitcase full?" I replied innocently.

"May we stop at the house we saw this morning with all the boulders, the one that's under construction?" Marjory asked. "I'd like to take a picture of those boulders all over the lot."

"If Eleanor won't ask us to take one home for her," Mack teased.

When we reached the house in Salmon Cove, I volunteered to tell the man working in the driveway what we were up to. Well, nothing would do but we must all come in and look at the home he has been building in his spare time for the past two years.

"Back the car in the driveway. My woman's plastering

241

upstairs. She'll want to meet you." All over the peninsula, he explained, boulders some four or five feet in diameter lie just below the surface. Every builder has to dig them out to lay a foundation. As he talked he led us over the precarious jumble of cracked rocks, with a strong hand here and a supportive arm there, into the skeleton basement, which someday will be a garage, one room, and a bath.

"Now up the stairs," our host directed.

I knew what Marge was thinking of the see-through, rail-less, wall-less stairs, but with our host's taking her hand and steadying her elbow, she was soon upstairs. We wandered between the studs of the wall-less rooms except for the wall his wife was plastering.

He is doing all the construction himself—electricity, plumbing, sceptic tank, carpentry. He's a fisherman by profession. Is there any other in Newfoundland?

"Make the ladies some coffee," he said to his wife, indicating a one-burner unit propped on a plank between two joists. But we protested.

Back in the driveway, he hammered a piece of quartz into smaller bits. "Take some," he urged and Eleanor did take a piece for a special memory in her garden.

"What will become of all these boulders?" Marjory asked him.

"Much of it will be broken up for fill. The rest will have to be carried away." When we tried to thank him for his hospitality, he replied, "We're flattered when Americans are interested in us."

That evening we were playing contract rummy when O'Leary called.

"Brendan O'Leary?" I asked hesitantly.

"Yes, you were at my hoose this afternoon," he said with that tinge of Scottish dialect we hear so often, "and we dinna think 'til you were gone, but would you please send m' woman 'n' me a postcard from Florida?"

We wondered how he'd tracked us down until Marjory remembered he'd asked her where we were staying. The Floridians at the Fongs' were all the clues he needed.

Sunday, June 26

From 1919 to 1936, several attempts to fly the Atlantic took off from Harbor Grace, the next town to Carbonear, where we've been staying. These included Amelia Earhart's solo flight in 1932. The site is marked today by a Memorial Garden dedicated to those valiant pioneers. At the far end of the garden, a simple, flowing piece of sculpture reaches out toward Conception Bay and the Atlantic. At the other end, the old red Custom House is a museum. One room displays photos, letters, stories, and newspaper accounts of those early flights, several of which fared far less well than Amelia Earhart's. Some were aborted. Others were plagued with breakdowns. One picture of three jovial aviators standing by their plane is captioned "Never heard from."

In another room sits Peter Eastern, a life-sized, lifelike figure of the pirate who terrorized Harbor Grace and the Conception Bay for years in the eighteenth century. I pressed a button at the table where he's reading his Bible. He told me something of his adventures. Late in life he acknowledged his notorious reputation and begged forgiveness of James I. When James refused the request, Peter retired to France, and I could almost see the smirk on his face when he added "with considerable wealth."

Strains of "Rock of Ages" were coming from the Memorial Coughlin United Church across the street when we emerged from the museum. A woman came clicking along the sidewalk in her high heels. Although Mack and I were zipped to our chins, this Newfie in an elegant, low-cut dress three inches above her knees gave no clue other than the blowing of her skirt that a stiff wind was whipping off the bay.

Mack asked her a question, always enough to start a conversation in Newfoundland. A few minutes later, I interrupted with, "May I take a picture of you two?"

"Yes, of course. Coom on, love, stand close," she said, putting her arm around Mack. Such friendly folk!

This afternoon we went to Salmon Cove Sands. Brendan O'Leary had said its beach is as pleasant as Northern Bay and more accessible. He was right. We walked directly from the car to soft, powdery sand. Except for a woman walking her dog, the gulls and we owned the beach. As we explored a quiet cove, four Least Sandpipers skimmed the water and settled on the next sandbar from us. A cameo moment.

Monday June 27

After three days of venturing in and out of Carbonear, the time has come to return to St. John's. South we drove, down the western coast of Conception Bay, resolving not to investigate *every* side road and cove. But Brigus would be an exception. It is supposed to be different, more like an English village. Realizing she had missed the turn for Brigus, Mack pulled off the road to turn around. The car behind us followed, pulled up beside us, and one of the men asked, "You looking for Brigus?"

"As a matter of fact, I am," Mack said.

"We thought so. Back two miles where you were looking off to the bay, you should have taken a left. 'Twill be your second right now as you go back." At least Big Brother is hospitable. Mack thanked him and we went our separate ways.

Brigus did suggest a British village. Its several streets, all with neatly lettered street signs, did not edge the harbor. The village was, so to speak, set to one side. Lilacs bloomed in the dooryards. Green grass filled the space between home and sidewalk. A Canadian flag flew over the post office. We visited two craft shops and contributed once more to the Canadian economy.

I was taking pictures of crab nets piled on the wharf when a man stopped to speak. After some preliminaries, mostly about the weather and where I come from, he asked, "D'ya know aboot the hole in the rock?"

"No, I don't."

"It's warth a look. Jis o'er the bridge thar," pointing to my right, "un tarn left un front of tha chorch thar. Ya sae tha wite chorch? Tak tha next roight. Ya'll sae the hole."

Cliffs rose abruptly either side of the narrow harbor where we stood. The harbor itself is too shallow for anything bigger than a lobster boat to dock. Long ago, my informant wasn't quite sure when, the townsfolk excavated a tunnel, "the hole," about six feet wide, eight feet high, and forty feet long through the solid rock of one of those cliffs out to deeper water. Through it they were able to unload cargo manually from larger ships. It was indeed worth a visit and several pictures.

By then it was time to head for St. John's in earnest.

While we were registering at the Airport Inn, Eleanor said she and Marjory wanted to take Mack and me to dinner but didn't want to disclose where ahead of time. The surprise was the name of the restaurant, Journey's End. How appropriate since we'll be parting tomorrow.

Marjory had reserved a table by the window overlooking the harbor. As dusk turned to dark, twinkling lights came on along the shore and around the city off toward Signal Hill. A cargo ship was unloading sand 'n' salt in anticipation of winter. Winter? The temperature today had been in the eighties. I sent compliments to the chef for my salmon fettucini Alfredo.

Tuesday, June 28

After breakfast we left Marjory and Eleanor to explore St. John's another day on their own, and Mack and I took a meandering, waterside route back to Whitebourne and the Moorland Motel. Tomorrow morning we will leave early to catch the ferry at Argentia.

Wednesday, June 29

Another pea soup crossing. We didn't see one sea bird. But we treasure the Iceland Gull, our only lifer, and the thousands of other birds we've seen in Newfoundland.

Wednesday, July 12

Returning through Maine we spent an evening with our Boulder, Colorado, friends, Wally and Jenny Kate. They were on their way to Newfoundland, following our itinerary. Today we received a card, which I quote in its entirety:

> Did you see whales at St. Vincent's? I hope you did—it was a sight to behold! 25 humpbacks not twenty yards from shore—blowing, diving, calling! Gadzooks! jk

The capelin must have come in.

Polar Bears and Snowy Owls

Though you have no song to sing
worth my stopping work to hear,
still your constant, thankless effort
brings its bit of winter cheer.
And for that, aspiring wight,
breadline forms upon the right.

—Alma Roberts Giordon
(to a winter sparrow)

The Boeing 737 pierced the cloud cover, touched down on the gravelled runway, and roared to a stop. I followed Jean and Mack down the cold metal steps and shivered to the shed where Bonnie, our host and guide for the weekend, was waiting.

"Are there any bears?" I asked as we sloshed through the slush to the outdoor baggage claim.

"Lots of bears—and hares, foxes, minks, and," she paused teasingly, "Snowy Owls."

We had come to Churchill this time ostensibly to photograph polar bears. However, our hopes were pinned, too, on finding the Snowy Owl, which had eluded us on two summer visits. Now it was late October, and Bonnie's report was encouraging.

"Maybe it will be life bird six hundred," Mack rhapsodized.

"We'll have to find two more first," I noted, keeping the record straight.

Bonnie was gathering up the dozen or so others who had

247

flown in for her weekend safari. Introductions were hurriedly made, duffel bags stashed at the back of the bus, and we were on our way to various hostels to don the heaviest clothes we had brought for an almost immediate visit to blustery Cape Merry.

"What are all those little birds flying close to the ground?" Mack asked as we turned onto the Highway.

"Snow Buntings," Bonnie replied matter-of-factly.

"SNOW BUNTINGS!" Mack shrieked. "Five-ninety-eight! Five-ninety-eight! Five-ninety-eight!"

"What's 'five-ninety-eight'?" a man across the aisle asked.

"It's our five hundred and ninety-eighth lifer."

"What's a 'lifer'?"

"A *life* bird. I've never seen a Snow Bunting before in my *life.*"

"But you've seen five hundred and ninety-seven other birds?"

"Right!"

"Amazing."

Obviously, unlike our previous visits to Churchill, we had fallen among nonbirders. October is for polar bears, and I was as eager as the next to see the bears.

Mack and I had crossed the country last year, looking for twenty-seven new birds to reach the magic six hundred on our life list, but returned seven short. Last January we flew one weekend to Texas to chalk up the Blue-footed Booby that had somehow gone badly astray and was living on a diving board at Lake LBJ in Granite Shoals. We sleuthed the next two lifers out in Florida, a Lesser Black-backed Gull and a stray Eurasian Wigeon. The Iceland Gull in Newfoundland this past summer had left us only three short when we set out for Churchill this time.

"What do you have to offer for five-five-nine if we save six hundred for the Snowy?" Mack asked.

"What do you need?" Bonnie countered.

"A Rock Ptarmigan," I answered quickly.

"Rock Ptarmigans *should* be here now, but the weather has been so warm they haven't shown up yet. One of my drivers saw a Gyrfalcon a few days ago."

"That would do," I said in my usual monotone.

"Would *do!*" Jean exclaimed. "I should think it would."

"But don't count on it," Bonnie said. "They are recluses. We'll keep our eyes open on the tundra tomorrow."

"I'll be back for you guys in about twenty minutes," Bonnie said the next morning about daybreak as she left to collect her crowd from their several B and Bs—Roseanne and Sheri (sisters from Milwaukee) and a contingent from the Detroit Zoo Travel Club. "Coffee's made and you'll find sweet rolls."

"I've one more," Bonnie said as we climbed aboard, "waiting at the railroad station. I hope." A woman with a knapsack looked relieved when she saw Bonnie's blue bus. She had traveled two and a half days by train from Winnipeg to see the bears. John had gone ahead with the lunch to warm up the tundra bus waiting at the end of the road. He'd be our driver today.

"This fog may lift," Bonnie said as we barreled down the Highway to the tundra bus, "but whatever the weather, I promise you bears. I'm glad we have a warm day." The temperature hovered close to freezing.

I was surprised the ground was bare. Jean and I had pictured white bears on glistening snow when we bought our film. Oh, well, white bears would show up better against gray rocks and brown grass.

After an hour of jostling and jouncing over rough terrain and splashing through stony ponds, John called, "Bear ahead on the right." We would have to wait our turn, though. Traffic was heavy. Three vehicles ahead of us had first divvies on photographing the first polar bear most of us had ever seen in the wild.

Transportation varied in size from vans with sun tops to huge tundra buggies standing six feet off the ground on tires taller than the passengers. In between were yellow school busses and the blue-and-white busses of Bonnie's Wilderness Encounter fleet.

While we waited, an Arctic fox in its winter white loped through the grasses at some distance. It stopped now and then to sniff or investigate something in the grass, but we were of no concern to it. We watched it disappear across the tundra.

Eventually our turn came to pull up to the bear stretched out beside a bush not ten feet off the track. He appeared to be asleep, yet as we drew close, his eyes blinked disinterestedly. For the twenty minutes we had taken to reach him, he had remained outwardly oblivious to the traffic moving past his nose. Or worse yet, to the cameras pointing in his face.

"Will they all be that sleepy?" someone asked Bonnie.

"I don't think so."

We drove on. John pointed out at some distance a bear that looked like a rock. Then we began seeing bears that John decreed *were* rocks.

"Ptarmigan on the left," Bonnie called out.

"Rock Ptarmigans?" I asked hopefully. Both Rock and Willow would be all white this time of year.

"Willow," Bonnie said, checking with her binoculars. Again she reminded us it is still too warm for Rock Ptarmigans. It began to snow lightly. Just a flurry, but through the flurry flew a flock of Willow Ptarmigans looking like large snow-flakes.

A half hour later, Mack asked, "Are we going to see any more bears?"

"I promise," John called from the front of the bus. And soon we did begin to see them close enough to tell them from rocks. As we neared the bay and the mobile motel, they became more numerous. The mobile motel, three or four tundra buggies connected to each other, provides accommodations for those who want to spend an overnight with the bears. Tourists and bears enjoy a silent sociability here on the banks of Hudson Bay. By noon seven or eight vehicles had arrived from town. A dozen or more bears roamed placidly in and out around the huge tires. The curious stretched up the sides of the bigger vehicles, pointing their noses toward the cameras behind the windows. Nor were the smaller busses spared their curiosity.

The upper sections of our windows could be lowered for picture taking. But we were warned to close those windows fast if a bear began showing interest in making friends.

"Never underestimate how fast a bear can move or how far it can reach," John cautioned.

One bear sat beside a school bus, looking like a Saint Bernard puppy being left behind when his master boarded the bus. As my camera clicked rapidly, he stretched and put one paw gently on the door as if to say, "Please take me, too." They appear so soft, so docile, so slow moving we tend to forget how powerful and dangerous they can be.

But the show didn't end at the terminal. Only after we pulled away from the mobile motel did the bears seem less interested in us and more and more involved in their own activities. A group of four stood idly in a circle. I could imagine one's saying, "Whose deal is it?" Before I finished photographing them, another came swimming across a pond and loped up to the others. We didn't have to take John's word for it that they could travel fast. I've titled that picture "Deal Me In."

For another hour John moved slowly among the bears, stopping whenever we came upon a good gathering. One fairly small fellow sat pensively, chewing twigs on a low shrub.

A bigger bear approached, paused, and queried, "May I join you?"

"Be my guest," the little one replied.

The newcomer sat down on his haunches, looked around, yawned, lay down, and rolled over onto his back—belly up. "Call me when the ice freezes," he said and went to sleep. He must have stretched ten feet from the bottom of his bare bear feet to the tip of his pointed ears. I didn't lie down beside him for an exact measure.

Some livelier bears sparred, romped, rolled, or put half nelsons on each other. Two stood on their hind legs in a struggle that looked more like dancing than quarreling. I didn't witness any ill-naturedness among any of them. But these were all males. The females and cubs stay away until the males have returned to the ice. Make of that what you will.

John allowed plenty of time for pictures. He said, "I figure anyone who doesn't shoot twenty rolls isn't having a good time." It was a great day for Kodak and Fuji.

While two bears played mumbletypeg on one side of the bus, an Arctic fox dug a hole on the other. At the rate he was digging, if he didn't catch his lemming, he'd be halfway to China by sunset. Great photo opportunities!

"Are you watching for Snowy Owls?" Mack asked Bonnie.

"You bet I am," she assured her.

John finally said, "I'm going to start back by way of Gordon Point. If some of you want to get out and stretch, Gordon Point is *relatively* safe."

We hadn't lacked fresh air. The windows had been open more than closed despite the bitter wind, and within limits we had been able to move up and down the narrow aisle, but no one but no one had been allowed to open the door for any reason. Now after six hours we were released with the caution, "*If* you see a bear, don't be the last person back on the bus."

The view extended for miles across the flat, bleak, rocky

landscape. We huddled around the bus, clapped our hands to keep warm, and tried to take pictures in an impossible wind. Soon everyone was aboard again. John headed the bus toward Churchill.

But we weren't through with bears. Waiting down the trail was a mighty monarch, the most photogenic of the day. He was alone with nothing on his mind but his solitude and a curiosity about us, philosopher that he was. John stopped and waited. The bear approached from perhaps a hundred feet . . . slowly, deliberately, maybe meditatively. He was a beauty. At fifty feet he almost dismissed us, paused, and then continued toward the bus. At twenty-five feet, he sat down and raised his nose skyward. He sniffed. He posed.

"You'll never get a better picture than that," someone said. Every window was chock-a-block with cameras.

"Do you want another angle?" the bear asked, standing and resuming his progress toward us, one slow, pigeon-toed step at a time, 'til John called, "All arms, hands, and cameras inside. And be prepared to close the windows." Reacting to such inhospitality, the bear dropped to the ground, rested his jaw on his paws, and went to sleep not fifteen feet from us. John started the motor and headed for the setting sun.

Wanting her guests to have a different wilderness experience the next day, Bonnie took us to Twin Lakes in the opposite direction from the bears' haunt.

"First I'm going to make a short detour along the coast road. We'll pick up the Highway down a few miles," she explained. We were scarcely out of town when she slowed and said, "There's your Snowy Owl on the right."

"Five hundred and ninety-nine!" Mack cried. And this time, Dalen, leader of the Detroit Zoo Club, knew what she meant. Everyone seemed happy for us, and admittedly, Jean, Mack, and I had stirred some interest (or curiosity) in birding over the past thirty-six hours. Did they have a choice? The owl perched on a low bush too far away for pictures. Of course that didn't keep us from taking them. See that white spot?

Another half mile, Jean called, "Ptarmigan on the left!" It was at a distance also but stood out on the gray boulder.

"Rock or Willow?"

"Willow, probably," Bonnie replied patiently, "but let's scope it." Several of us piled out and had it in our binoculars when Bonnie exclaimed, "It *is* a Rock Ptarmigan," almost as excited as we.

Everyone who wanted had a chance to look through the scope while Mack and I did our victory dance in the road. Several joined in the dance, including the Milwaukee sisters, who were amused by our enthusiasm for birds. We received a card from them after we got home, saying they had seen a flock of over forty Willow Ptarmigans after we left. They included also a photo of Mack with six fingers raised at the moment of victory.

As the euphoria waned, I asked Bonnie, "How do you tell the difference between Rock and Willow? They look so much alike."

"Chiefly by the bill," she said. "The bill is a little smaller and definitely narrower."

Someone asked about Arctic hares. "You have to look among the rocks and boulders for them," Bonnie said. For the next hour, she drove in, out, and around the boulders that line the Coast Road until she said, "Enough of this. We must get on to Twin Lakes. I want to share some of the flora as well as the fauna of Churchill."

Bonnie drove west away from the bay and bears. She described as we went along the taiga, the transition from the tundra to the forests of both white and black spruce. We noted the willows and fireweed (long gone to seed but beautiful) along the road. We saw two more Snowy Owls, one in a bush and another in flight. She left the road and drove down a trail into the woods. Parking, she said, "Let's walk a little way." As Bonnie left the bus, she took the rifle from its hooks and put it over her shoulder. "We are not *likely* to see bears, but let's stay together."

The narrow trail looked as though it had a frosting of snow, but the snow was caribou, or palgonia, moss. She identified low bush juniper with its bluish berries, red berry-berry, and baked-apple berry growing with the caribou moss and meskeg among the black spruces and larches. Meskeg, she explained, is low plant life that has not yet broken down. It is very spongy, as is the caribou moss. With that botany lesson tucked away, we headed back to the bus. On the way a Gray Jay posed by the trail, and Jean was there to take the picture.

The next morning before our plane left, Bonnie drove Jean, Mack, and me out again to the rocky ridge that lines the bay. A light snow had fallen overnight, changing the face of the coast.

Bonnie said, "You knew I wasn't looking for an Arctic hare when I wasted that hour down here yesterday morning. One of my drivers phoned he'd seen a Gyrfalcon, and I was hoping we could find it." We still hadn't found it when we had to leave for the airport.

"But if we hadn't come down the coast road, we wouldn't have found the Rock Ptarmigan," Mack said.

"What have we missed besides the Gryfalcon?" Bonnie asked as we waited for the plane.

"The Northern Lights," I said.

"Oh, you won't see those until it gets cold. Come in January next time."

Something in Memory

Goodnight! and sweetest dreams be thine
   Through all their shining way
Till darkness goes, and bird and rose
   With rapture greet the day.

—Edna Dean Procter

I touched the key for PRINT DOCUMENT and the screen flashed NOTHING IN MEMORY. What a dreadful thought: nothing in memory. Praises be to Saint Francis that my memory is studded with memorable moments like the time Mack and I finally caught a glimpse of the endangered Black-capped Vireo in the bushes beside Travis Lake near Austin or the Kirtland's Warbler in the jack pines of Michigan. We had searched several springs for the former; the latter we came upon, never having looked for it, quite by accident. Such are the vagaries of birding.

Kirtland's Warbler breeds in an area no larger than a pencil-point dot on a map of Michigan's Lower Peninsula. Returning from our first trip to Churchill, we camped one night in Grayling, Michigan, unaware we were sitting on the edge of that pencil-point dot.

"You've come for the Kirtland's Warbler?" our neighbor across the way assumed, having learned we were birders.

"The . . . uh? Er, what?"

"Are we in Kirtland's territory?" I asked in surprise.

"'Bout dead center."

These birds come every spring from the Bahamas to

breed in the jack pines. And not just any jack pines, if you please. They must be between fifteen and eighteen feet tall to keep the Kirtland's happy—and propagating. To that end the Forest Service maintains a burn and reforestation program throughout the few counties where jack pines grow and closes the breeding grounds to the public once the nesting begins. Mack and I had arrived two days after the property was posted.

Not easily put off when a life bird is at stake, Mack began sleuthing and learned one breeding area bordered a public highway, which the forestry office was loath to identify. And rightfully so. We had no quarrel with their desire to protect the birds. We'd have to do this on our own.

Luck went with us the next morning when we met a binoculared couple on a morning stroll. Yes, they had seen a Kirtland's Warbler that morning without leaving the highway. They gave us specific directions to the spot less than a mile away.

We heard him first. Then we saw him on a bare branch about twenty feet above the ground, a gray-backed, tail-wagging chap who lived up to his reputation of being sociable. He was not in the least put off by our pausing to enjoy the cheery notes he carolled to the world. We sent our regards to Mrs. Kirtland's, who was doubtlessly sitting on her nest close by, thanked him for his song, and went on.

I remember another morning. This time in Arizona. Bob had picked us up at six. A huge red sun on the horizon forecast another hot day. We drove thirty miles west of Phoenix, parked the car, and walked along the desert road.

"We'll probably have to get away from the road," he said. "We may encounter some briars." He had been recommended as the best birder in Arizona. Surely he would find a Leconte's Thrasher for us. A few briars were no problem. He played a tape of the LeConte's call, and we waited.

We wandered on through the saltbush and among the

sparse mesquite bushes—stopping, scanning. The stubble snapped under my feet. Seeds from the dry grasses clung to my jeans. Every sprig was crisp in the desert heat. Each time Bob played the tape, we stopped and listened. Nearly an hour passed.

"Guess we'll have to go deeper into the saltbush," he said. Mack and I followed. He played the tape again. Nothing. We walked on. *The search is all* popped up on my computer screen. Then I heard the call. Or was it the tape? No, the bird had answered. Ah, Emily, "It *is* a lonesome glee . . . a bird to overhear . . . arrestless as invisible . . ."

"Over there," Bob muttered, moving to the left.

We were looking for a bird a little bigger than a robin, a bird with a dark bill, a dark tail, and a gray body lighter than other thrashers. It is uncommon even within its range, which is a narrow strip running from the southern tip of Nevada down the western edge of Arizona into Mexico. And down the Baja of southern California. We scanned the ground as well as bushes.

We waited. We listened. We pushed farther into the desert crispness. The zzzzz of an insect accentuated the silence. A lone steer lowed in the distance. Again the thrasher responded, and Mack caught a glimpse of it in flight. We branched out in three directions. Shortly Mack called, "There's a bird in a bush about fifty feet beyond the cactus with the yellow blossoms," and then added quickly, "Forget it," as the bird flew, showing the white wing patches of a mockingbird.

The sun was getting hot. I stooped to tie my sneaker and pick some stickers from my socks. *Patience is a birder,* I thought to myself. A streak of bird crossed our vision.

"That was it," Bob called. "It's here. It's coming closer." He played the tape once more. We scanned every bush to the distant fence posts.

"Is that it on the third post to the right of the tall mesquite bush?" Mack asked.

"Too far to tell."

I enjoy birding, but I am not addicted. Sometimes at a crucial moment a diverting phrase jumps into my head like a jumping cholla spine:

> Have you heard
>   that elusive bird?
> The thrasher
>   won't ansher.

This is no place for Ogden Nash, I scolded myself. Nevertheless, I reached into my hip pocket for my note pad to record these avian aphorisms that were accumulating in my head. At such a moment, the bird in question (I can count on it) always shows. How many times have I been caught with my binoculars down, and this was one of them.

"There it is," said Bob, pointing.

"I have it," Mack said, so excited she choked on her whisper.

"Where?" I asked, stuffing the pad back into my pocket and picking up my binoculars. "Oh, there." It sat fairly conspicuously in a mesquite bush close enough and long enough for a definite identification. I distinctly heard it say as it flew away, "Guess I toyed with those folks long enough."

As we trudged back through the saltbush, ebullient with our success, Bob commented, "I wasn't overconfident of that one."

We snared LeConte's Thrasher, one of the birding world's more elusive birds, in about two hours. We had been looking for an American Dipper, one of the birding world's more common birds, for over two years. Also called Water Ouzel, it has the distinction of being the birding world's only aquatic songbird. Plump and short-tailed like a starling, it sings like a wren and dives like a kingfisher. It feeds on aquatic insects and larvae on the bottom of mountain streams and is fairly common along mountain streams in the West from Mexico to Nome, Alaska.

"The ouzel's easy," Wally said. "Come to Colorado."

"I'll find you one," Martha countered. "Come to Arizona."

"Look into the streams coming off the Kenai Range into Kachemak Bay when you are in Homer," Dick advised.

"Come to Twin Falls," Judy, the naturalist on the cruise into the Kenai Fjords, offered.

"You'll see one in the stream outside Marian's dining room window when we go to North Bend," Ginny promised.

"You'll even see the nest on the cliff's edge beside the waterfall on the Catwalk Trail," Myra at Bear Mountain Guest Ranch directed. But it was too well camouflaged.

"Now let's get serious about this ouzel," I said. We were in Idaho and remembered Judy's offer.

"We're looking for Canyon Wrens and American Dippers," Mack told her on the phone.

"I'll take you out to Shoshone Falls tomorrow evening for the wren. In the meantime I'll tell you three places to look for the ouzel. You can't miss."

"Yeah, we've heard that before."

"They are all in Sun Valley, and if you don't find one, you're no birders."

So off Mack and I went the next morning seventy-five miles to Sun Valley. The first river had everything a respectable ouzel could want. We strolled along the bank of the tumbling stream. We crossed the bridge and followed the opposite bank for a hundred yards or so. The river rushed and splashed—cool on a hot day, refreshing to linger beside. But no bird showed. Ditto the next stream. Drat!

"Our reputations are at stake," I warned. "Let's move on."
We took our stands at either end of a bridge about twice the
length of the motor home—seventy-five feet?

Everything an ouzel could want was there. Crystal-clear
water rushed over a river full of rocks. I checked every stone,
noticed every movement of twig or falling leaf, and resisted
the hypnotic power of the foaming torrent under the hot sun.

I had stood like this some fifty years ago on a much larger,
heavily traveled bridge joining the twin cities of Auburn and
Lewiston, Maine, overlooking the Androscoggin River. I was
a student in college. Heavy rains in recent days had swollen
the river. Someone reported a bridge upstream had been
washed out and masses of logs were floating down the river.
We crazy kids were standing there, waiting to see the logs go
by, wagering whether they would clog at the dam, wash over,
or more dramatically knock the dam out—an unlikely sce-
nario. Someone cried, "Here they come!" I could see the logs
tossing in the roiling water. But they never came.

Stop daydreaming, I warned myself. Okay, let's make one
more systematic survey—little rocks, big rocks, pebbles,
stones. I practically willed an American Dipper to be sitting
on a rock midstream, bobbing up and down, ready to dive for
a delectable lunch of caddisfly larvae. Wet stones, gray stones,
dry stones, brown, rust, and variegated stones . . . smooth
rocks, lumpy rocks. I paused, puzzled over a dry, gray stone at
the far edge. It was about a foot in diameter, fairly flat. Resting
on it was a smaller gray stone, maybe six inches in diameter
. . . roundish. But wait a minute. Did the breeze jar it? *Was* it
a rock? Could it be? Sitting motionless? Shouldn't it be bobbing?

"Maaaack," I whispered, as though any sound I could
make would disturb a bird over the splashing and the dashing
of the river below. "Mack!" I called again, tentatively but

261

louder. I motioned for her to come. "See that gray bump on that gray rock?"

"Is it . . . " she started to ask, raising her binoculars. "It *is*!" she shouted. We watched, hoping to see it walk underwater. We continued to wait. It didn't fly, it didn't bob, it didn't dive, it didn't sing its melodious song with trills and repetitions, but no one could mistake that squat body with the stubby tail and sooty plumage. What a nondescript little bird to create such a charged moment.

In the evening Judy took us up the canyon to the falls to find a Canyon Wren. She played a tape of its song. In no time it emerged from the rocks to see who had invaded its territory. How it scolded. It sat on a boulder not fifteen feet from me and told my camera in no uncertain terms where it could go. Its language was scurrilous.

Abert's Towhee was similarly long sought and finally found on our third visit to Arizona. Bird books say it is "fairly common" in the brushlands of the arid Southwest. We should have found one in the mesquite thickets along the Santa Cruz River or around the sewage ponds in Tucson.

"You should have found one at the San Xavier Mission," a guide told us after we had left Tucson far behind.

"They are all over Tucson," Martha, who lives there, said.

"They breed in my backyard," Bob Bradley wrote from Phoenix.

"Come to Montezuma Castle," Marion, a friend and ranger there, said. And so we did. The rest was easy.

Marion was on the trail below the cliff dwellings, answering tourists' questions when we arrived. Ravens, Cliff Swallows, and White-throated Swifts, all of which nest in the cliffs, flew in and out of the dwellings. Marion drew our attention to a beehive. Suspended from the great arch over the main dwellings, it was clearly visible to us on the path hundreds of feet below. She walked with us back to the visitors center, pointing out a Mountain Bluebird and its nest in a cottonwood tree along the path.

"Are you still looking for an Abert's Towhee?" she asked.

"You remembered," I said.

"I'll take you to the feeders behind my cottage. If I can wangle an early lunch, I'll watch with you, though I guarantee you won't have to wait long for an Abert's."

Her backyard feeders were busier than Sea World during school vacation. Hooded Orioles, Black-chinned Hummingbirds, House Finches thick as flies, Phainopeples, a Gila Woodpecker, and, ah yes, one Abert's Towhee darted even at high noon in and out of her many feeders.

Montezuma Quails didn't show at Montezuma Castle National Monument, but that doesn't mean they were not there. These quails are prized not because they are so rare but because they are so difficult to spot. When approached, instead of running they hunker down and remain motionless almost to the point of being stepped on. Looking for Montezuma Quail is like looking for lumps on the road. Mack and I did finally find a pair at Fort Davis State Park in Texas. Then as happens so often, a few days later as we were RVing from Alpine to Big Bend in Texas a pair scooted right across the road in front of us.

Another moment stored in my memory bank takes me back to Silver City, New Mexico. Mack and I were staying at Myra's Bear Mountain Guest Ranch on the east edge of the Continental Divide. Black-chinned Hummingbirds darted around the feeders strung outside the dining room windows. Black-headed Grosbeaks and squirrels shared a larger feeder farther from the house. A flock of noisy birds flew by without stopping.

"Let's go for a walk before dinner," I suggested. As we started down the drive, the noisy flock flew over again.

"What's that haunting call?" Mack asked. "Have we heard

it before?" It wasn't the raucous scream of crows or Blue Jays, but more of a high mewing, almost musical in its dissonance. They settled briefly in a tree to our left. We walked in that direction, but they didn't wait. They flew off helter-skelter like a crowd of kids released from school. With more distraction than direction. A half mile down the road, they paused again, restlessly selecting perches in a tree closer to us this time—close enough for the steel blue of their feathers to shimmer in the light of the late afternoon sun.

"What *are* they?" Mack asked, a bundle of excitement and frustration. They flew again in a disorderly array so unlike the flights of blackbirds, grackles, or skimmers. Two flew directly over our heads. "Ev!" Mack screamed. "They're Pinyon Jays."

Now we'd been looking for Pinyon Jays longer than the Water Ouzel. I needed a picture to complete my series of jays—Blue, Stellar's, Scrub, Gray-breasted, Gray, Green. Yes, I even had a Brown Jay, the biggest and probably the shiest of them all. We had promised ourselves not to go home from this trip without a Pinyon Jay, but they were far from our thoughts when we set out on that walk.

I was still excited at dinner. When we told Myra of our find, she said, "I thought I heard them. You're lucky. Pinyons are unpredictable and not common around here, though they do pass through now and then."

"They remind me," I told her, "in their erratic dashing about of children on a playground."

"Children!" she scoffed. "They are marauders! Full-blown pirates. In winter they descend on farmers' fields in huge flocks, rattling and shaking their sabers."

Pinyon Jays are so unpredictable it is almost useless to search for them. The best advice is to find the right habitat, put yourself into a receptive mood (which is what we unwittingly did with the Pinyon Jays), and go about your other business. At the other extreme are the birds that carry a business card with a given address like the Red-whiskered Bulbul. It lives at

Royal Palms Tennis Court
Corner of Ninety-eighth Street and Seventy-second Avenue
South Florida, Miami,

Ignoring the MEMBERS ONLY sign, Mack and I entered the parking lot. A woman getting into her car noticed our binoculars and said, "You've come for the bulbul?" When we agreed, she added, "It's been around this morning. You might ask someone over at the courts."

It sounded as though we were meeting someone for tennis. As we approached a groundsman, he greeted us, "Lookin' fer the bulbul? Come with me." He put down his rake. We followed him back through the parking lot to a utility line. There the resident bird sat. He flicked his tail and turned from side to side so every aspect could be admired—his dark, high-pointed crest, bright red ear patches, and red whiskers. He tipped forward on the line as though losing his balance, but I knew he was showing off the red splotch under his tail.

Two years later we took Jean to see the Red-whiskered Bulbul. Not finding him at home, we drove a couple of blocks to Southwest Ninety-sixth Street, the address of the Spot-breasted Orioles. Maybe they were having a kaffe klatch. Betty, of Art and Betty who feed the "locally common" birds, said, "The bulbul? It's been in and out this morning. I'm surprised you didn't find him at the tennis courts." She whistled his song softly, and within seconds he flew in to the birdbath. As he had done originally for Mack and me, he presented several postures without a smidgen of modesty.

Believed once to have been caged birds, the bulbul, the Spot-breasted Oriole, the Canary-winged Parakeet, and other varieties of parrots have been flying free around South Miami for over thirty years, long enough for the American Birding Association to agree they really are wild birds. Such predictable birds may not be as memorable as long-sought ouzels, but they would have to be high on anyone's Dependable List.

But for all-time dependability, give me an owl. Give me the little screech owl in the primitive campground at Bentsen State Park or the six-inch Elf Owl near our campsite there in Bentsen. Give me the Great Horned Owl in the crotch of a tree in Choke Canyon Campground in Callahan, Texas, or the Burrowing Owl beside County Road 330 near Manatee Springs State Park in Florida. And if I can have only one owl in my memory bank, I'll take the Whiskered Screech Owl in Madera Canyon, Arizona.

"When you reach the picnic area at the head of the canyon—just before Santa Rita Lodge," a birder told us, "turn left toward Bog Springs campground. Look for where the utility lines cross the road. The Whiskered Screech Owl lives in a hole in the utility pole on the left side of the road. He comes out, reliable as an alarm clock, between 7:20 and 7:30 every evening." We were waiting at 7:10. He might wake up early.

The sun set. Dusk was turning to dark. A thousand mosquitoes were honing their needles on me. At 7:23 I heard the owl. Or did I? A rattling burst of Morse code dots and dashes came from somewhere in or on the pole. I could hardly believe one wee owl, smaller than a robin, was making that commotion. Surely some cicada had gone mad. After a short pause and what must have been a remarkably deep breath, the owl appeared in person at the entrance of the hole and did the whole Morse code routine again for the doubting Thomases. And in a flash, too fast for some human eyes in the fading light, he was gone . . . into the forest to hoot and hunt the night away. But tucked away forever in my memory.